HELLBOY ™

CONQUEROR WORM

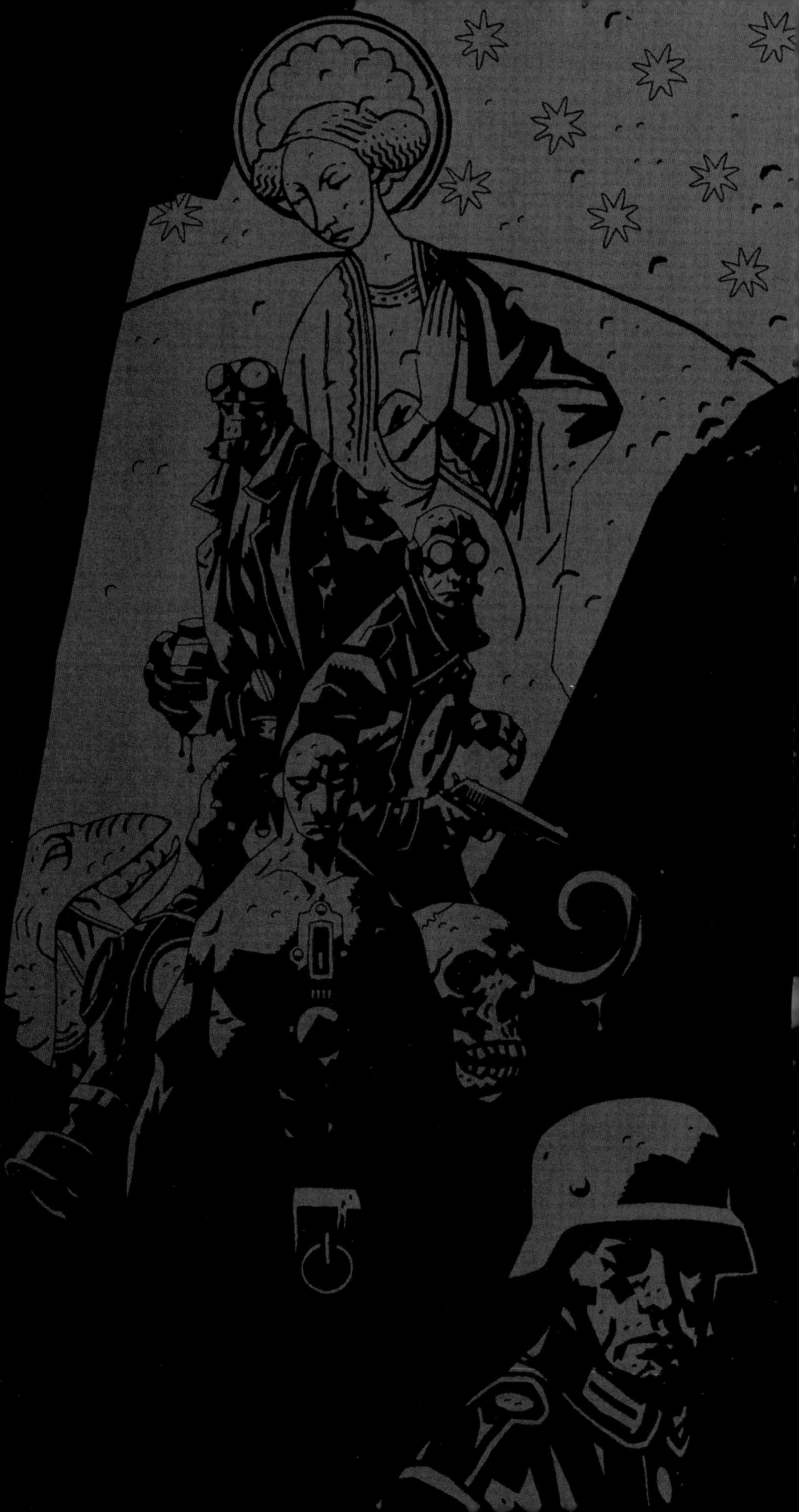

CONQUEROR WORM

by
MIKE MIGNOLA

Colored by
DAVE STEWART

Lettered by
PAT BROSSEAU

✠

Introduction by
GUILLERMO DEL TORO

Edited by
SCOTT ALLIE

Hellboy logo designed by
KEVIN NOWLAN

Collection designed by
MIKE MIGNOLA & CARY GRAZZINI

Published by
MIKE RICHARDSON

DARK HORSE BOOKS™

Published by Dark Horse Books
A division of Dark Horse Comics, Inc.
10956 SE Main St.
Milwaukie, OR 97222
www.darkhorse.com

First Edition: February 2002
Second Edition: November 2003
ISBN: 1-59307-092-6

This volume collects the four-issue series published by Dark Horse Comics.

10 9 8 7 6 5 4 3

PRINTED IN CHINA

MIKE MIGNOLA IS A GENIUS
An unapologetically subjective introduction

by GUILLERMO DEL TORO

Yes, Mike Mignola is a genius.
Right off the bat, we can agree on it. That's what makes writing an intro like this so easy. Especially if you were—like me—a groveling fan already. After all, Mike Mignola conjured up a perfect character in Hellboy, and his latest adventure, *Conqueror Worm*, is compelling and beautiful.

Nosiree, Bob. No problem: this introduction—like all of its kind—will merely point the reader to a few more reasons for grovelling at the feet of a comic-book demi-God like Mr. Mignola, here.

As a naïve young geek, I was fascinated by Mignola's legendary inking and penciling. I leafed through the art and drooled over the sensuous lines, bathed in those deep pools of blackness that appear in most every vignette Mike creates. And, like many heathens, I thought for a few issues that Hellboy was wearing goggles on his forehead. Then, at the end of *Wake the Devil*—when his horns sprout out—I realized what they were. I hurried back and actually re-read every story, searching out those issues that I was missing.

I was hooked. Or rather, I fell in love. Truly, madly, deeply in love.

As a matter of fact, my rediscovery of *Hellboy* is one of the happiest memories I have of shooting *Mimic* in Toronto. In spite of a grueling schedule, I often found myself waiting patiently for Silver Snail Comics to open. Once inside, I would browse through the bins hoping for a *Dark Horse Presents* issue that I somehow had missed. I loved reading a newly-found issue at 5:00 A.M. while my family slept and I prepared to storyboard that day's scenes.

I humbly confess that many a time I have aspired to imitate Mignola's mysterious style in the design of my films, especially the cold, velvet backdrop of darkness from which his characters emerge. Alas, his hyper-expressionistic lighting is—I've found out—almost impossible to reproduce in a 3-D world.

And then there are the moments of quiet, almost elegiac horror juxtaposed with a kinetic energy only hinted at by the best of Kirby. And then—and then—above all!—an irritating simplicity. A perfect, effortless line that reduces all us amateur illustrators to nothing but salivating Salieris prostrate before a Mozart symphony.

A few years ago, I had the pleasure of developing a *Hellboy* screenplay. I tried to honor and expand upon the universe created by Mike in his series and in his masterful short stories.

Mike's body of work is firmly anchored in the comic-book and literary traditions of Machen, Lovecraft, Toth, and Kirby. Yet what has been emerging from them is a species all its own.

In discussing the characters with Mike, I suggested that their fascinating, comforting immutability would need to yield to a more three-dimensional dramatic approach. In addition, a complete, self-contained screen drama would need to tie things up a bit more in the end.

I say this without a hint of criticism, for we work in parallel but separate arenas. In the illustrated stories, Mike finds a way to give us a calm, unfazed Hellboy, a quiet, always dignified Abe (my favorite character), or a tormented, almost biblical Rasputin.

And now ... now ... *Conqueror Worm* gives us something new, something more subtle and complete. We finally get an explanation of those Kirbyesque aliens in *Seed of Destruction*. At last, Hellboy lashes out at his benign captors at the BPRD. Lobster Johnson's origin and feats are expanded upon. In my fevered reading, all the characters seem more nuanced and evocative. Hell, even Roger the Homunculus becomes a brooding, almost Miltonian figure, conflicted by his origins and searching for an identity and purpose in life. Kriegaffe aside, the only character who remains delightfully one-dimensional is Lobster Johnson, and with a crazy-ass name like that, we shouldn't ask for more.

So, move in and explore these pages. They draw us into a deeper, richer universe; they crown all past work and signal a new promising future for the character, all while still giving us the pulp beauty, cheap thrills, and cosmic horrors that have become Mignola's signature.

A work of genius.

(Did I already mention that Mike Mignola is a genius?)

For Doc Savage, the Shadow,
the Spider, G-8, and the men who wrote them.
And for the original 11 1/2-inch G.I. Joe.

CHAPTER ONE

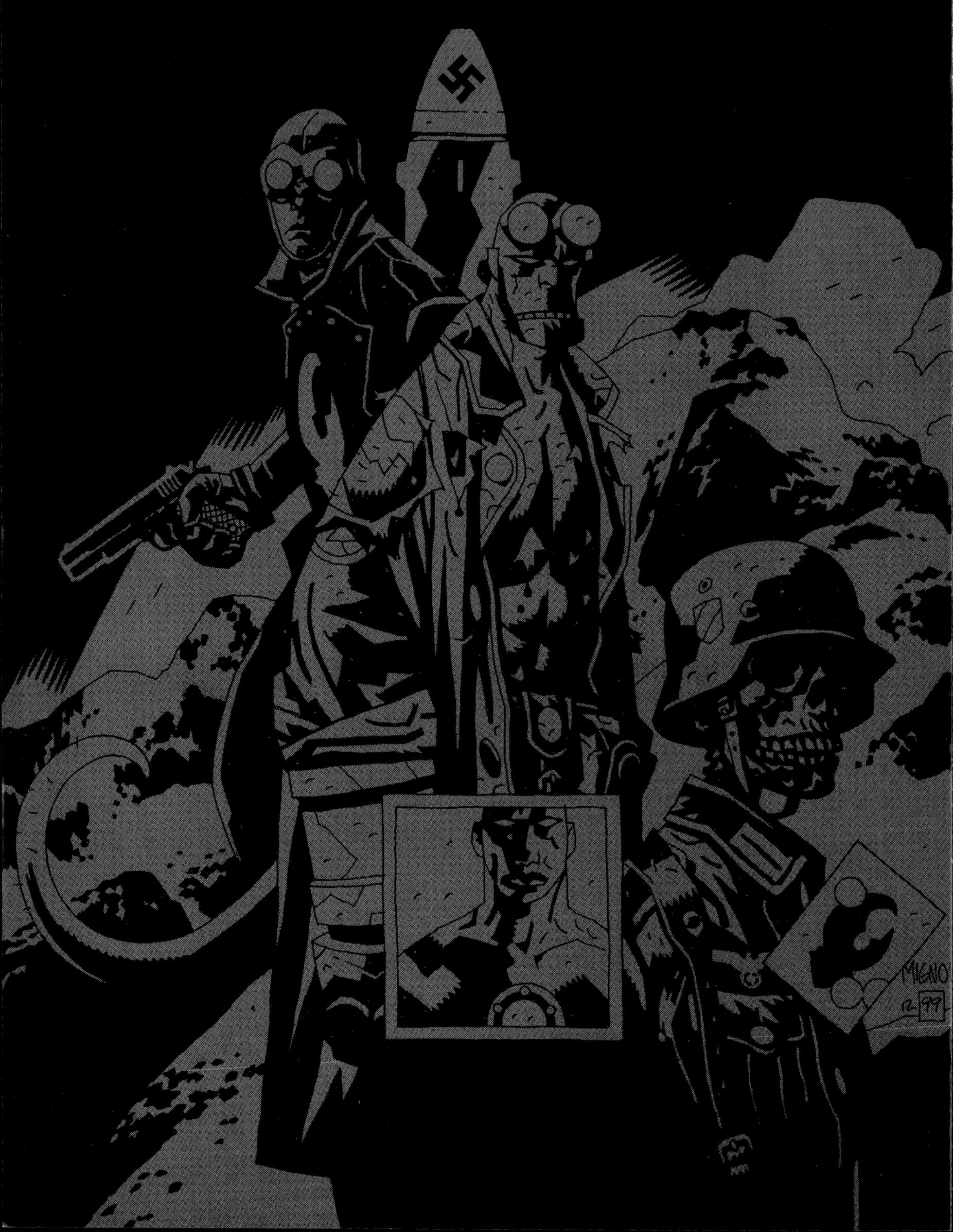
MIGNO
12 99

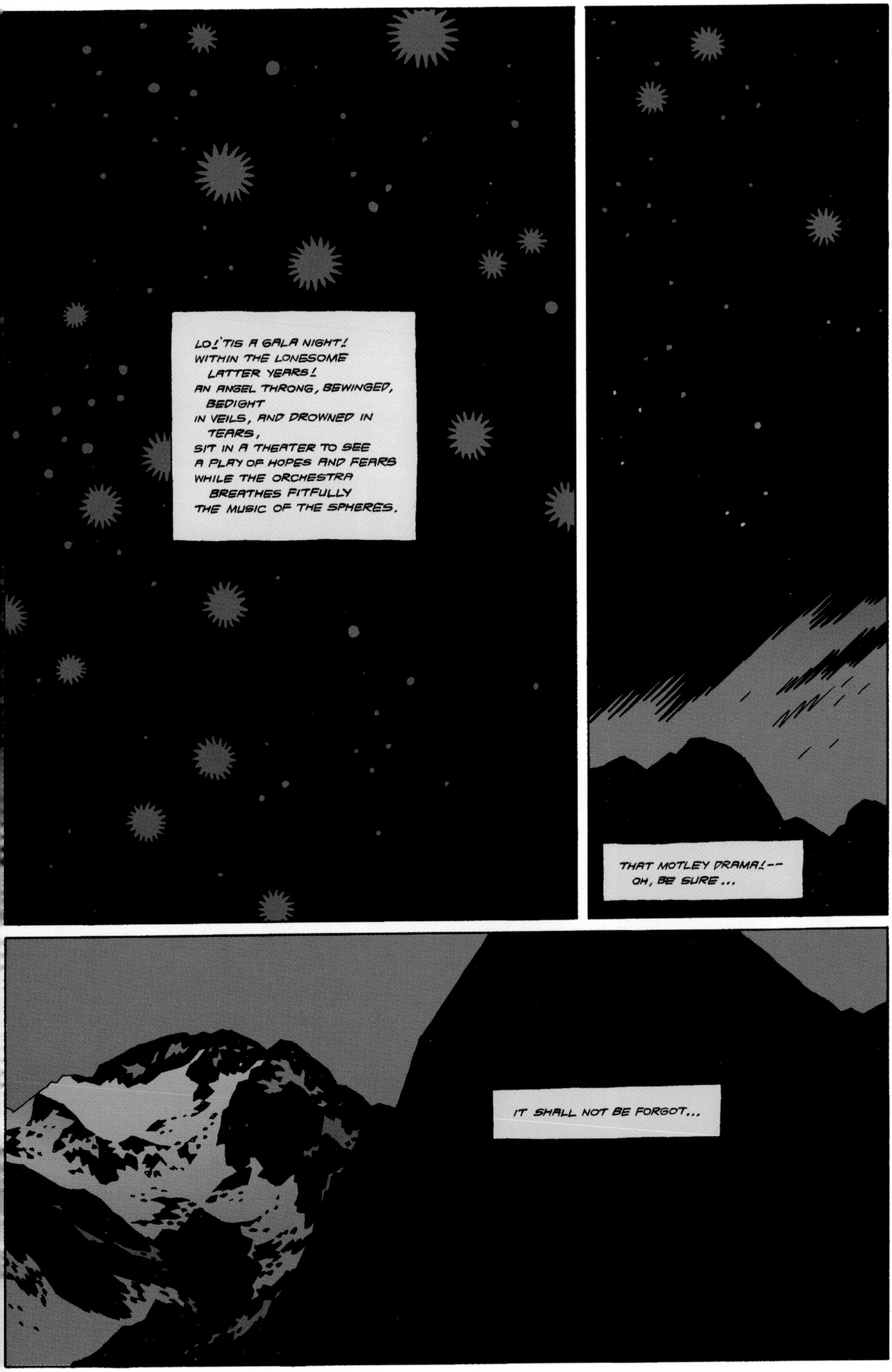
LO! 'TIS A GALA NIGHT!
WITHIN THE LONESOME LATTER YEARS!
AN ANGEL THRONG, BEWINGED, BEDIGHT
IN VEILS, AND DROWNED IN TEARS,
SIT IN A THEATER TO SEE
A PLAY OF HOPES AND FEARS
WHILE THE ORCHESTRA BREATHES FITFULLY
THE MUSIC OF THE SPHERES.
THAT MOTLEY DRAMA!-- OH, BE SURE...
IT SHALL NOT BE FORGOT...

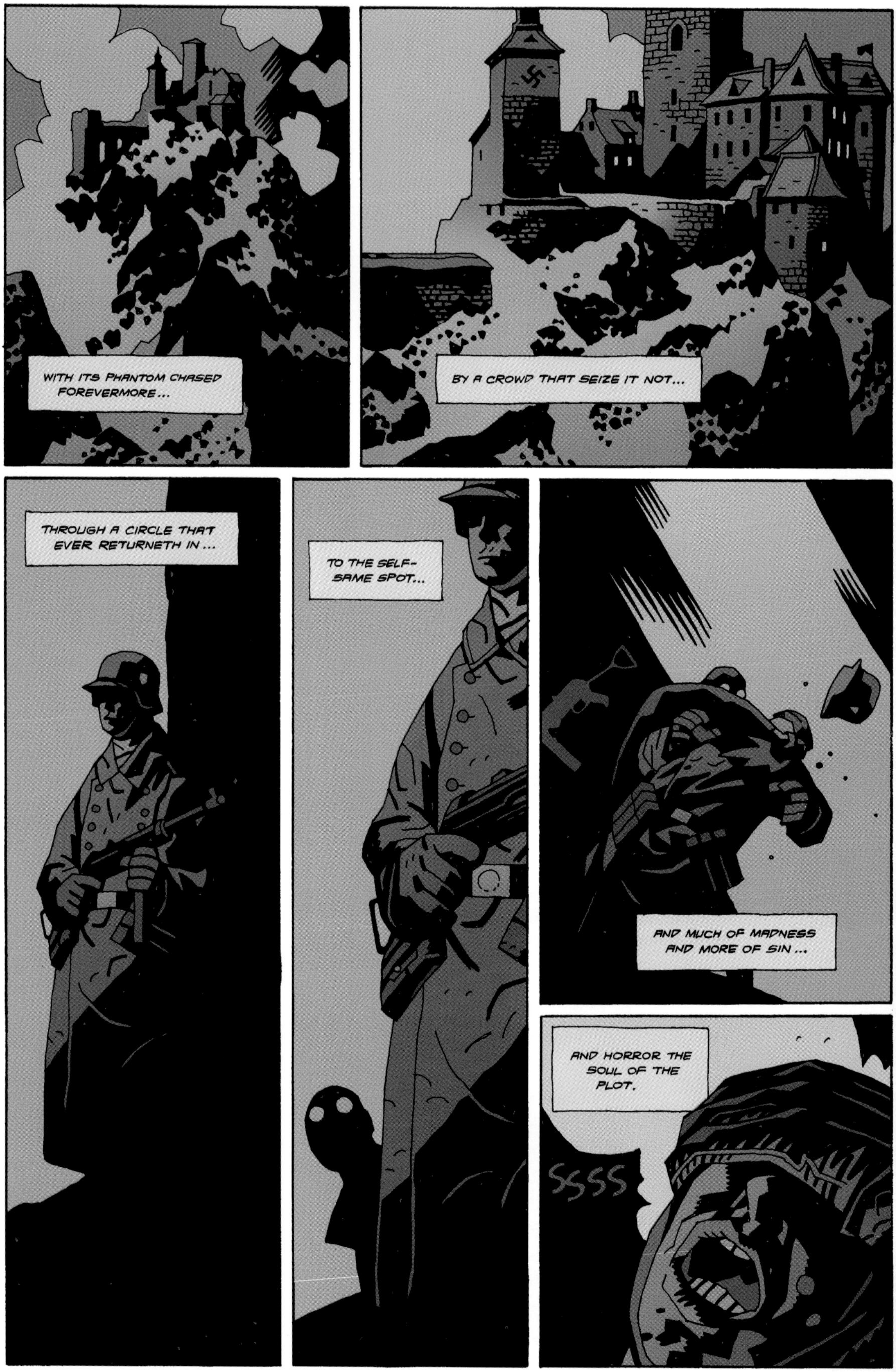
WITH ITS PHANTOM CHASED FOREVERMORE...
BY A CROWD THAT SEIZE IT NOT...
THROUGH A CIRCLE THAT EVER RETURNETH IN...
TO THE SELF-SAME SPOT...
AND MUCH OF MADNESS AND MORE OF SIN...
AND HORROR THE SOUL OF THE PLOT.
SSSS

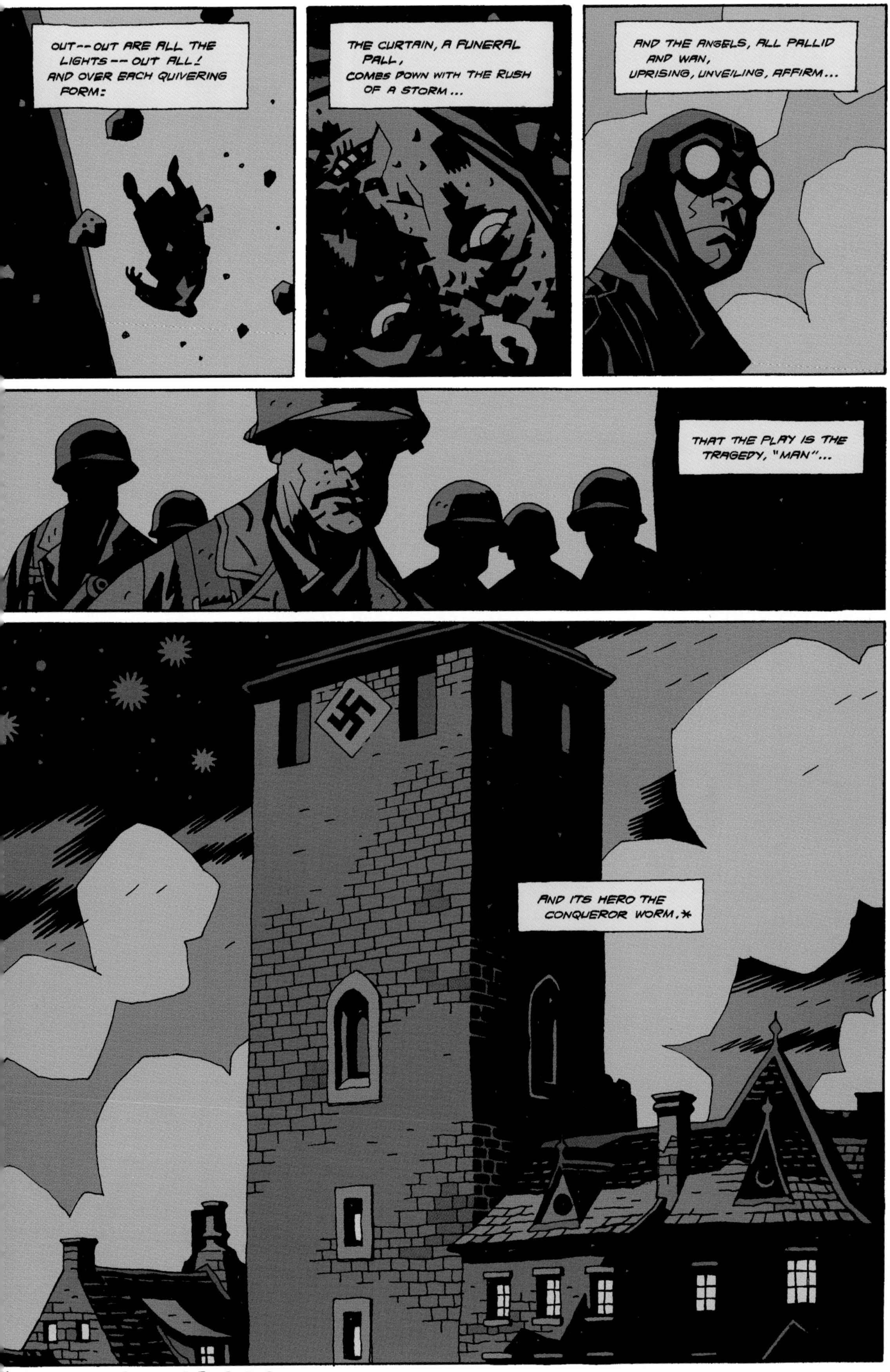
OUT--OUT ARE ALL THE LIGHTS--OUT ALL! AND OVER EACH QUIVERING FORM:
THE CURTAIN, A FUNERAL PALL, COMES DOWN WITH THE RUSH OF A STORM...
AND THE ANGELS, ALL PALLID AND WAN, UPRISING, UNVEILING, AFFIRM...
THAT THE PLAY IS THE TRAGEDY, "MAN"...
AND ITS HERO THE CONQUEROR WORM.*

* FROM "LIGEIA" BY EDGAR ALLAN POE

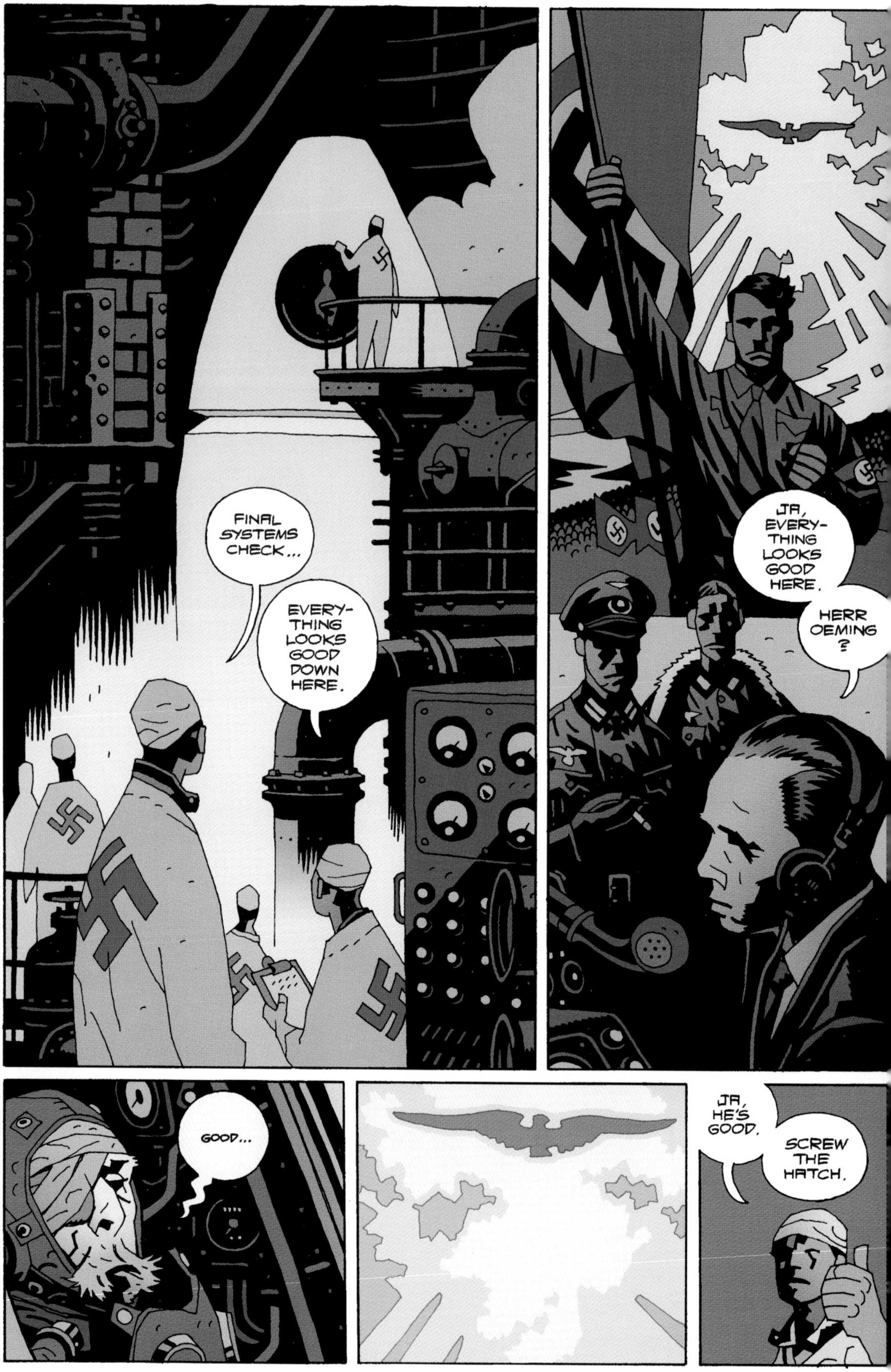
FINAL SYSTEMS CHECK...
EVERY-THING LOOKS GOOD DOWN HERE.
JA, EVERY-THING LOOKS GOOD HERE.
HERR OEMING?
GOOD...
JA, HE'S GOOD.
SCREW THE HATCH.

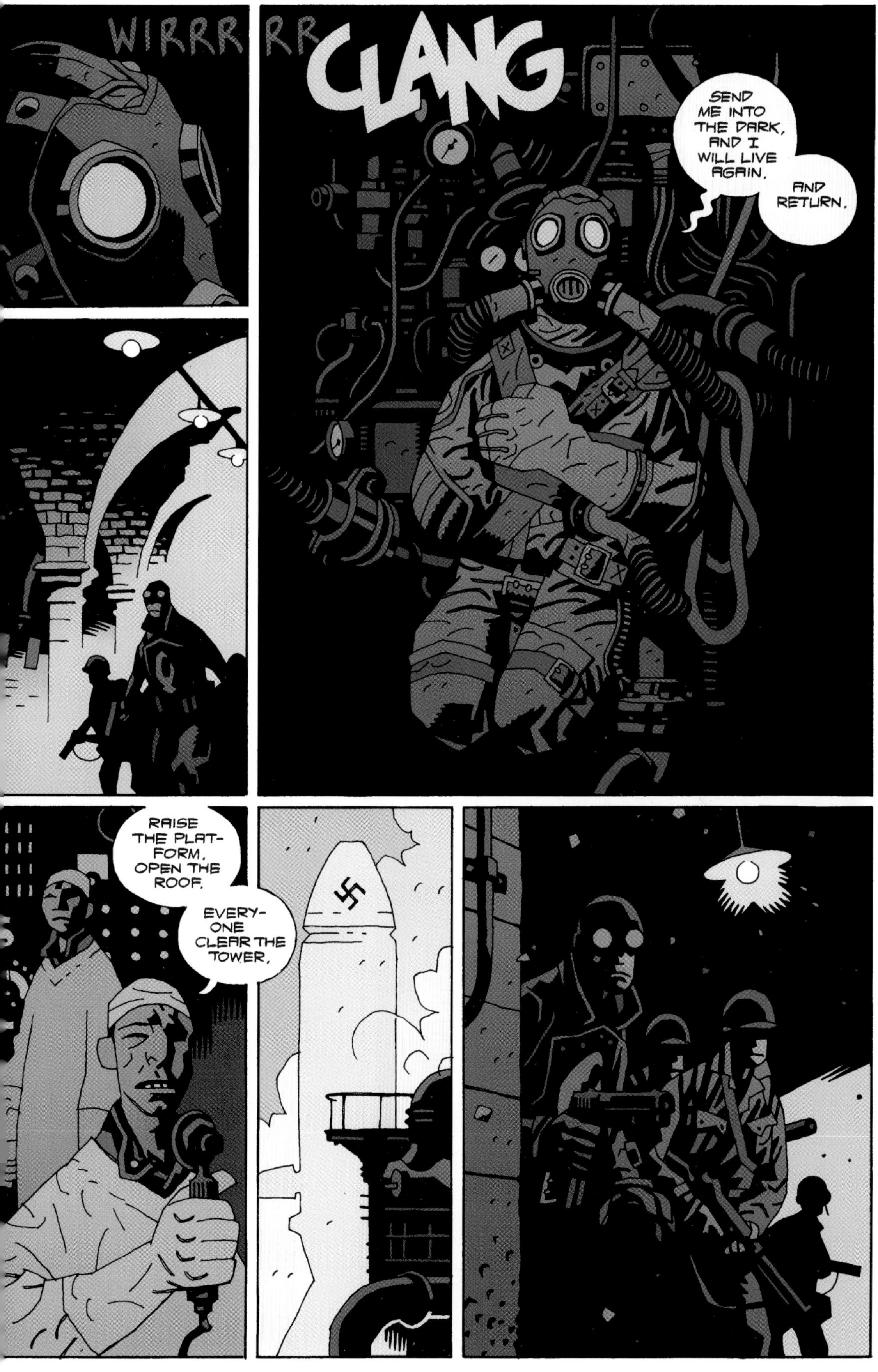
WIRRRRRR
CLANG
SEND ME INTO THE DARK, AND I WILL LIVE AGAIN.
AND RETURN.
RAISE THE PLATFORM. OPEN THE ROOF.
EVERYONE CLEAR THE TOWER.

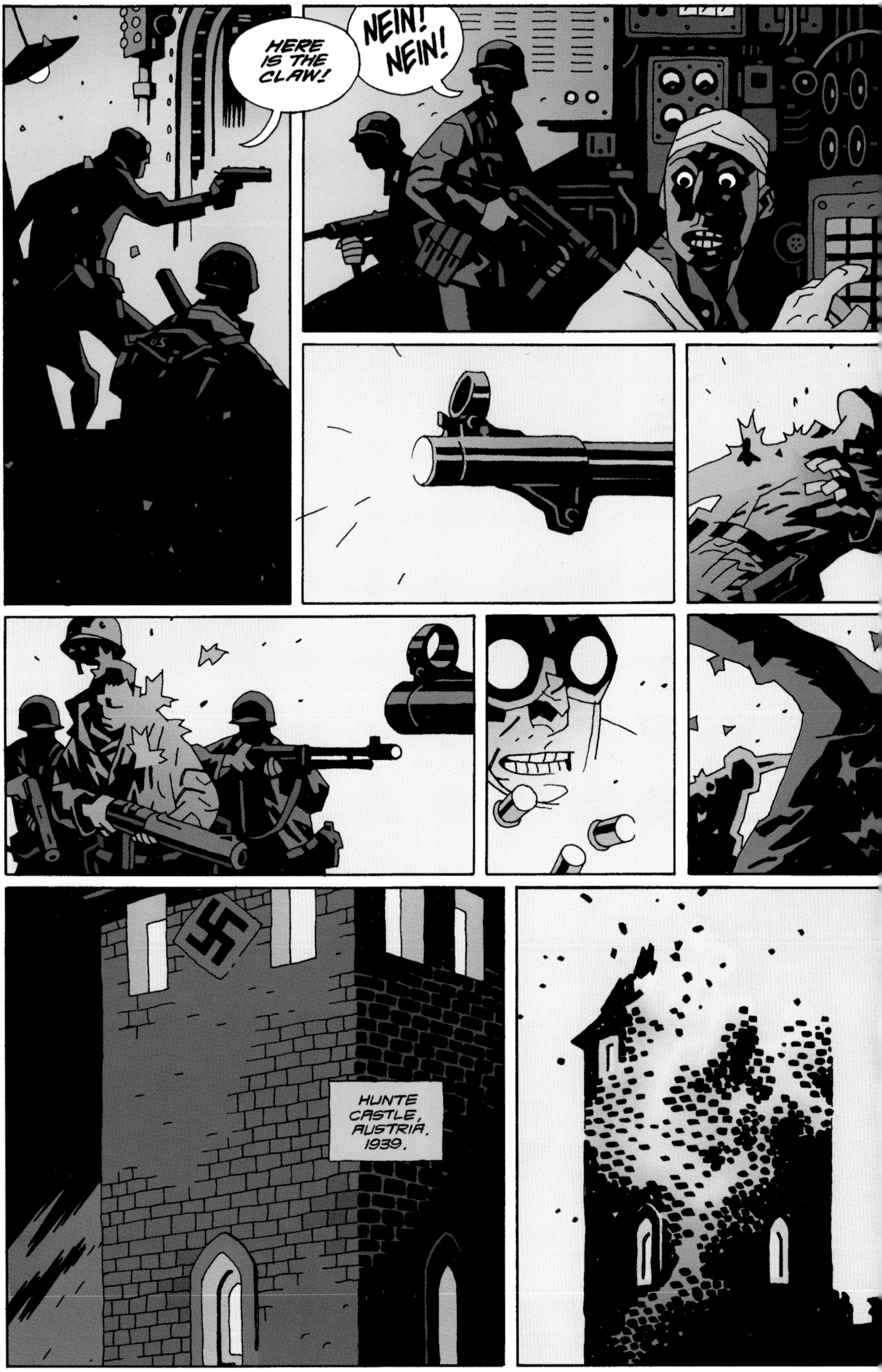
HERE IS THE CLAW!
NEIN! NEIN!
HUNTE CASTLE, AUSTRIA. 1939.

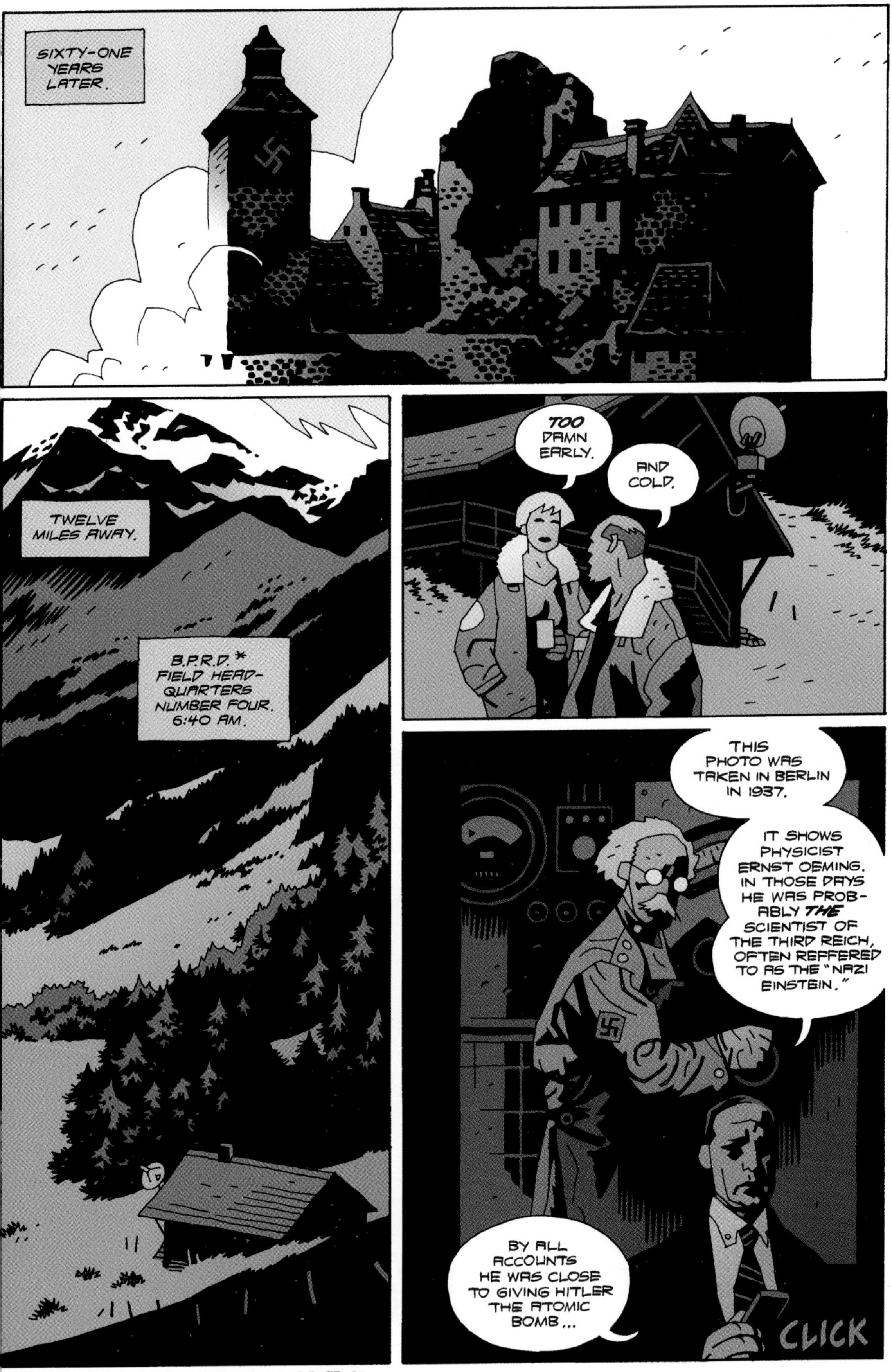
SIXTY-ONE YEARS LATER.
TWELVE MILES AWAY.
B.P.R.D.* FIELD HEAD-QUARTERS NUMBER FOUR. 6:40 AM.
TOO DAMN EARLY.
AND COLD.
THIS PHOTO WAS TAKEN IN BERLIN IN 1937.
IT SHOWS PHYSICIST ERNST OEMING. IN THOSE DAYS HE WAS PROB-ABLY THE SCIENTIST OF THE THIRD REICH, OFTEN REFFERED TO AS THE "NAZI EINSTEIN."
BY ALL ACCOUNTS HE WAS CLOSE TO GIVING HITLER THE ATOMIC BOMB...
CLICK

* BUREAU FOR PARANORMAL RESEARCH AND DEFENSE

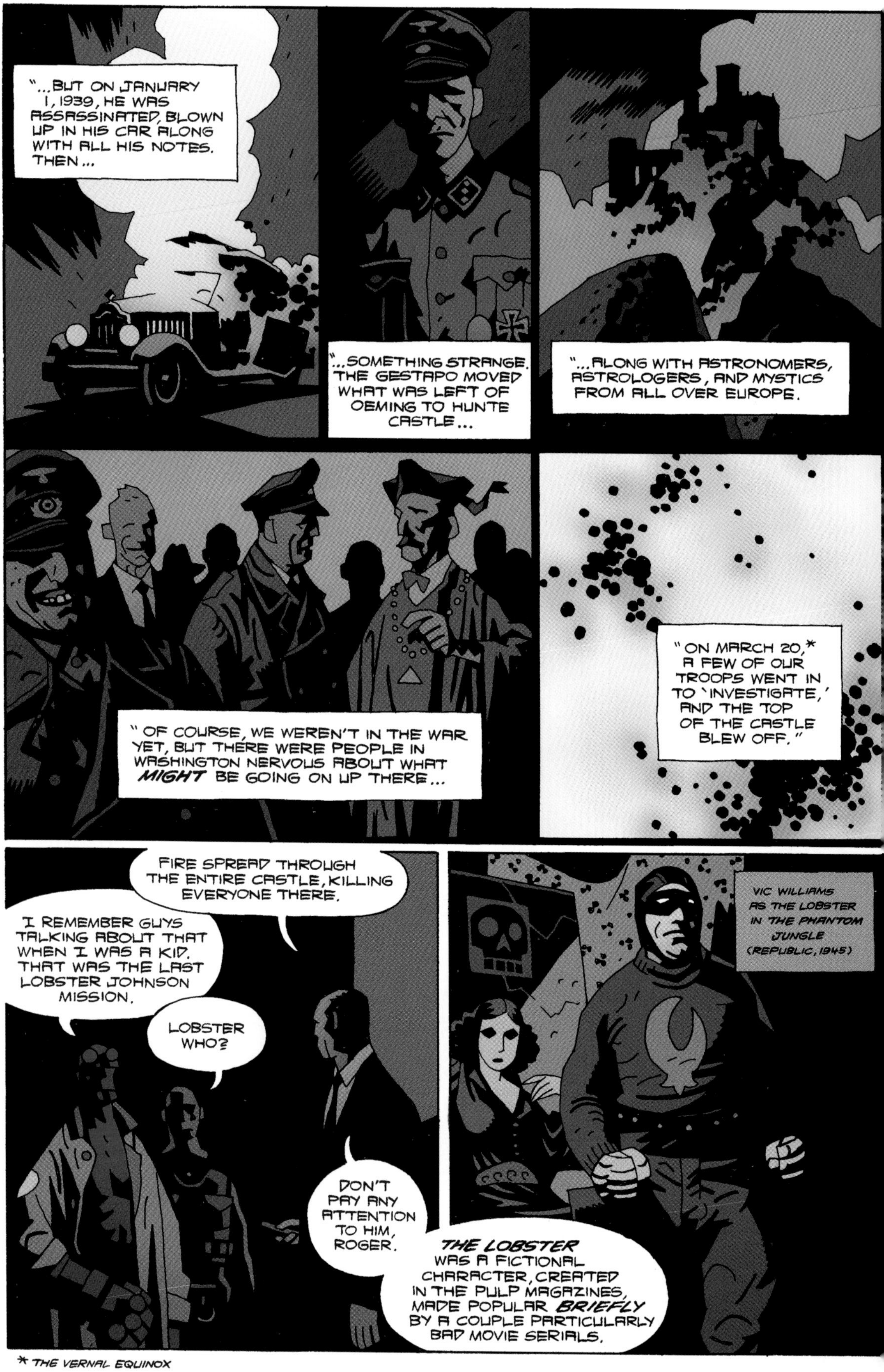
"...BUT ON JANUARY 1, 1939, HE WAS ASSASSINATED, BLOWN UP IN HIS CAR ALONG WITH ALL HIS NOTES. THEN...
"...SOMETHING STRANGE. THE GESTAPO MOVED WHAT WAS LEFT OF OEMING TO HUNTE CASTLE...
"...ALONG WITH ASTRONOMERS, ASTROLOGERS, AND MYSTICS FROM ALL OVER EUROPE.
"OF COURSE, WE WEREN'T IN THE WAR YET, BUT THERE WERE PEOPLE IN WASHINGTON NERVOUS ABOUT WHAT *MIGHT* BE GOING ON UP THERE...
"ON MARCH 20,* A FEW OF OUR TROOPS WENT IN TO 'INVESTIGATE,' AND THE TOP OF THE CASTLE BLEW OFF."
FIRE SPREAD THROUGH THE ENTIRE CASTLE, KILLING EVERYONE THERE.
I REMEMBER GUYS TALKING ABOUT THAT WHEN I WAS A KID. THAT WAS THE LAST LOBSTER JOHNSON MISSION.
LOBSTER WHO?
DON'T PAY ANY ATTENTION TO HIM, ROGER.
VIC WILLIAMS AS THE LOBSTER IN *THE PHANTOM JUNGLE* (REPUBLIC, 1945)
THE LOBSTER WAS A FICTIONAL CHARACTER, CREATED IN THE PULP MAGAZINES, MADE POPULAR *BRIEFLY* BY A COUPLE PARTICULARLY BAD MOVIE SERIALS.

* *THE VERNAL EQUINOX*

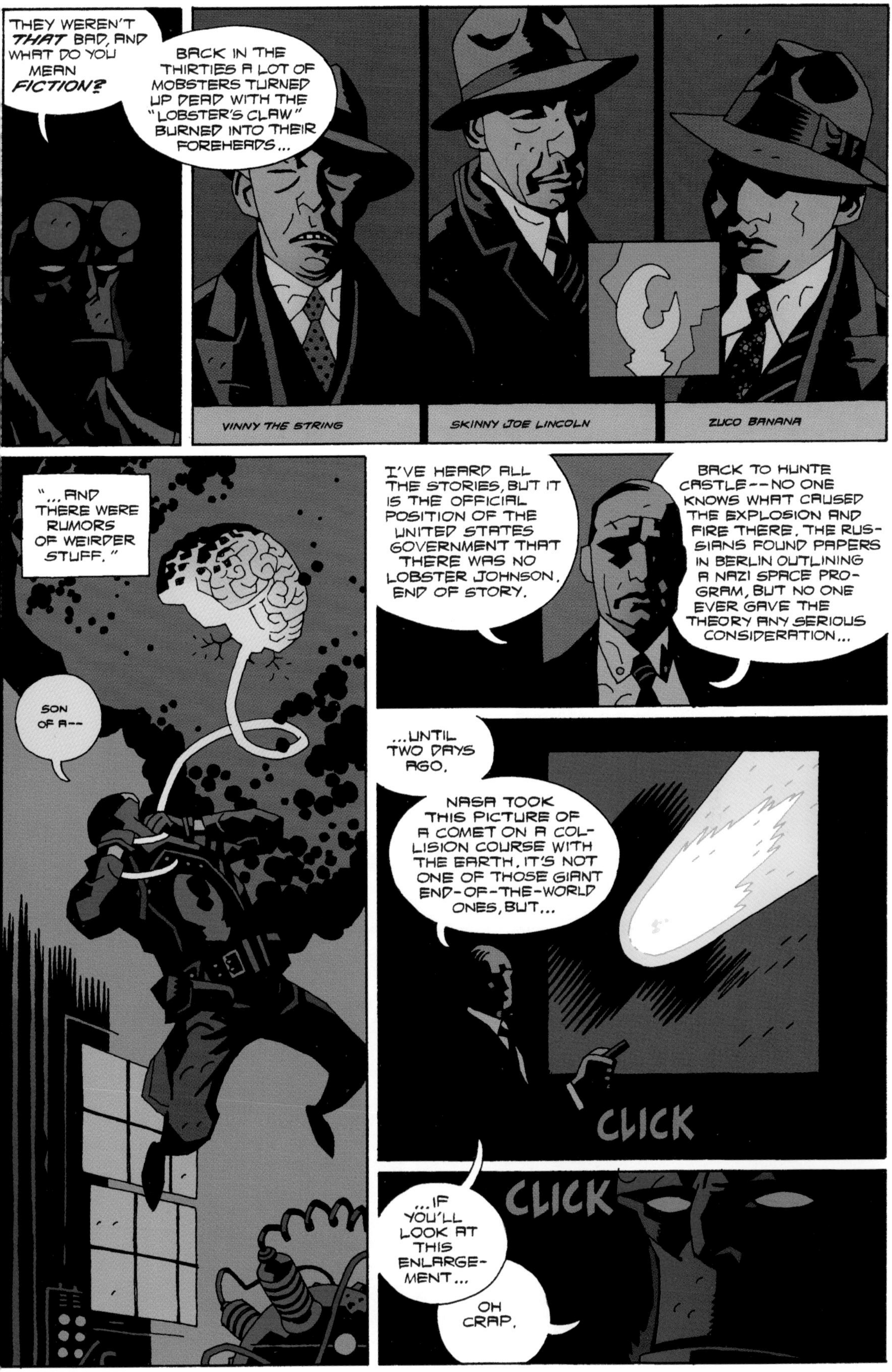
THEY WEREN'T *THAT* BAD, AND WHAT DO YOU MEAN *FICTION?*
BACK IN THE THIRTIES A LOT OF MOBSTERS TURNED UP DEAD WITH THE "LOBSTER'S CLAW" BURNED INTO THEIR FOREHEADS...
VINNY THE STRING
SKINNY JOE LINCOLN
ZUCO BANANA
"...AND THERE WERE RUMORS OF WEIRDER STUFF."
SON OF A--
I'VE HEARD ALL THE STORIES, BUT IT IS THE OFFICIAL POSITION OF THE UNITED STATES GOVERNMENT THAT THERE WAS NO LOBSTER JOHNSON. END OF STORY.
BACK TO HUNTE CASTLE--NO ONE KNOWS WHAT CAUSED THE EXPLOSION AND FIRE THERE. THE RUSSIANS FOUND PAPERS IN BERLIN OUTLINING A NAZI SPACE PROGRAM, BUT NO ONE EVER GAVE THE THEORY ANY SERIOUS CONSIDERATION...
...UNTIL TWO DAYS AGO.
NASA TOOK THIS PICTURE OF A COMET ON A COLLISION COURSE WITH THE EARTH. IT'S NOT ONE OF THOSE GIANT END-OF-THE-WORLD ONES, BUT...
CLICK
CLICK
...IF YOU'LL LOOK AT THIS ENLARGEMENT...
OH CRAP.

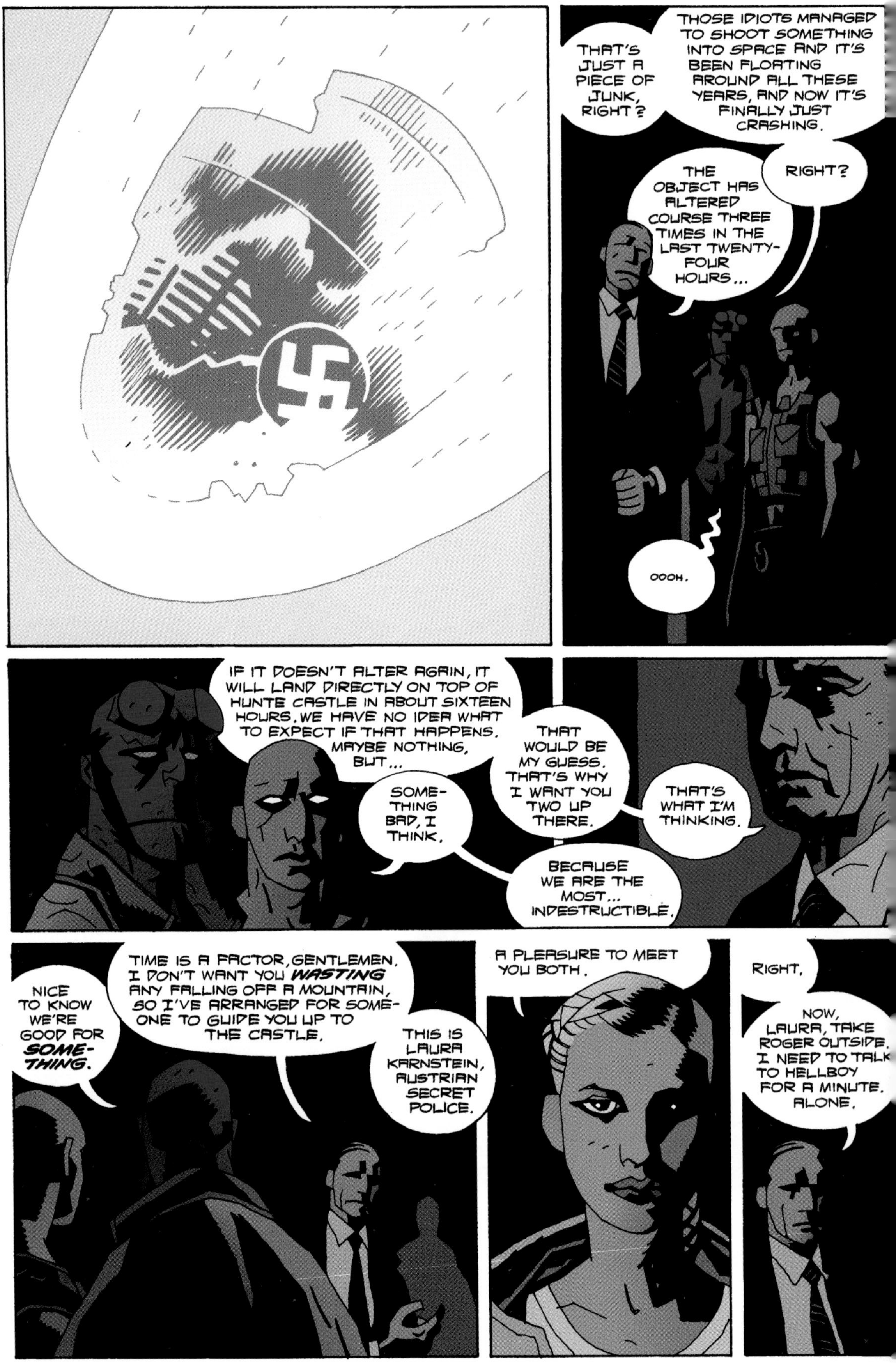
THAT'S JUST A PIECE OF JUNK, RIGHT?
THOSE IDIOTS MANAGED TO SHOOT SOMETHING INTO SPACE AND IT'S BEEN FLOATING AROUND ALL THESE YEARS, AND NOW IT'S FINALLY JUST CRASHING.
RIGHT?
THE OBJECT HAS ALTERED COURSE THREE TIMES IN THE LAST TWENTY-FOUR HOURS...
OOOH.
IF IT DOESN'T ALTER AGAIN, IT WILL LAND DIRECTLY ON TOP OF HUNTE CASTLE IN ABOUT SIXTEEN HOURS. WE HAVE NO IDEA WHAT TO EXPECT IF THAT HAPPENS. MAYBE NOTHING, BUT...
SOME-THING BAD, I THINK.
THAT WOULD BE MY GUESS. THAT'S WHY I WANT YOU TWO UP THERE.
BECAUSE WE ARE THE MOST... INDESTRUCTIBLE.
THAT'S WHAT I'M THINKING.
TIME IS A FACTOR, GENTLEMEN. I DON'T WANT YOU WASTING ANY FALLING OFF A MOUNTAIN, SO I'VE ARRANGED FOR SOME-ONE TO GUIDE YOU UP TO THE CASTLE.
NICE TO KNOW WE'RE GOOD FOR SOME-THING.
THIS IS LAURA KARNSTEIN, AUSTRIAN SECRET POLICE.
A PLEASURE TO MEET YOU BOTH.
RIGHT.
NOW, LAURA, TAKE ROGER OUTSIDE. I NEED TO TALK TO HELLBOY FOR A MINUTE. ALONE.

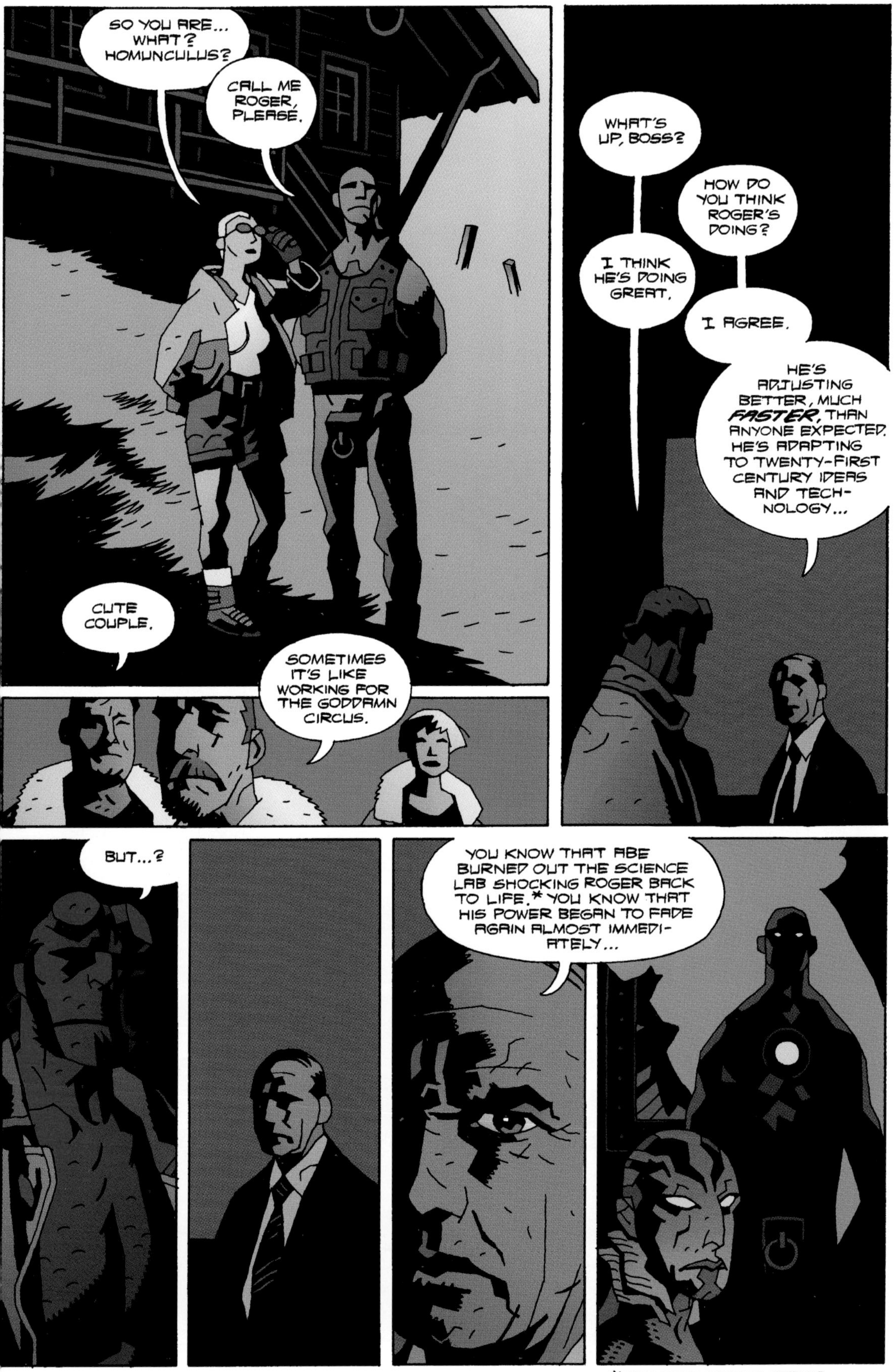
SO YOU ARE... WHAT? HOMUNCULUS?
CALL ME ROGER, PLEASE.
CUTE COUPLE.
SOMETIMES IT'S LIKE WORKING FOR THE GODDAMN CIRCUS.
WHAT'S UP, BOSS?
HOW DO YOU THINK ROGER'S DOING?
I THINK HE'S DOING GREAT.
I AGREE.
HE'S ADJUSTING BETTER, MUCH FASTER, THAN ANYONE EXPECTED. HE'S ADAPTING TO TWENTY-FIRST CENTURY IDEAS AND TECH-NOLOGY...
BUT...?
YOU KNOW THAT ABE BURNED OUT THE SCIENCE LAB SHOCKING ROGER BACK TO LIFE.* YOU KNOW THAT HIS POWER BEGAN TO FADE AGAIN ALMOST IMMEDI-ATELY...

*ABE SAPIEN VERSUS SCIENCE

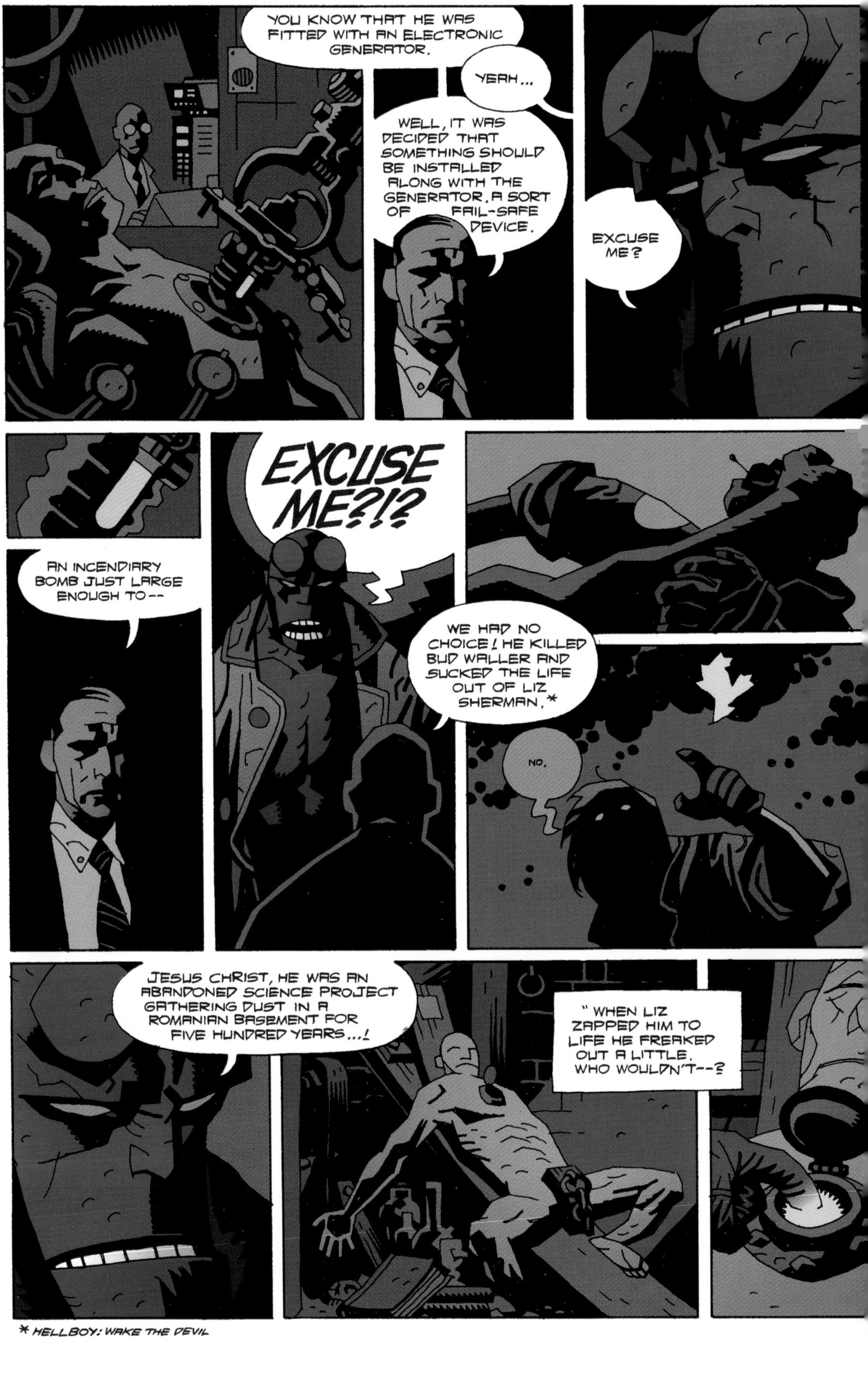
YOU KNOW THAT HE WAS FITTED WITH AN ELECTRONIC GENERATOR.
YEAH...
WELL, IT WAS DECIDED THAT SOMETHING SHOULD BE INSTALLED ALONG WITH THE GENERATOR. A SORT OF FAIL-SAFE DEVICE.
EXCUSE ME?
AN INCENDIARY BOMB JUST LARGE ENOUGH TO--
EXCUSE ME?!?
WE HAD NO CHOICE! HE KILLED BUD WALLER AND SUCKED THE LIFE OUT OF LIZ SHERMAN.*
NO.
JESUS CHRIST, HE WAS AN ABANDONED SCIENCE PROJECT GATHERING DUST IN A ROMANIAN BASEMENT FOR FIVE HUNDRED YEARS...!
"WHEN LIZ ZAPPED HIM TO LIFE HE FREAKED OUT A LITTLE. WHO WOULDN'T--?

* HELLBOY: WAKE THE DEVIL

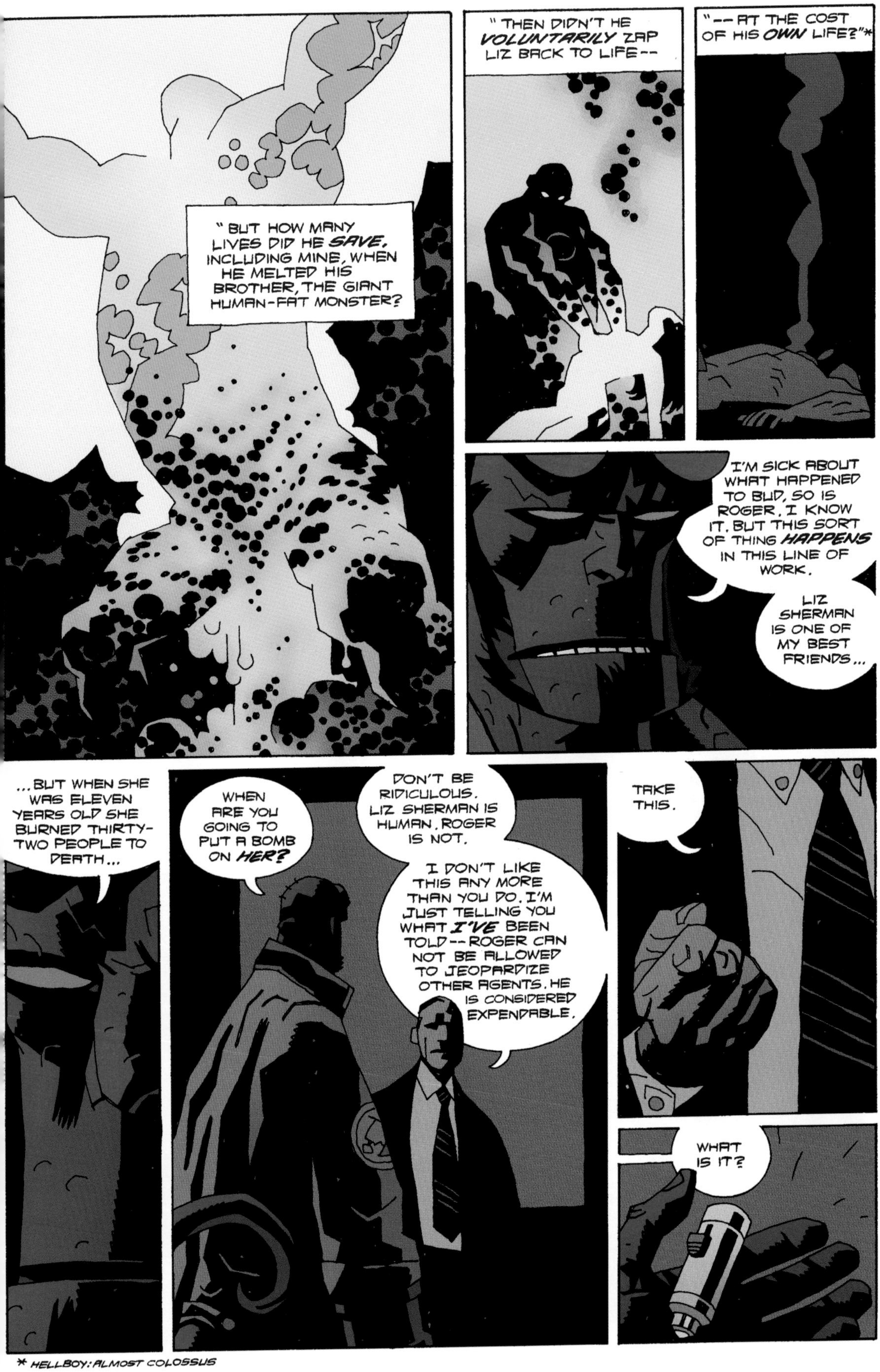
"BUT HOW MANY LIVES DID HE SAVE, INCLUDING MINE, WHEN HE MELTED HIS BROTHER, THE GIANT HUMAN-FAT MONSTER?
"THEN DIDN'T HE VOLUNTARILY ZAP LIZ BACK TO LIFE--
"--AT THE COST OF HIS OWN LIFE?"*
I'M SICK ABOUT WHAT HAPPENED TO BUD, SO IS ROGER. I KNOW IT. BUT THIS SORT OF THING HAPPENS IN THIS LINE OF WORK.
LIZ SHERMAN IS ONE OF MY BEST FRIENDS...
...BUT WHEN SHE WAS ELEVEN YEARS OLD SHE BURNED THIRTY-TWO PEOPLE TO DEATH...
WHEN ARE YOU GOING TO PUT A BOMB ON HER?
DON'T BE RIDICULOUS. LIZ SHERMAN IS HUMAN. ROGER IS NOT.
I DON'T LIKE THIS ANY MORE THAN YOU DO. I'M JUST TELLING YOU WHAT I'VE BEEN TOLD--ROGER CAN NOT BE ALLOWED TO JEOPARDIZE OTHER AGENTS. HE IS CONSIDERED EXPENDABLE.
TAKE THIS.
WHAT IS IT?

* HELLBOY: ALMOST COLOSSUS

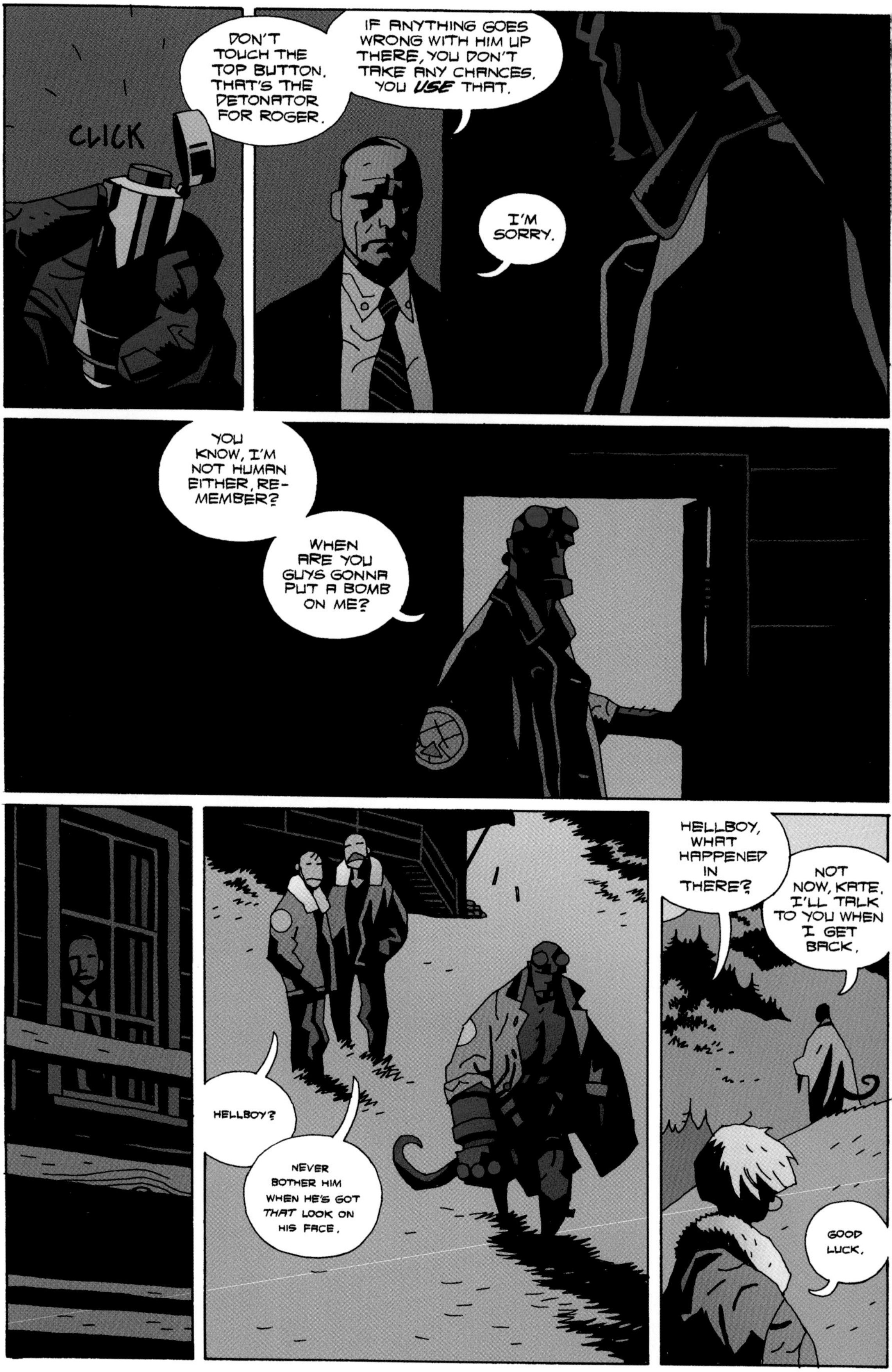
CLICK
DON'T TOUCH THE TOP BUTTON. THAT'S THE DETONATOR FOR ROGER.
IF ANYTHING GOES WRONG WITH HIM UP THERE, YOU DON'T TAKE ANY CHANCES. YOU USE THAT.
I'M SORRY.
YOU KNOW, I'M NOT HUMAN EITHER, RE-MEMBER?
WHEN ARE YOU GUYS GONNA PUT A BOMB ON ME?
HELLBOY?
NEVER BOTHER HIM WHEN HE'S GOT THAT LOOK ON HIS FACE.
HELLBOY, WHAT HAPPENED IN THERE?
NOT NOW, KATE. I'LL TALK TO YOU WHEN I GET BACK.
GOOD LUCK.

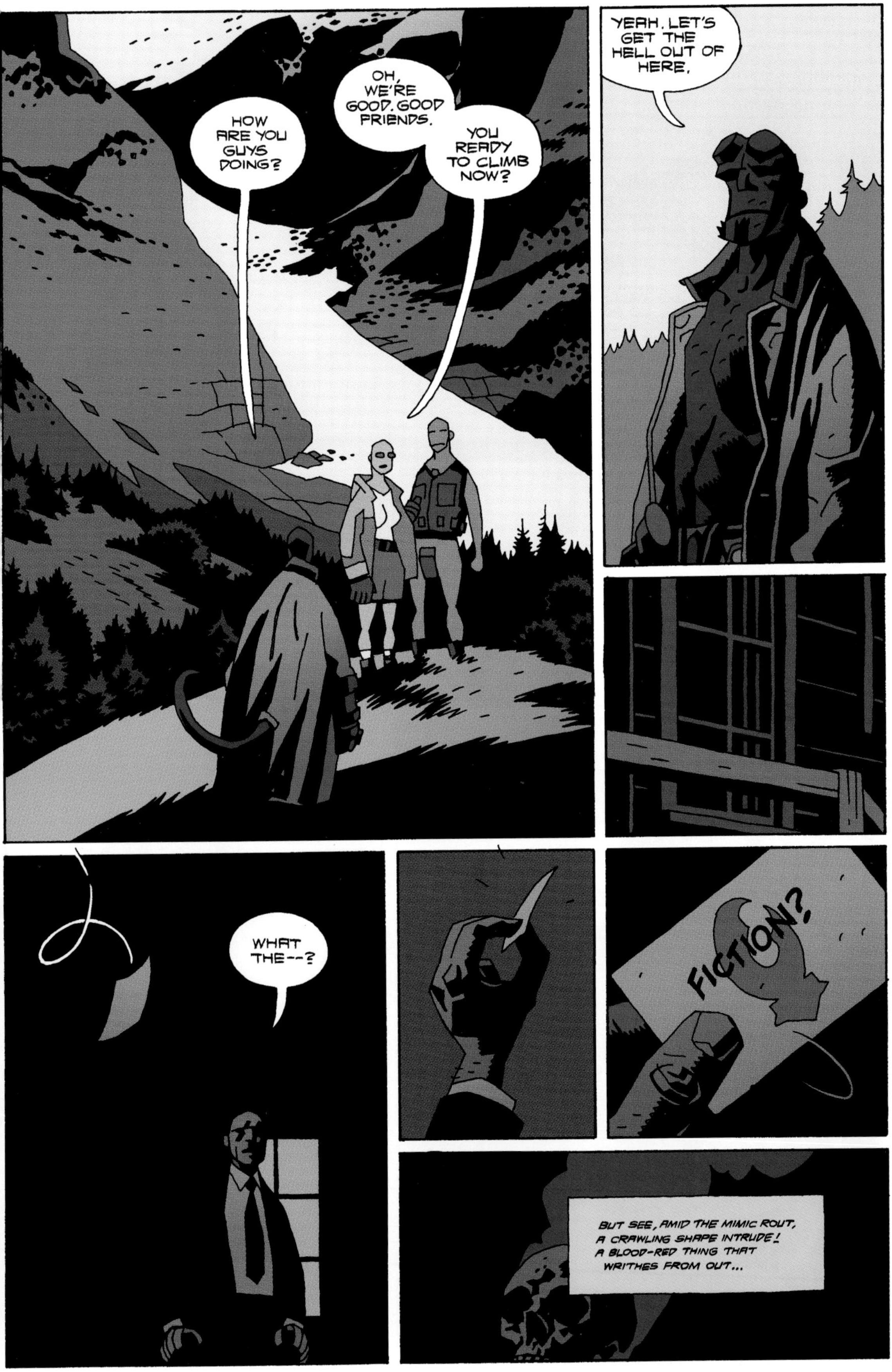
HOW ARE YOU GUYS DOING?
OH, WE'RE GOOD. GOOD FRIENDS.
YOU READY TO CLIMB NOW?
YEAH. LET'S GET THE HELL OUT OF HERE.
WHAT THE--?
FICTION?
BUT SEE, AMID THE MIMIC ROUT, A CRAWLING SHAPE INTRUDE! A BLOOD-RED THING THAT WRITHES FROM OUT...

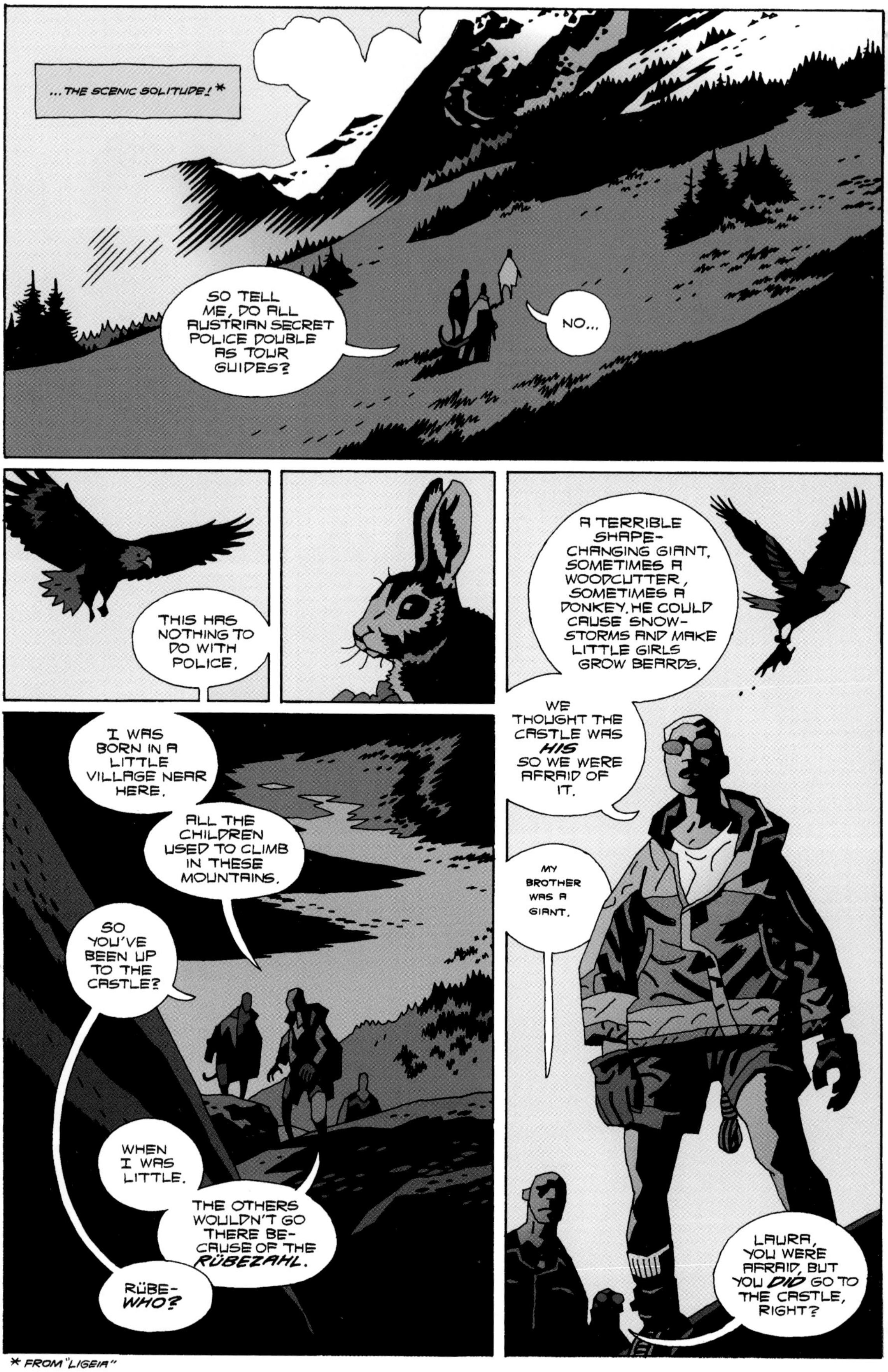
...THE SCENIC SOLITUDE! *
SO TELL ME, DO ALL AUSTRIAN SECRET POLICE DOUBLE AS TOUR GUIDES?
NO...
THIS HAS NOTHING TO DO WITH POLICE.
A TERRIBLE SHAPE-CHANGING GIANT, SOMETIMES A WOODCUTTER, SOMETIMES A DONKEY. HE COULD CAUSE SNOW-STORMS AND MAKE LITTLE GIRLS GROW BEARDS.
I WAS BORN IN A LITTLE VILLAGE NEAR HERE.
ALL THE CHILDREN USED TO CLIMB IN THESE MOUNTAINS.
SO YOU'VE BEEN UP TO THE CASTLE?
WHEN I WAS LITTLE.
THE OTHERS WOULDN'T GO THERE BE-CAUSE OF THE RÜBEZAHL.
RÜBE-WHO?
WE THOUGHT THE CASTLE WAS HIS SO WE WERE AFRAID OF IT.
MY BROTHER WAS A GIANT.
LAURA, YOU WERE AFRAID, BUT YOU DID GO TO THE CASTLE, RIGHT?

* FROM "LIGEIA"

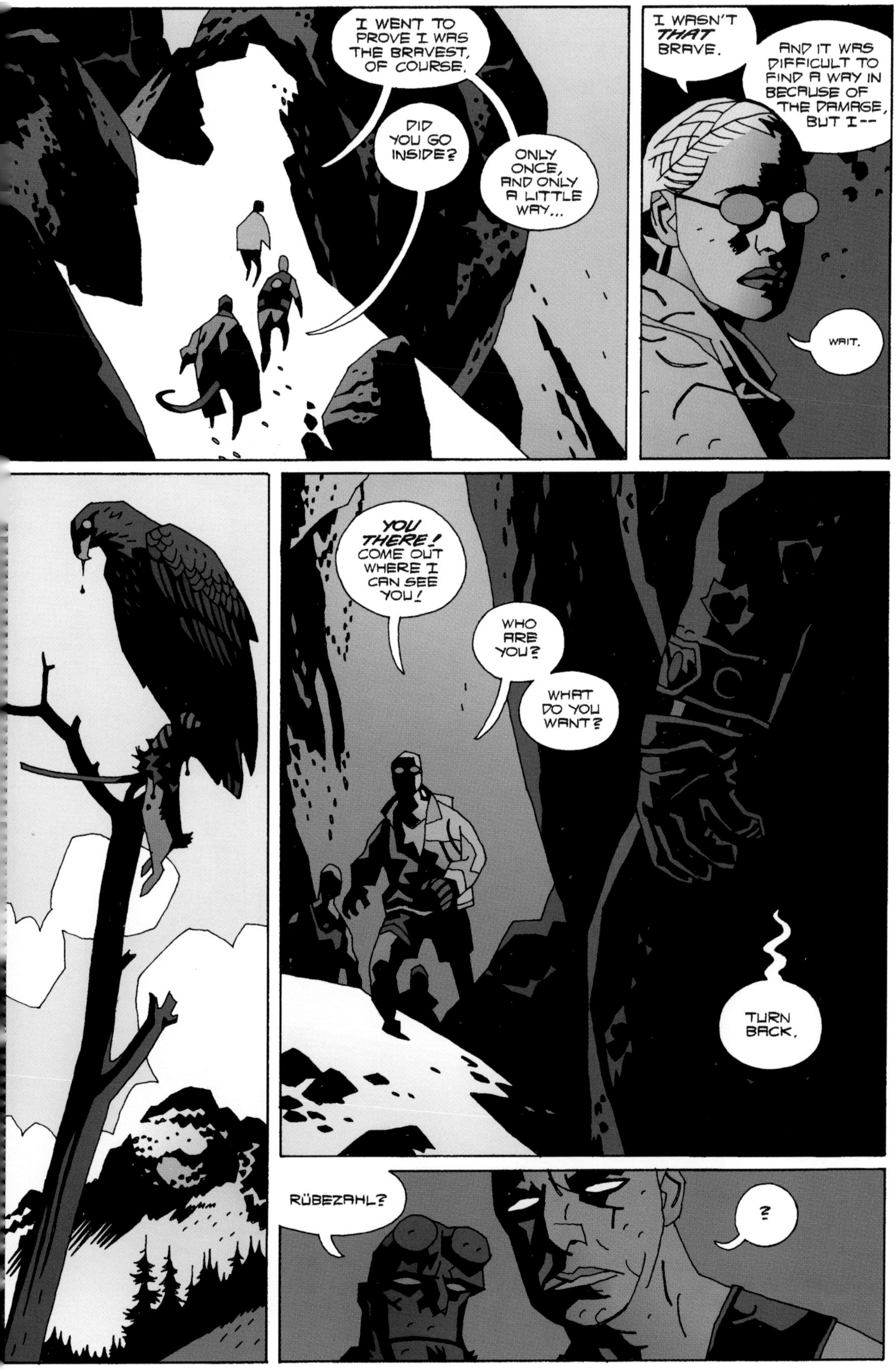

I WENT TO PROVE I WAS THE BRAVEST, OF COURSE.
DID YOU GO INSIDE?
ONLY ONCE, AND ONLY A LITTLE WAY...
I WASN'T THAT BRAVE.
AND IT WAS DIFFICULT TO FIND A WAY IN BECAUSE OF THE DAMAGE, BUT I--
WAIT.
YOU THERE! COME OUT WHERE I CAN SEE YOU!
WHO ARE YOU?
WHAT DO YOU WANT?
TURN BACK.
RÜBEZAHL?
?

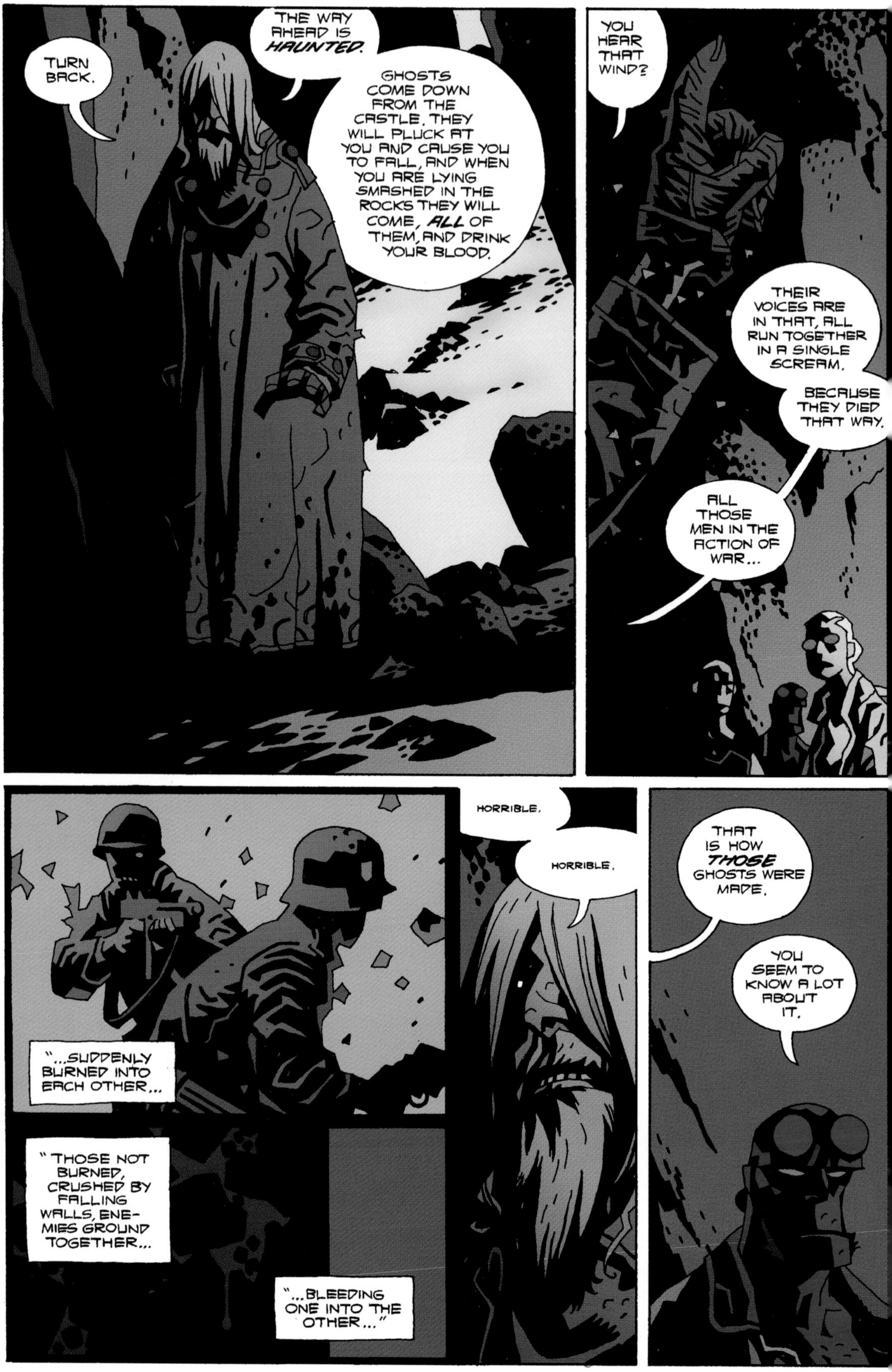
TURN BACK.
THE WAY AHEAD IS HAUNTED.
GHOSTS COME DOWN FROM THE CASTLE. THEY WILL PLUCK AT YOU AND CAUSE YOU TO FALL, AND WHEN YOU ARE LYING SMASHED IN THE ROCKS THEY WILL COME, ALL OF THEM, AND DRINK YOUR BLOOD.
YOU HEAR THAT WIND?
THEIR VOICES ARE IN THAT, ALL RUN TOGETHER IN A SINGLE SCREAM.
BECAUSE THEY DIED THAT WAY.
ALL THOSE MEN IN THE ACTION OF WAR...
"...SUDDENLY BURNED INTO EACH OTHER...
"THOSE NOT BURNED, CRUSHED BY FALLING WALLS, ENEMIES GROUND TOGETHER...
"...BLEEDING ONE INTO THE OTHER..."
HORRIBLE.
HORRIBLE.
THAT IS HOW THOSE GHOSTS WERE MADE.
YOU SEEM TO KNOW A LOT ABOUT IT.

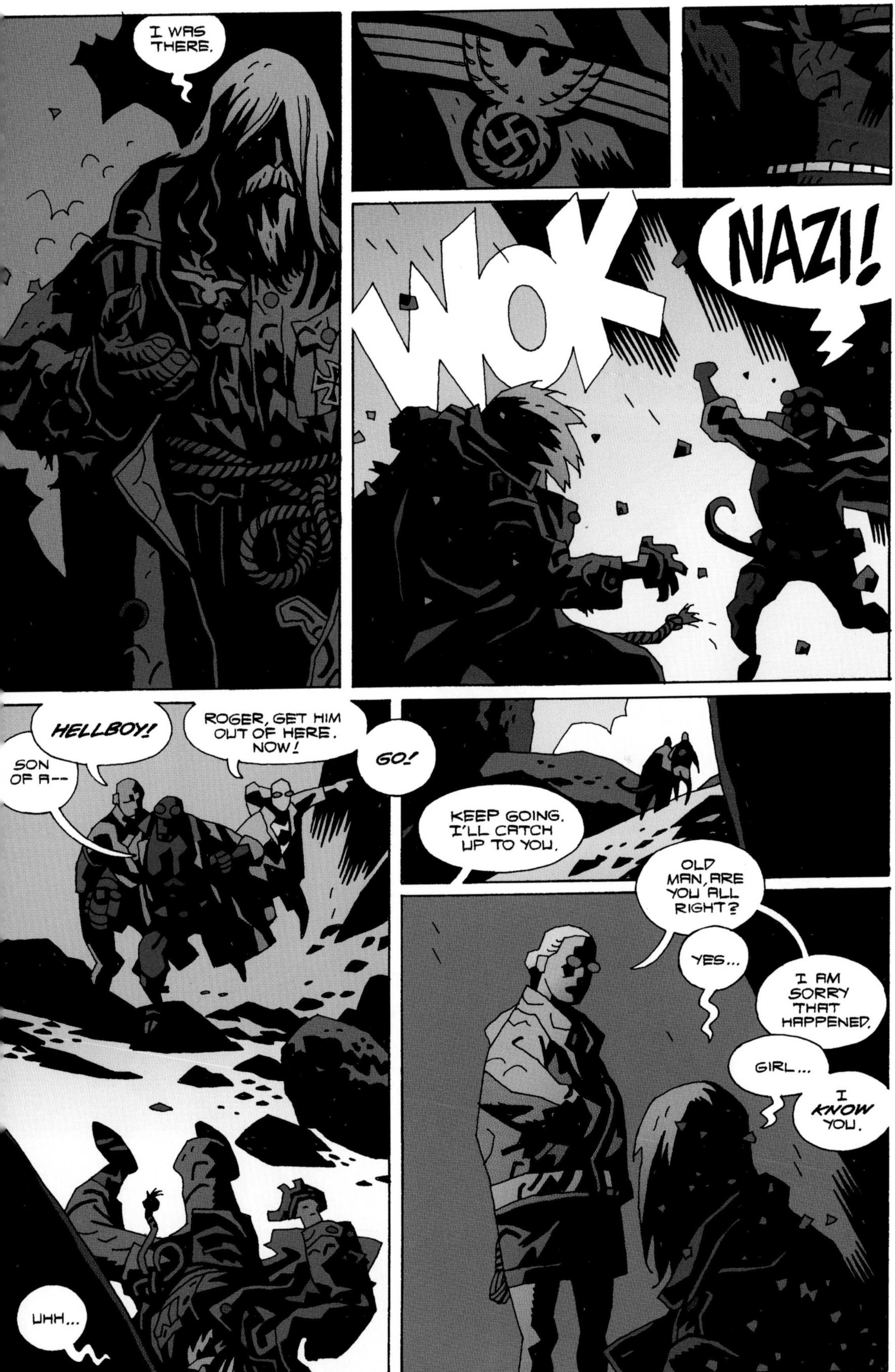
I WAS THERE.
WOK
NAZI!
HELLBOY!
SON OF A--
ROGER, GET HIM OUT OF HERE. NOW!
GO!
UHH...
KEEP GOING. I'LL CATCH UP TO YOU.
OLD MAN, ARE YOU ALL RIGHT?
YES...
I AM SORRY THAT HAPPENED.
GIRL...
I KNOW YOU.

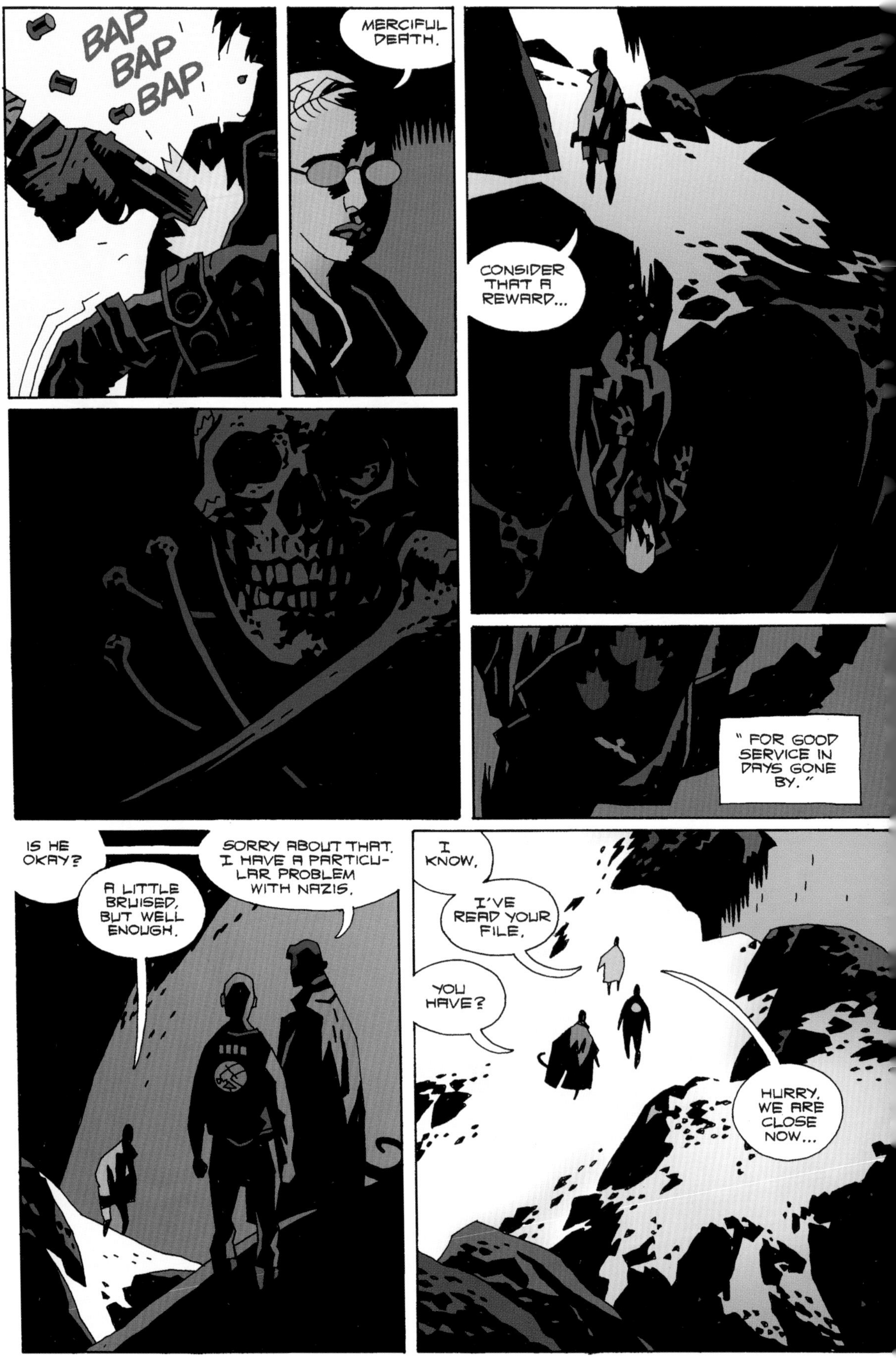
BAP
BAP
BAP
MERCIFUL DEATH.
CONSIDER THAT A REWARD...
" FOR GOOD SERVICE IN DAYS GONE BY. "
IS HE OKAY?
A LITTLE BRUISED, BUT WELL ENOUGH.
SORRY ABOUT THAT. I HAVE A PARTICU- LAR PROBLEM WITH NAZIS.
I KNOW.
I'VE READ YOUR FILE.
YOU HAVE?
HURRY, WE ARE CLOSE NOW...

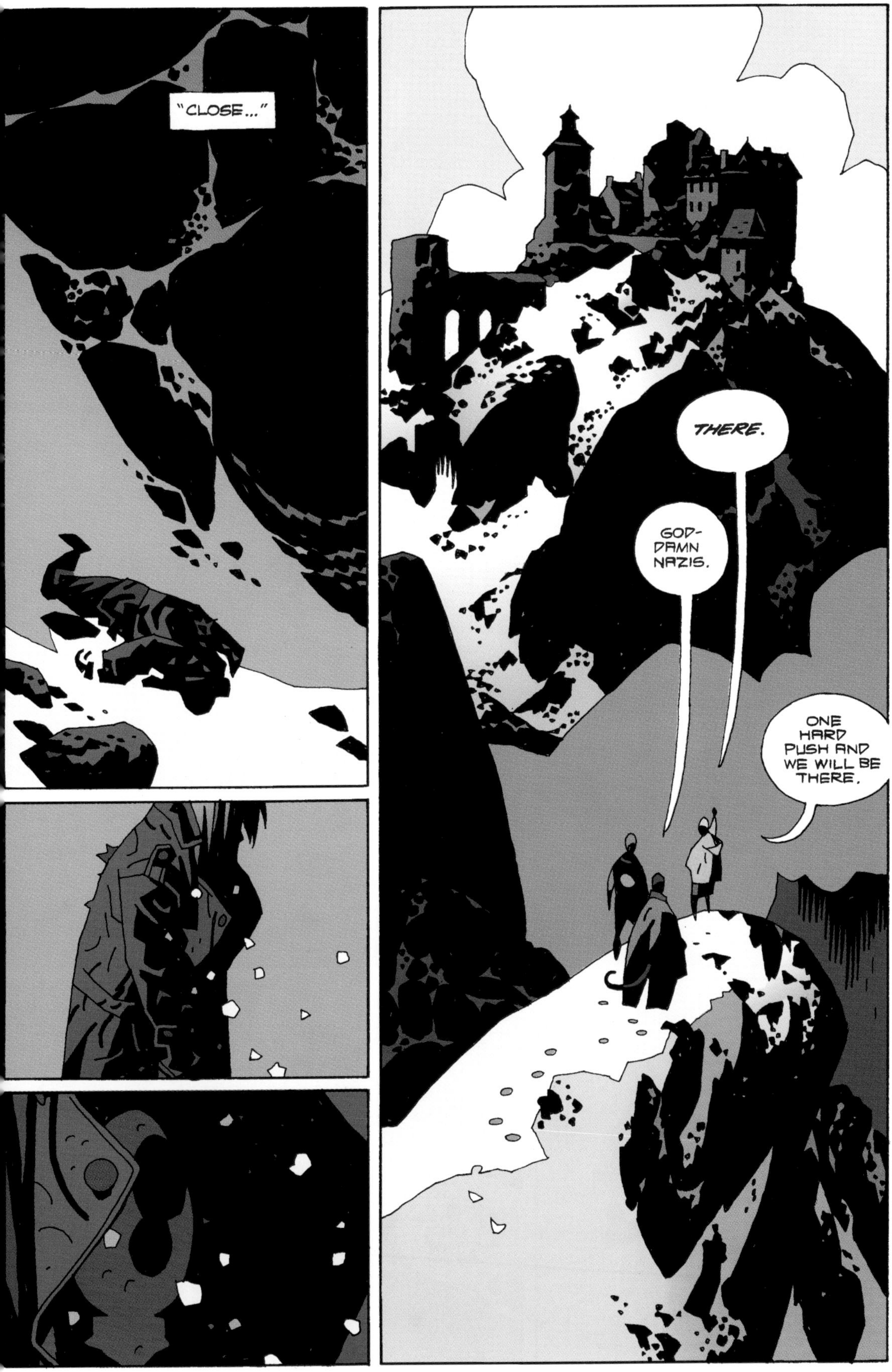
"CLOSE..."
THERE.
GOD-DAMN NAZIS.
ONE HARD PUSH AND WE WILL BE THERE.

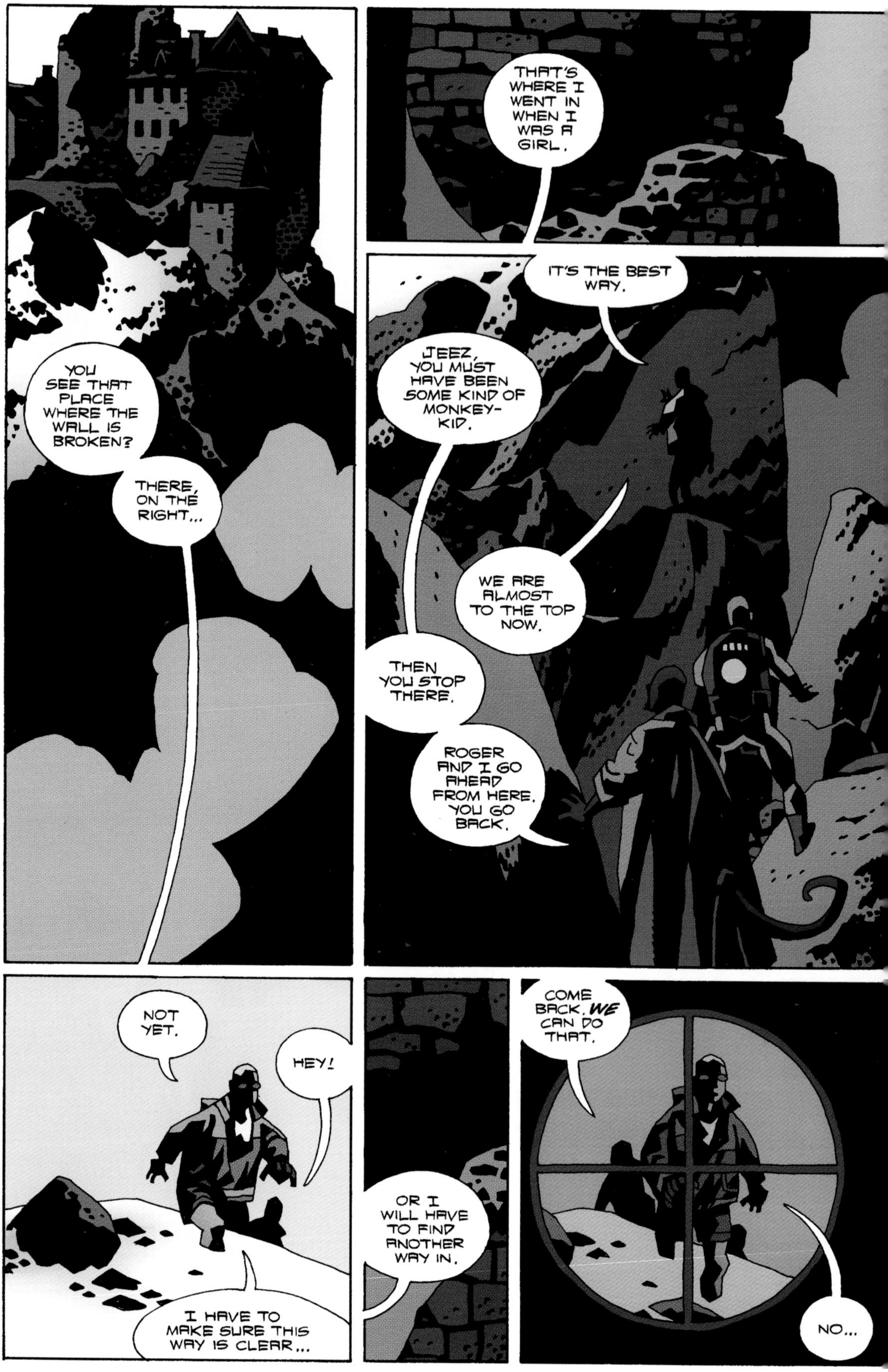
YOU SEE THAT PLACE WHERE THE WALL IS BROKEN?
THERE, ON THE RIGHT...
THAT'S WHERE I WENT IN WHEN I WAS A GIRL.
IT'S THE BEST WAY.
JEEZ, YOU MUST HAVE BEEN SOME KIND OF MONKEY-KID.
WE ARE ALMOST TO THE TOP NOW.
THEN YOU STOP THERE.
ROGER AND I GO AHEAD FROM HERE. YOU GO BACK.
NOT YET.
HEY!
I HAVE TO MAKE SURE THIS WAY IS CLEAR...
OR I WILL HAVE TO FIND ANOTHER WAY IN.
COME BACK. WE CAN DO THAT.
NO...

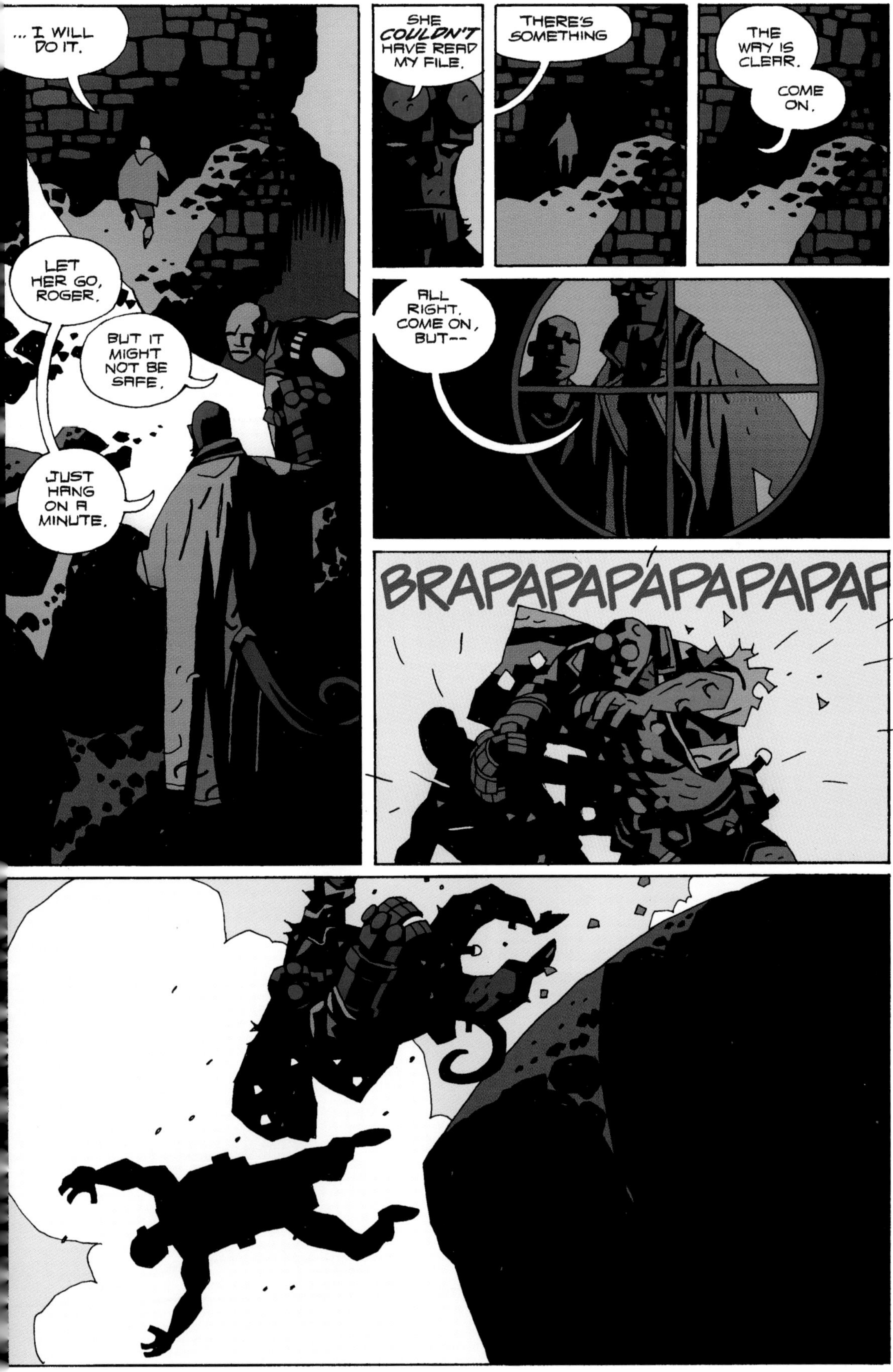
... I WILL DO IT.
LET HER GO, ROGER.
BUT IT MIGHT NOT BE SAFE.
JUST HANG ON A MINUTE.
SHE COULDN'T HAVE READ MY FILE.
THERE'S SOMETHING
THE WAY IS CLEAR.
COME ON.
ALL RIGHT. COME ON, BUT--
BRAPAPAPAPAPAPAPAP

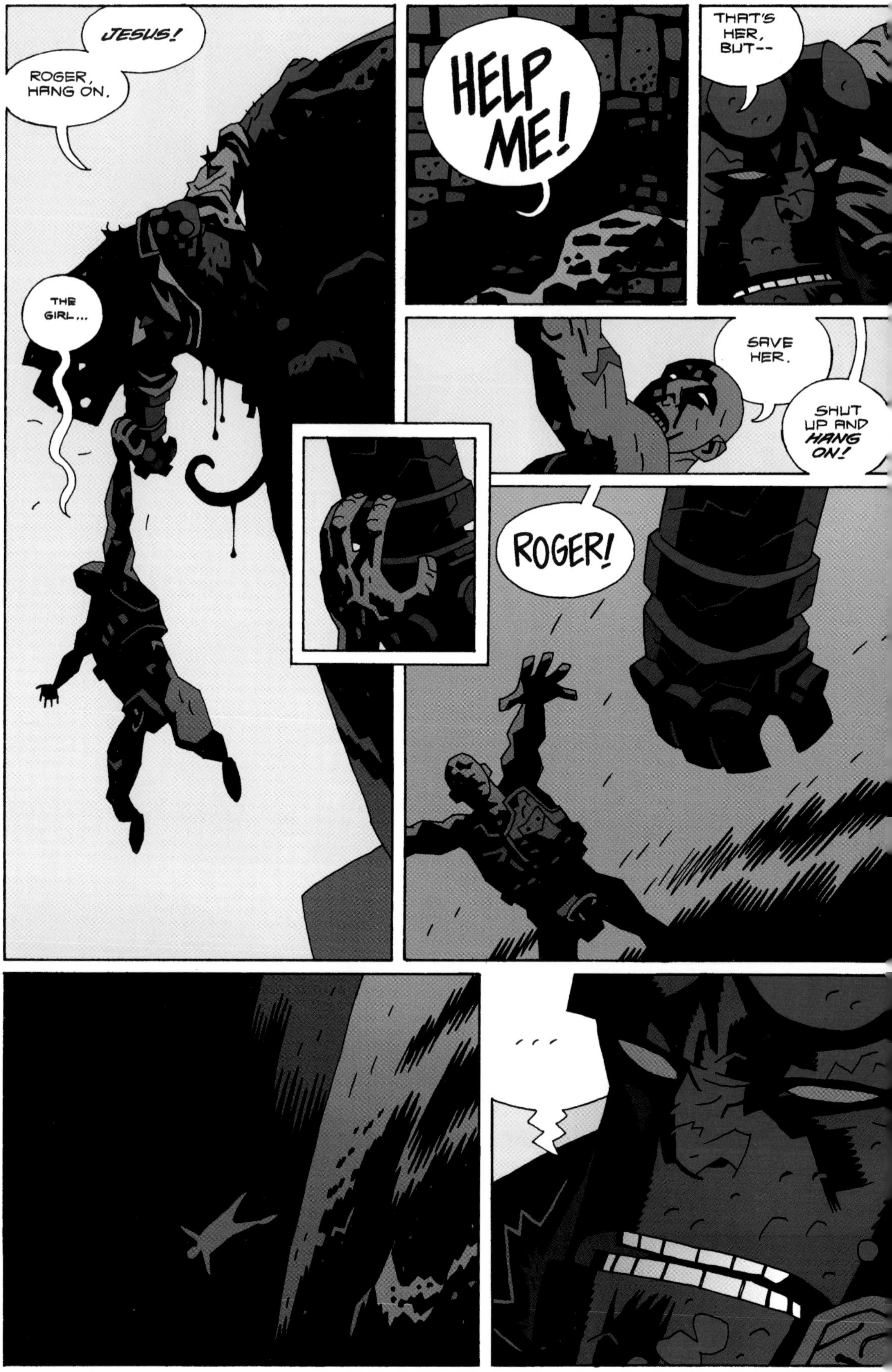
JESUS!
ROGER, HANG ON.
THE GIRL...
HELP ME!
THAT'S HER, BUT--
SAVE HER.
SHUT UP AND HANG ON!
ROGER!
...

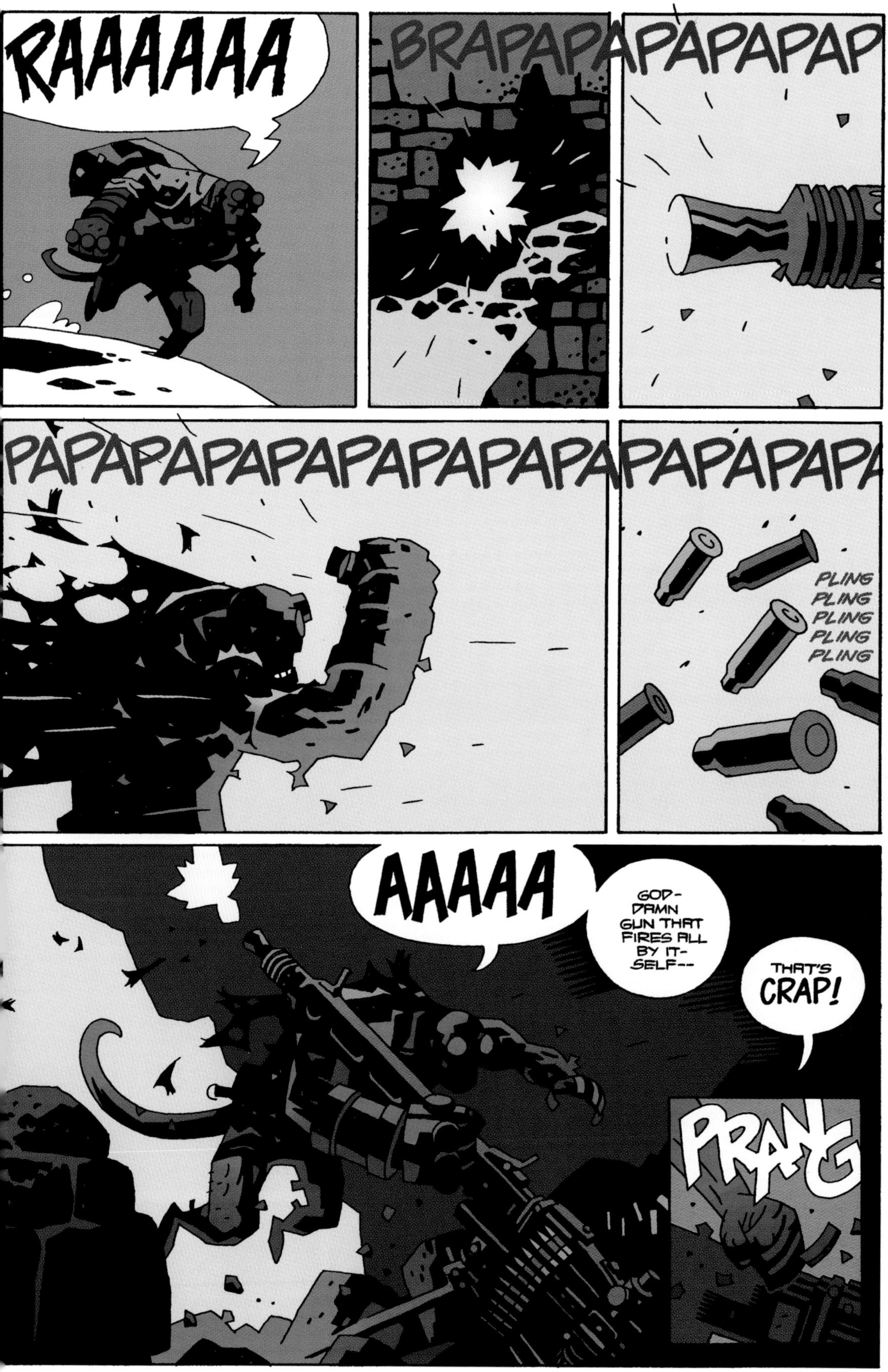
RAAAAAA
BRAPAPAPAPAPAPAP
PAPAPAPAPAPAPAPAPAPAPAPAPA
PLING
PLING
PLING
PLING
PLING
AAAAA
GOD-DAMN GUN THAT FIRES ALL BY IT-SELF--
THAT'S CRAP!
PRANG

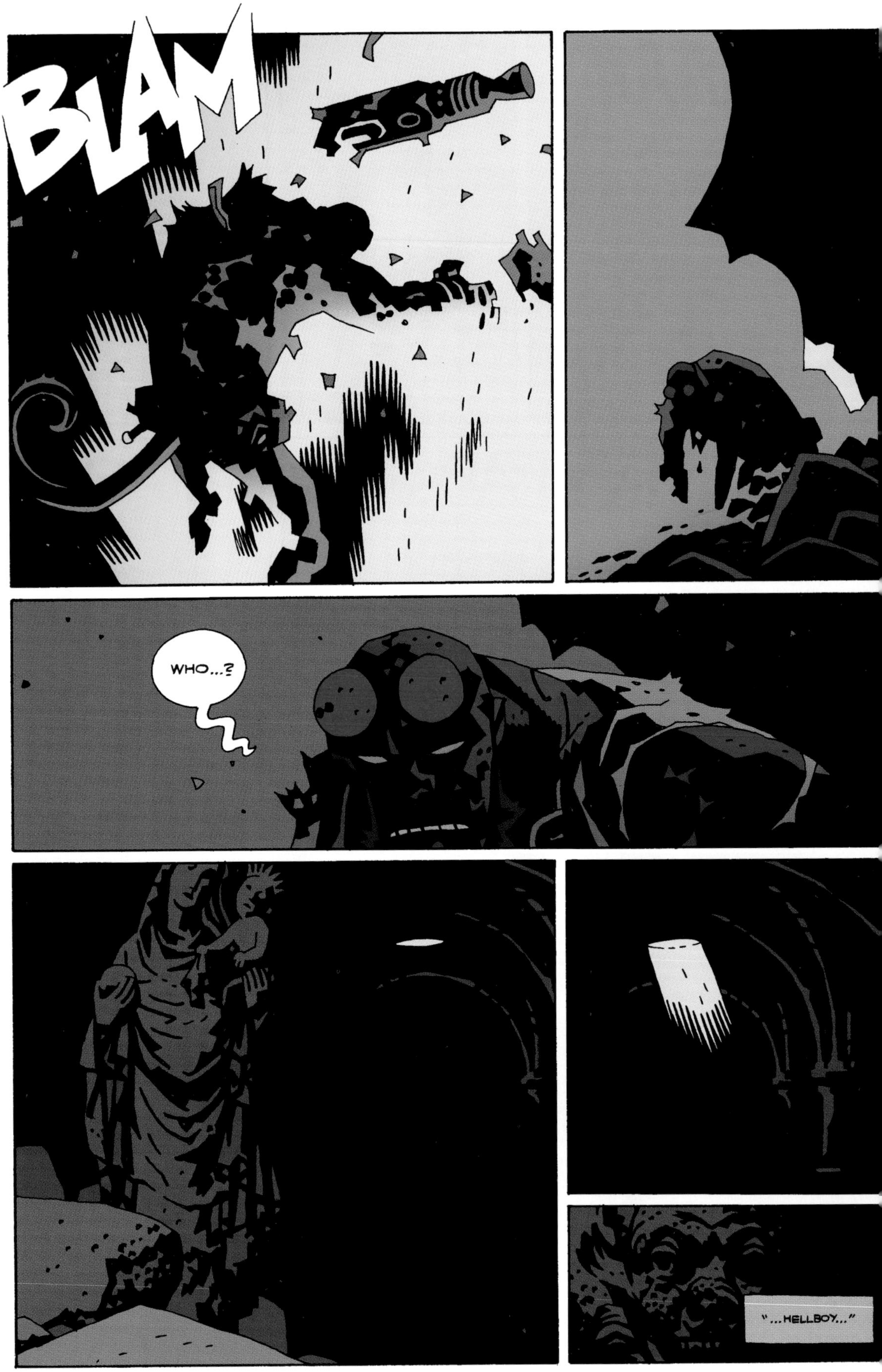
BLAM
WHO...?
"...HELLBOY..."

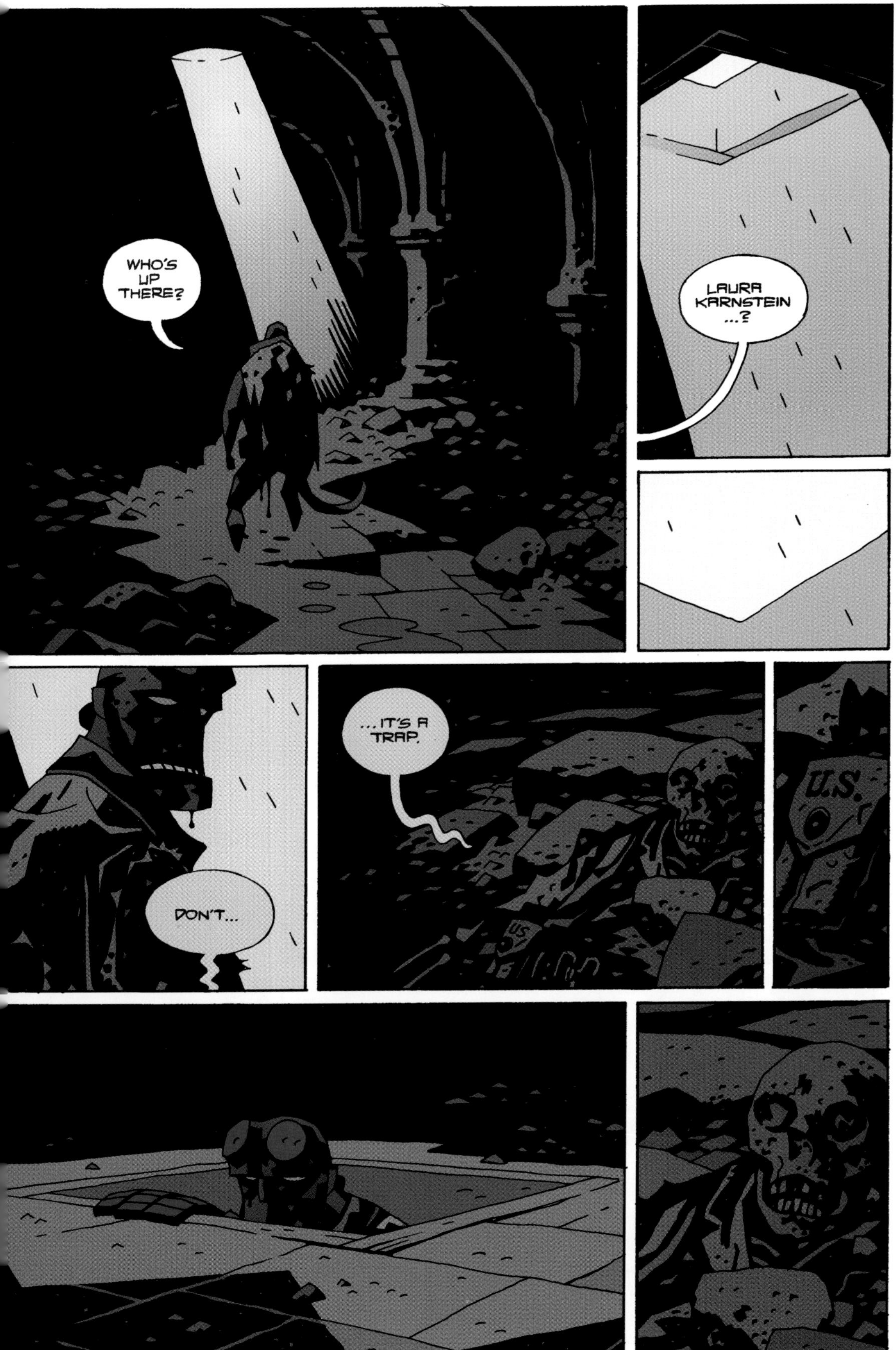
WHO'S UP THERE?
LAURA KARNSTEIN ...?
DON'T...
...IT'S A TRAP.
U.S.

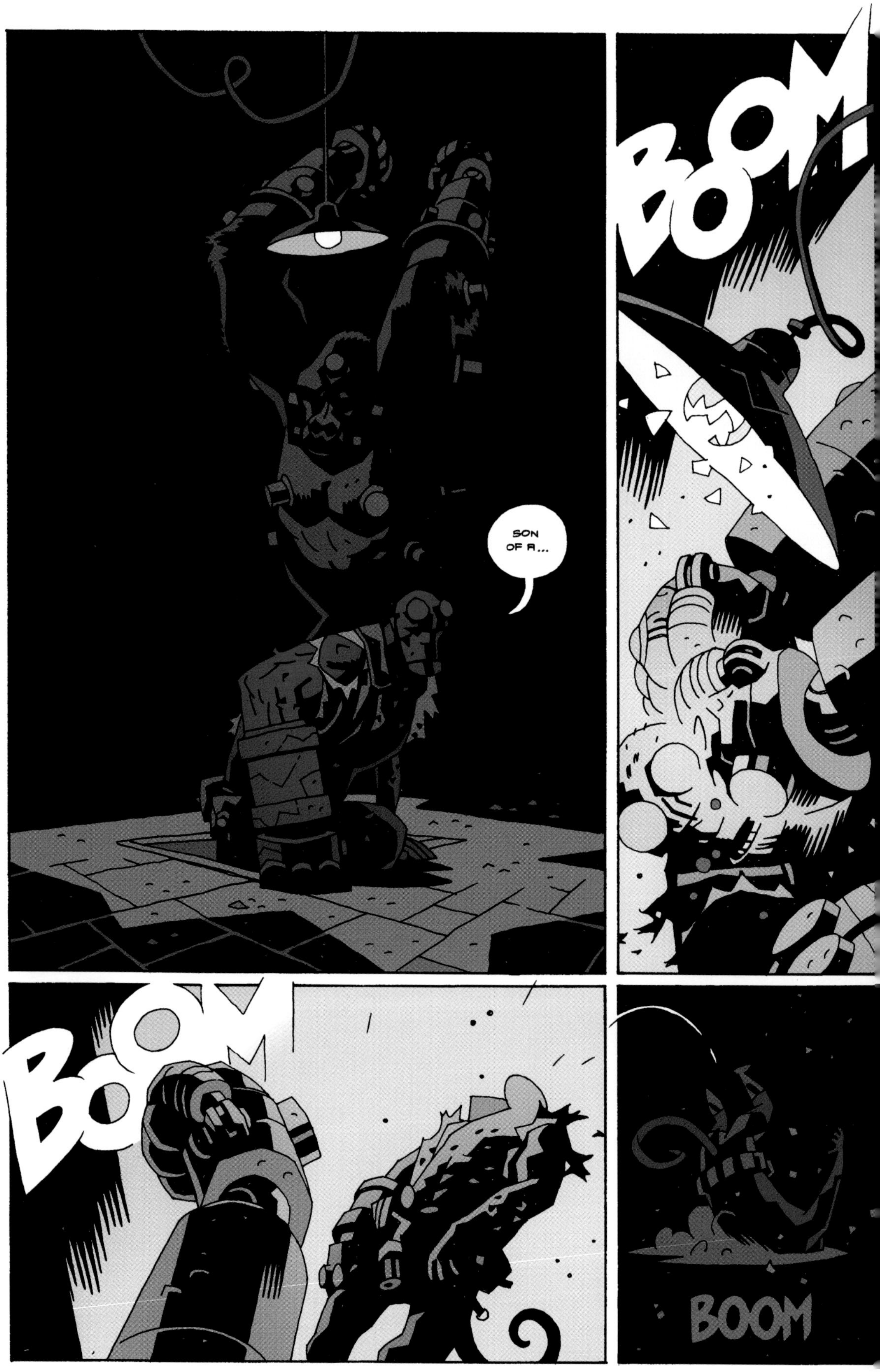
SON OF A...
BOOM
BOOM
BOOM

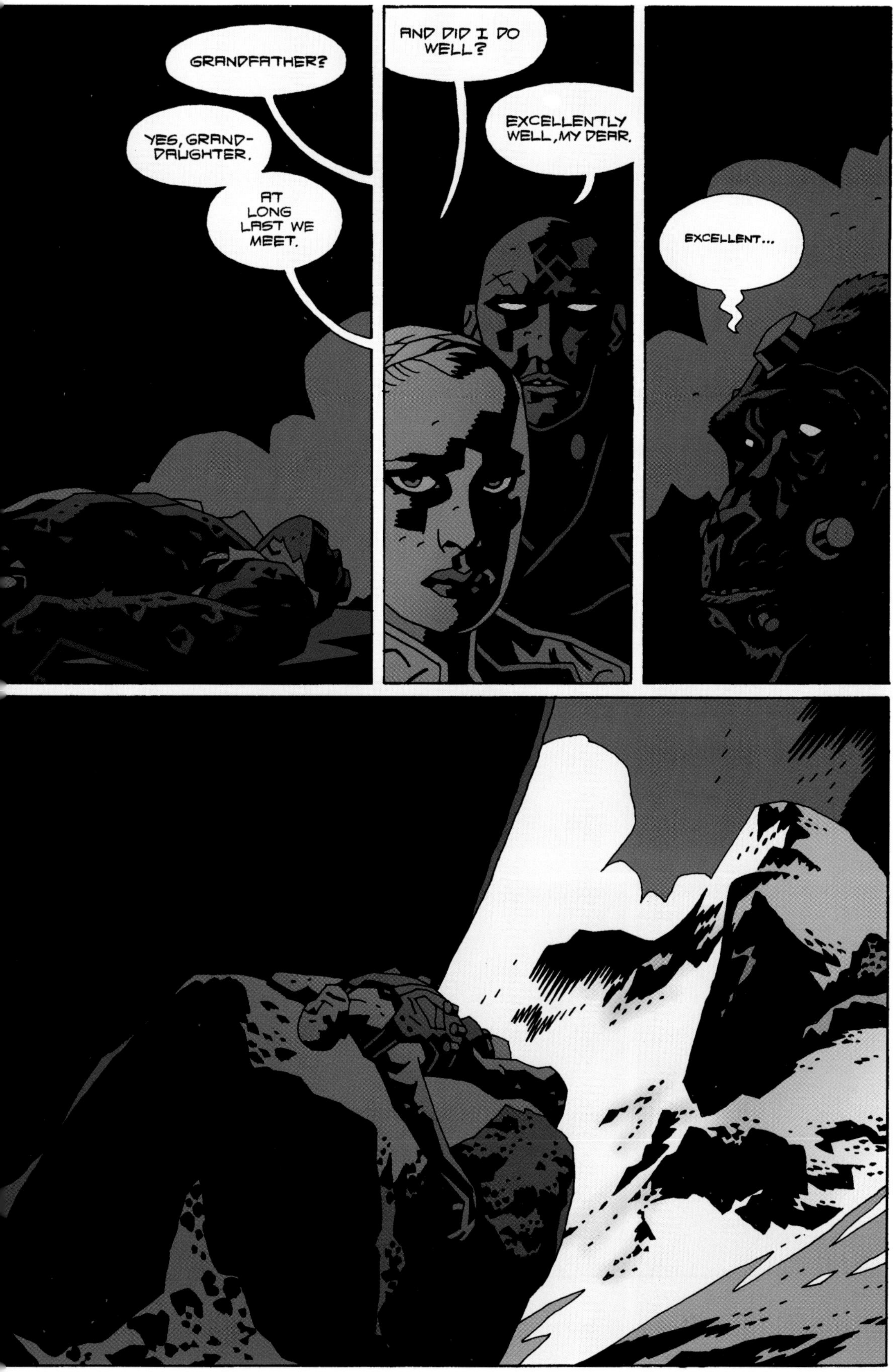
GRANDFATHER?
YES, GRAND-DAUGHTER.
AT LONG LAST WE MEET.
AND DID I DO WELL?
EXCELLENTLY WELL, MY DEAR.
EXCELLENT...

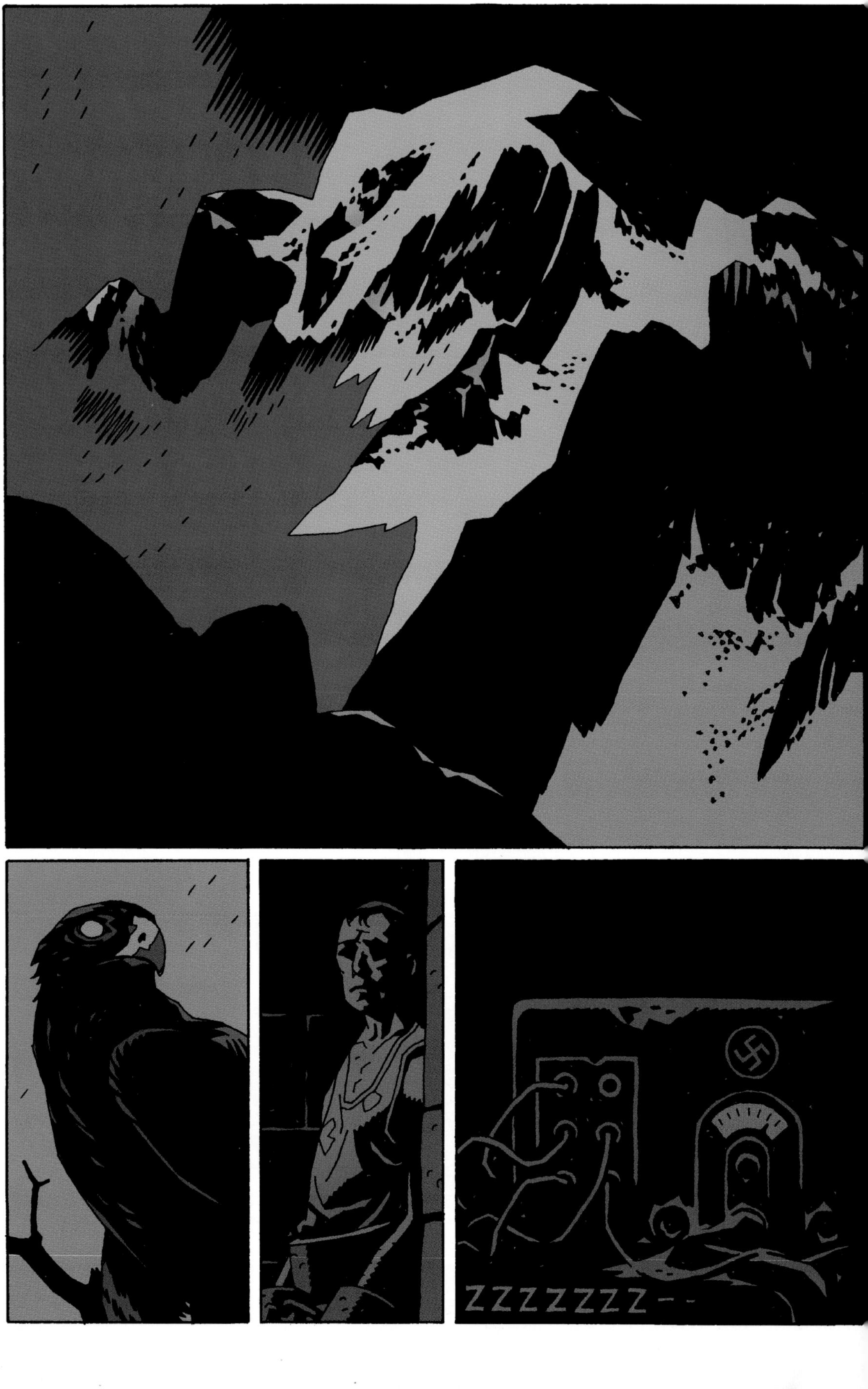
ZZZZZZZ--

CHAPTER TWO

MIGNOLA

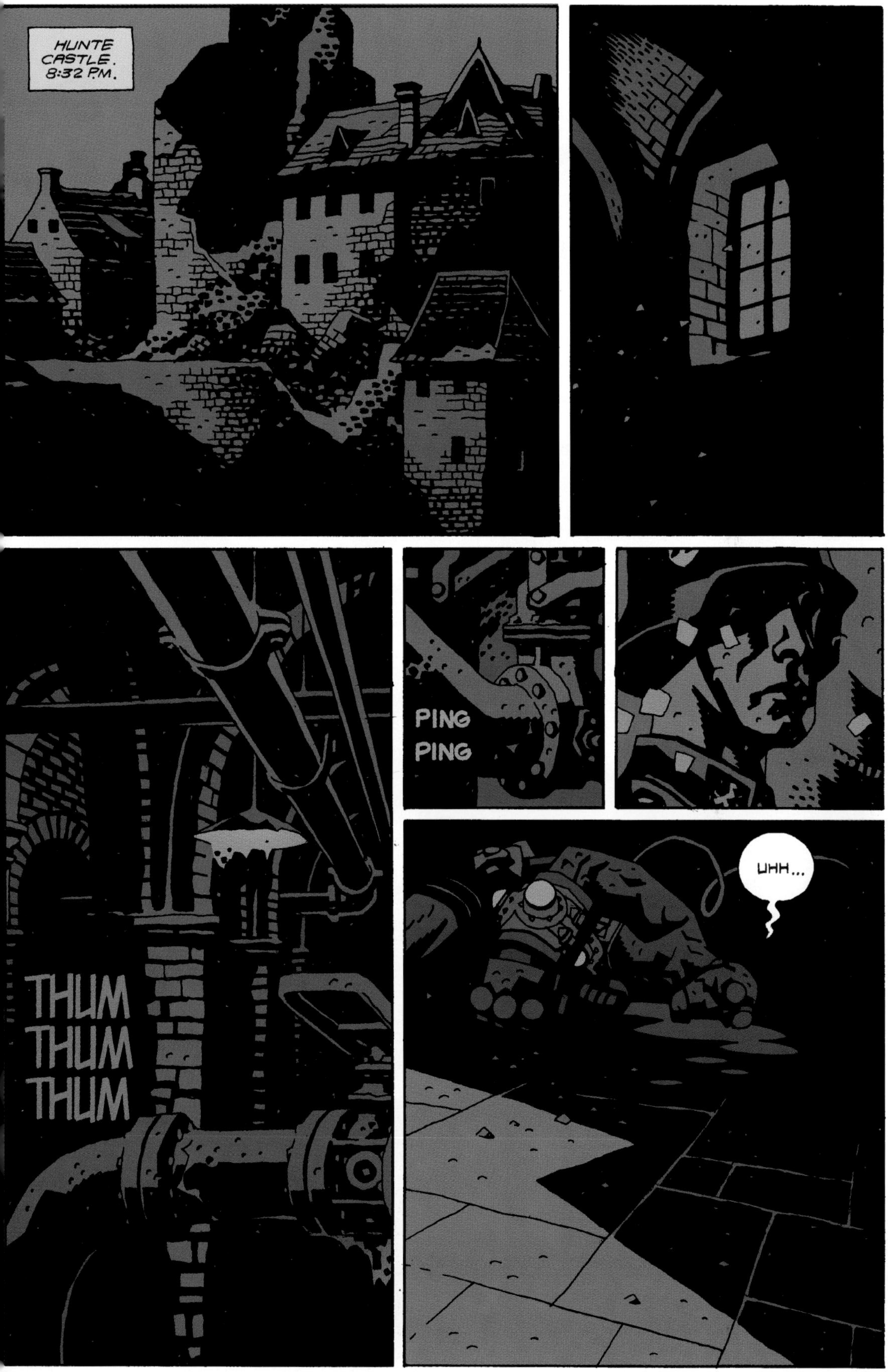
HUNTE CASTLE. 8:32 P.M.
THUM THUM THUM
PING PING
UHH...

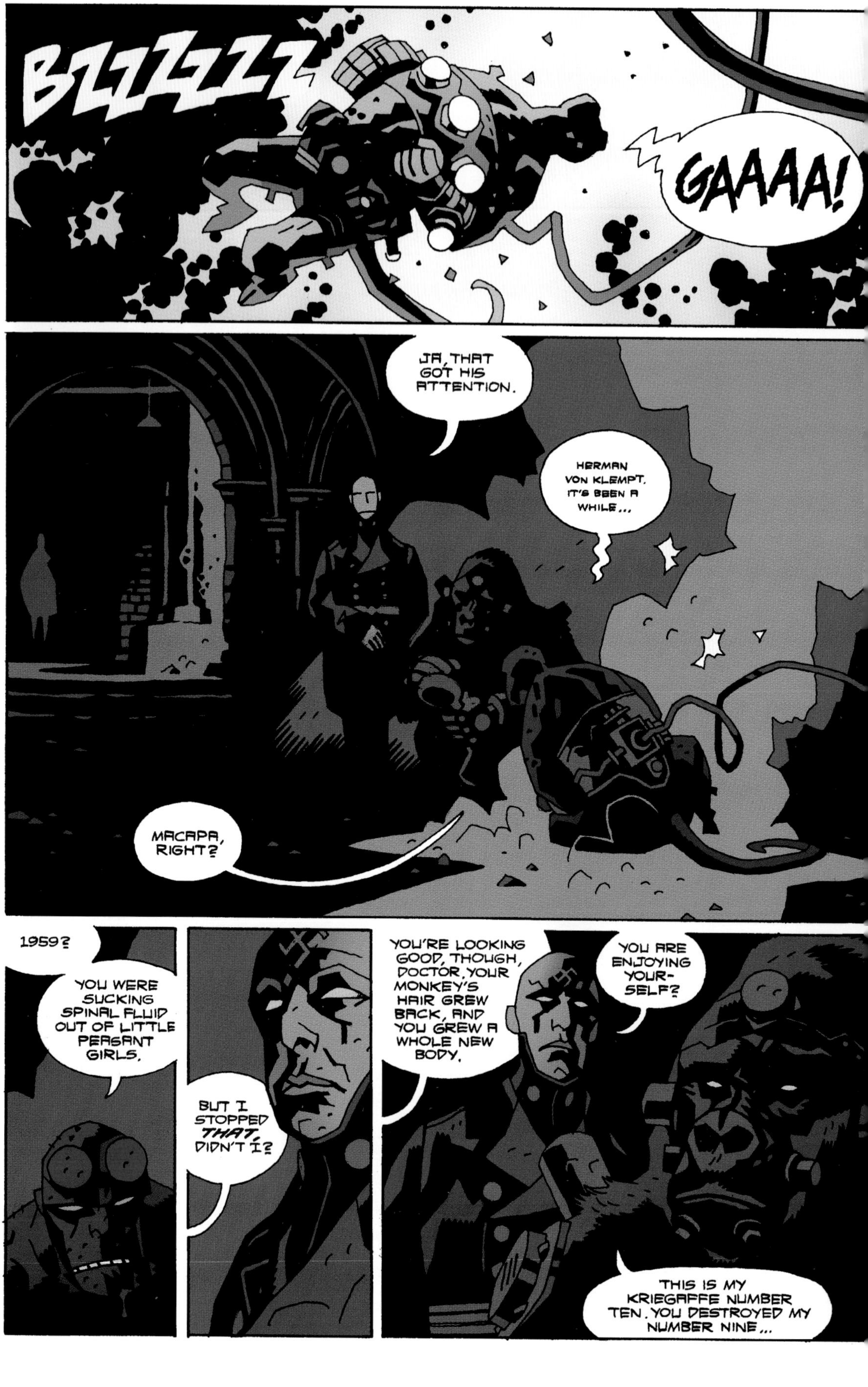
BZZZZZZ
GAAAA!
JA, THAT GOT HIS ATTENTION.
HERMAN VON KLEMPT. IT'S BEEN A WHILE...
MACAPA, RIGHT?
1959?
YOU WERE SUCKING SPINAL FLUID OUT OF LITTLE PEASANT GIRLS.
BUT I STOPPED THAT, DIDN'T I?
YOU'RE LOOKING GOOD, THOUGH, DOCTOR. YOUR MONKEY'S HAIR GREW BACK, AND YOU GREW A WHOLE NEW BODY.
YOU ARE ENJOYING YOURSELF?
THIS IS MY KRIEGAFFE NUMBER TEN. YOU DESTROYED MY NUMBER NINE...

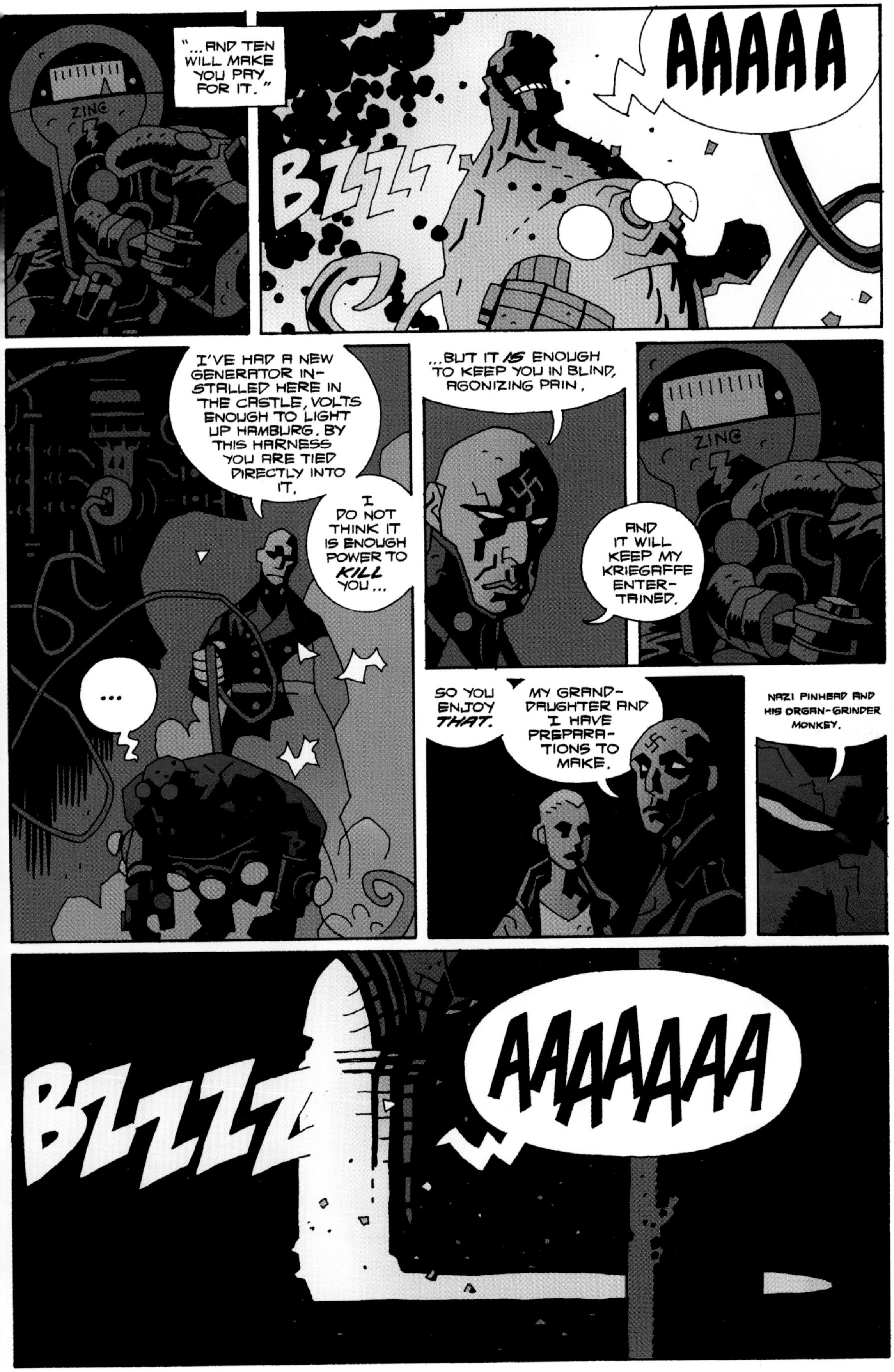
"...AND TEN WILL MAKE YOU PAY FOR IT."
AAAAA
BZZZZ
I'VE HAD A NEW GENERATOR IN-STALLED HERE IN THE CASTLE, VOLTS ENOUGH TO LIGHT UP HAMBURG. BY THIS HARNESS YOU ARE TIED DIRECTLY INTO IT.
I DO NOT THINK IT IS ENOUGH POWER TO KILL YOU...
...
...BUT IT IS ENOUGH TO KEEP YOU IN BLIND, AGONIZING PAIN.
AND IT WILL KEEP MY KRIEGAFFE ENTER-TAINED.
ZING
SO YOU ENJOY THAT.
MY GRAND-DAUGHTER AND I HAVE PREPARA-TIONS TO MAKE.
NAZI PINHEAD AND HIS ORGAN-GRINDER MONKEY.
BZZZZ
AAAAAAA

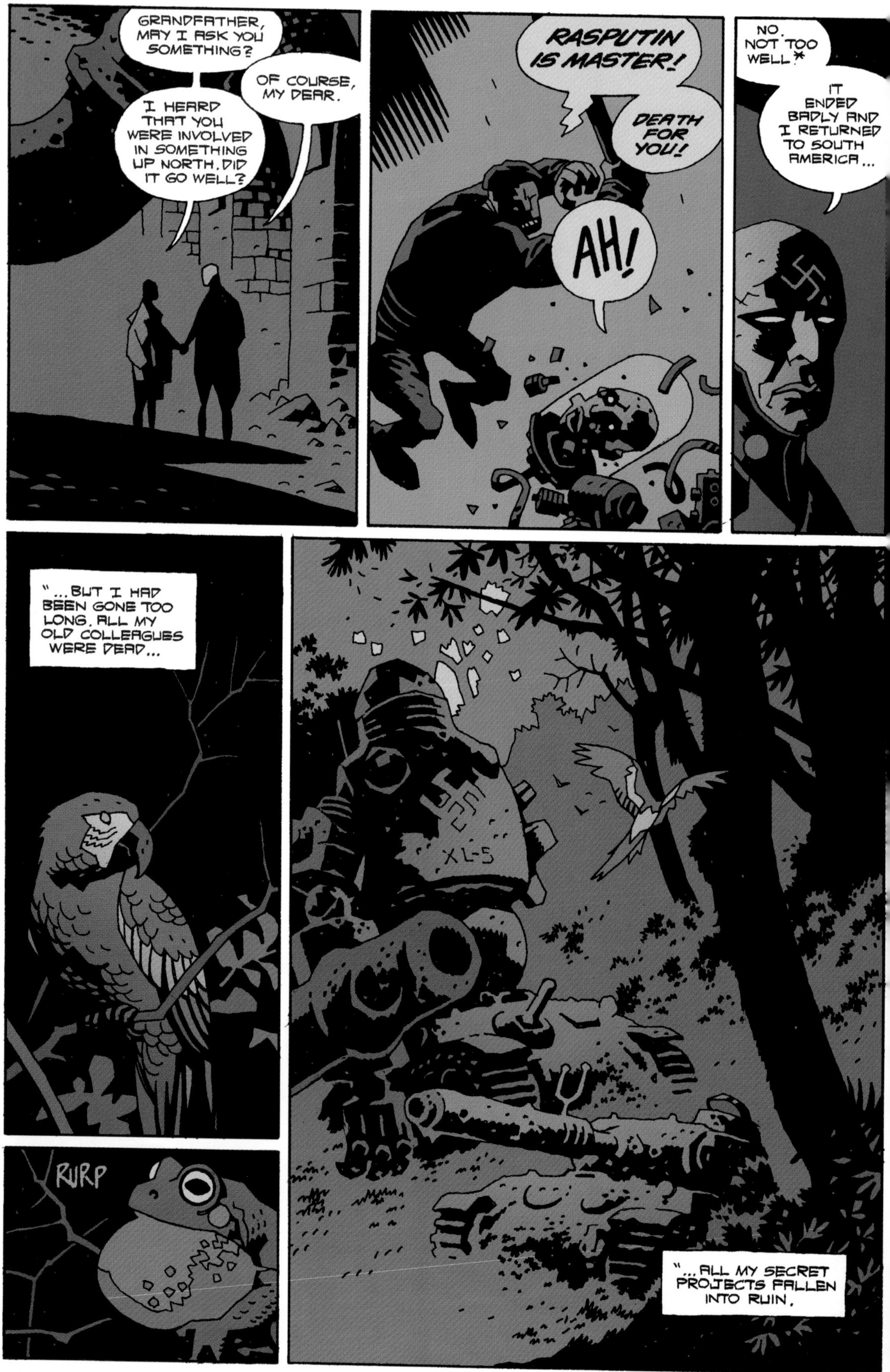
GRANDFATHER, MAY I ASK YOU SOMETHING?
OF COURSE, MY DEAR.
I HEARD THAT YOU WERE INVOLVED IN SOMETHING UP NORTH. DID IT GO WELL?
RASPUTIN IS MASTER!
DEATH FOR YOU!
AH!
NO. NOT TOO WELL.*
IT ENDED BADLY AND I RETURNED TO SOUTH AMERICA...
"...BUT I HAD BEEN GONE TOO LONG. ALL MY OLD COLLEAGUES WERE DEAD...
RURP
XL-5
"...ALL MY SECRET PROJECTS FALLEN INTO RUIN.

* HELLBOY: WAKE THE DEVIL

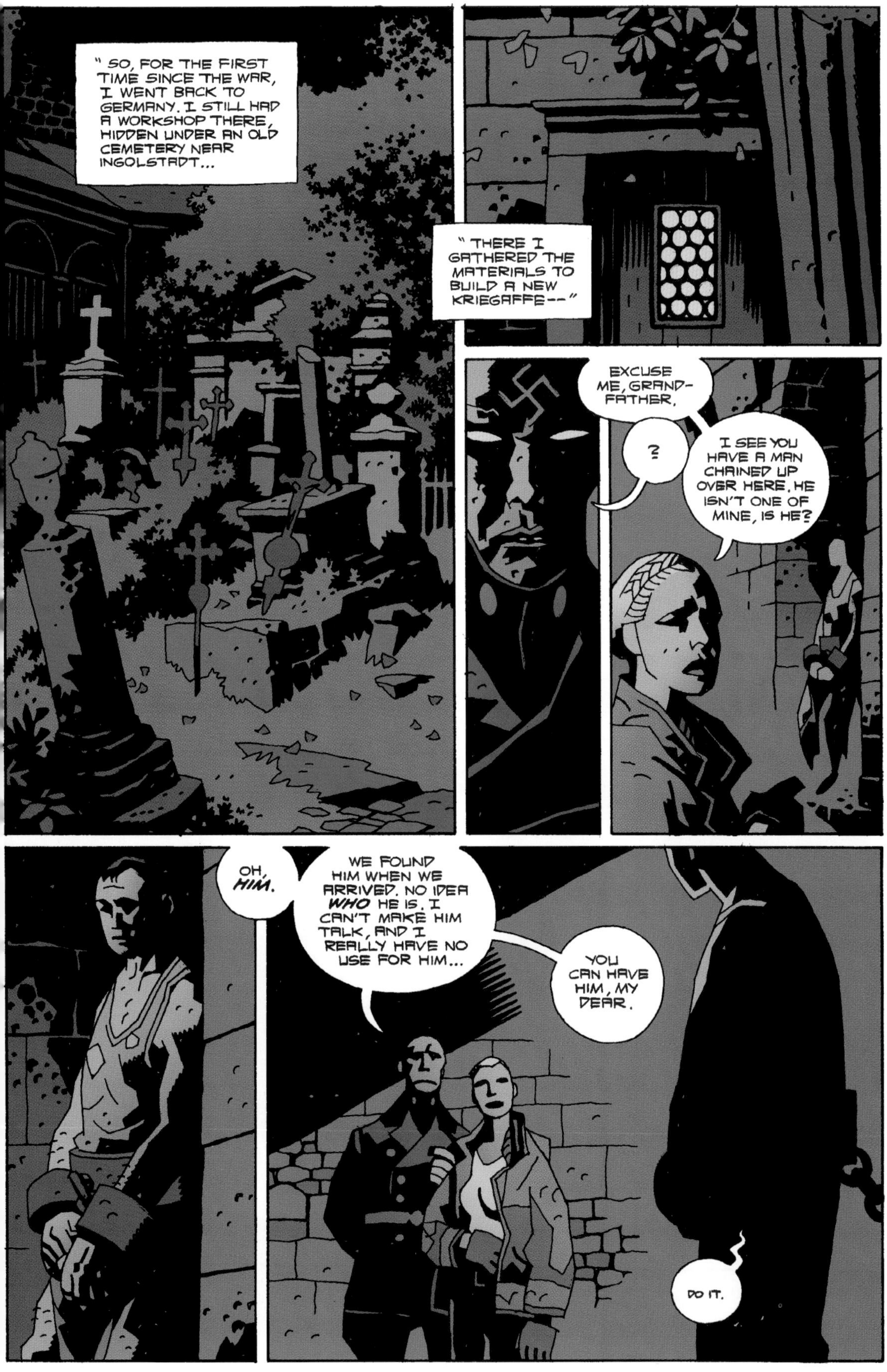
"SO, FOR THE FIRST TIME SINCE THE WAR, I WENT BACK TO GERMANY. I STILL HAD A WORKSHOP THERE, HIDDEN UNDER AN OLD CEMETERY NEAR INGOLSTADT...
"THERE I GATHERED THE MATERIALS TO BUILD A NEW KRIEGAFFE--"
EXCUSE ME, GRAND-FATHER.
?
I SEE YOU HAVE A MAN CHAINED UP OVER HERE. HE ISN'T ONE OF MINE, IS HE?
OH, *HIM*.
WE FOUND HIM WHEN WE ARRIVED. NO IDEA *WHO* HE IS. I CAN'T MAKE HIM TALK, AND I REALLY HAVE NO USE FOR HIM...
YOU CAN HAVE HIM, MY DEAR.
DO IT.

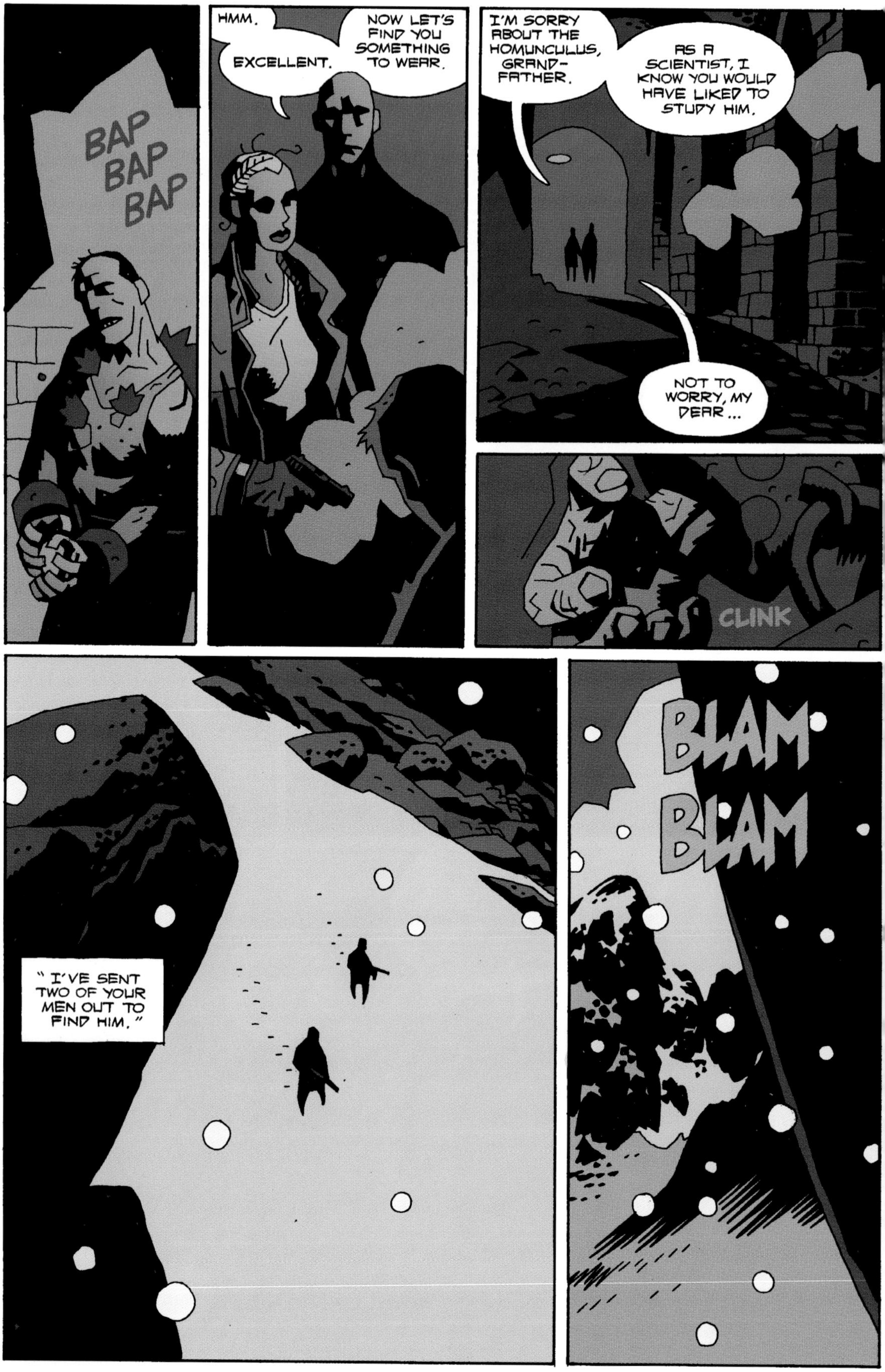
BAP
BAP
BAP
HMM.
EXCELLENT.
NOW LET'S FIND YOU SOMETHING TO WEAR.
I'M SORRY ABOUT THE HOMUNCULUS, GRAND-FATHER.
AS A SCIENTIST, I KNOW YOU WOULD HAVE LIKED TO STUDY HIM.
NOT TO WORRY, MY DEAR...
CLINK
" I'VE SENT TWO OF YOUR MEN OUT TO FIND HIM."
BLAM
BLAM

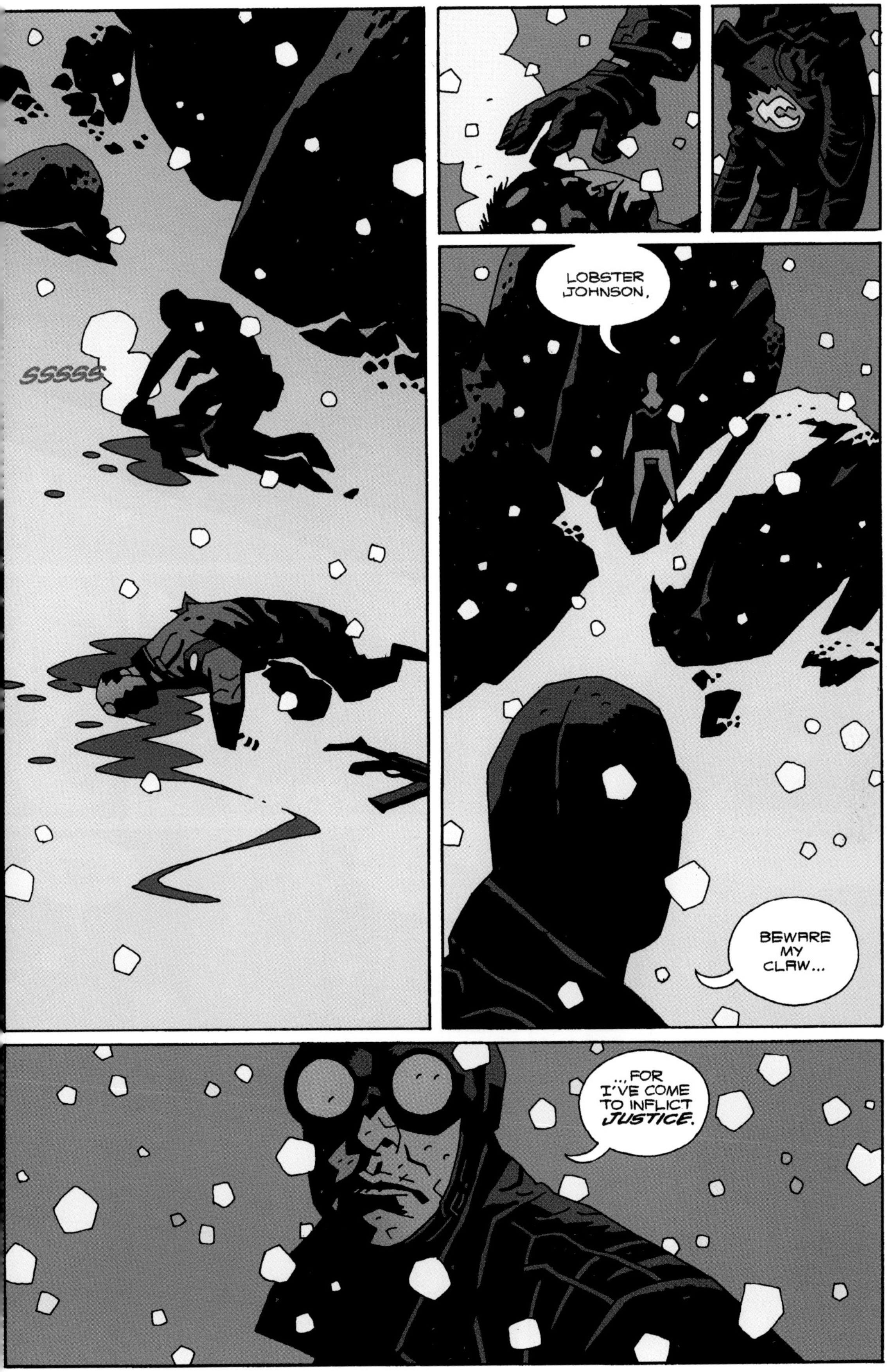
SSSSS
LOBSTER JOHNSON,
BEWARE MY CLAW...
...FOR I'VE COME TO INFLICT JUSTICE.

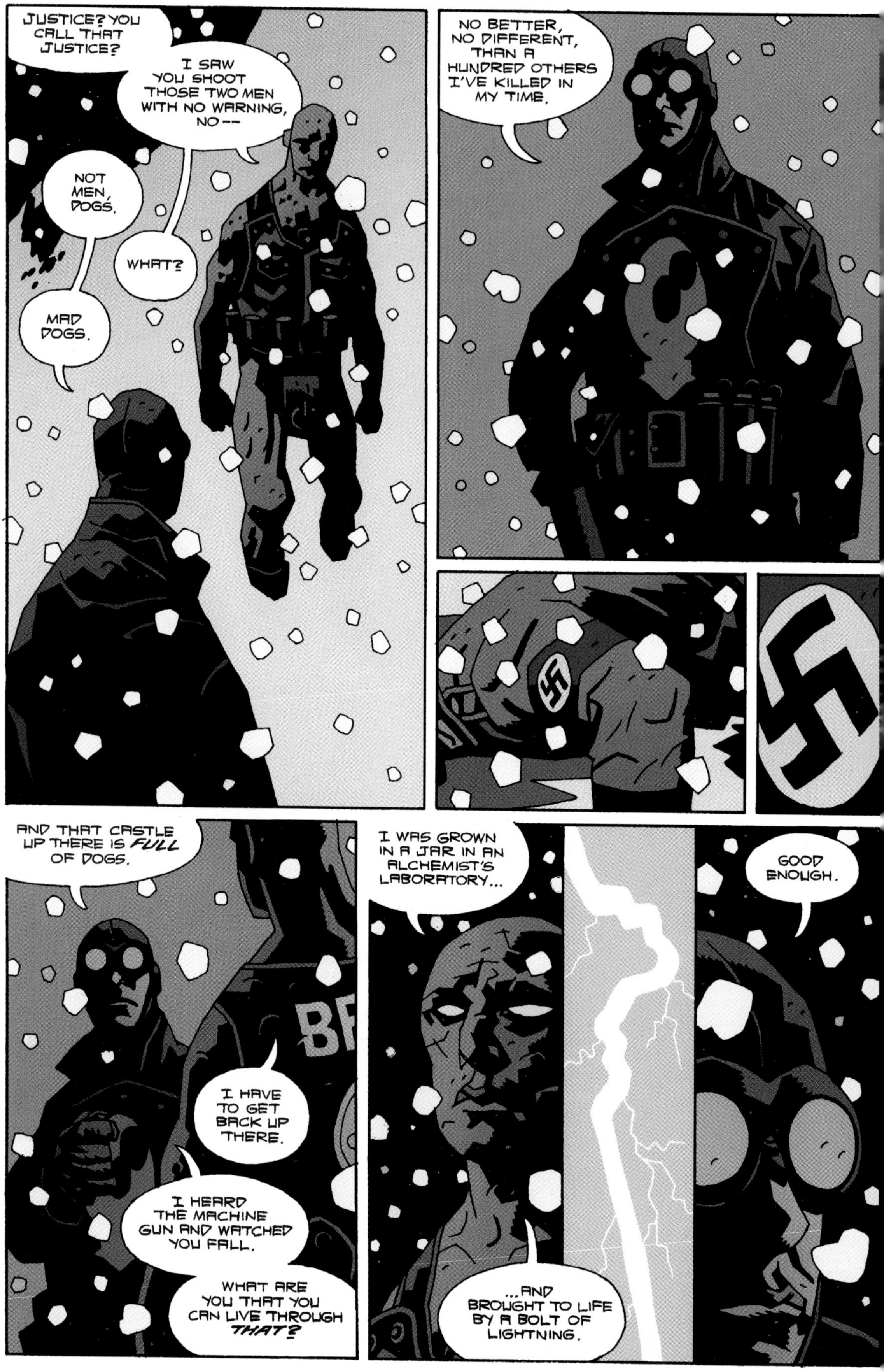
JUSTICE? YOU CALL THAT JUSTICE?
I SAW YOU SHOOT THOSE TWO MEN WITH NO WARNING, NO--
NOT MEN, DOGS.
WHAT?
MAD DOGS.
NO BETTER, NO DIFFERENT, THAN A HUNDRED OTHERS I'VE KILLED IN MY TIME.
AND THAT CASTLE UP THERE IS FULL OF DOGS.
I HAVE TO GET BACK UP THERE.
I HEARD THE MACHINE GUN AND WATCHED YOU FALL.
WHAT ARE YOU THAT YOU CAN LIVE THROUGH THAT?
I WAS GROWN IN A JAR IN AN ALCHEMIST'S LABORATORY...
...AND BROUGHT TO LIFE BY A BOLT OF LIGHTNING.
GOOD ENOUGH.

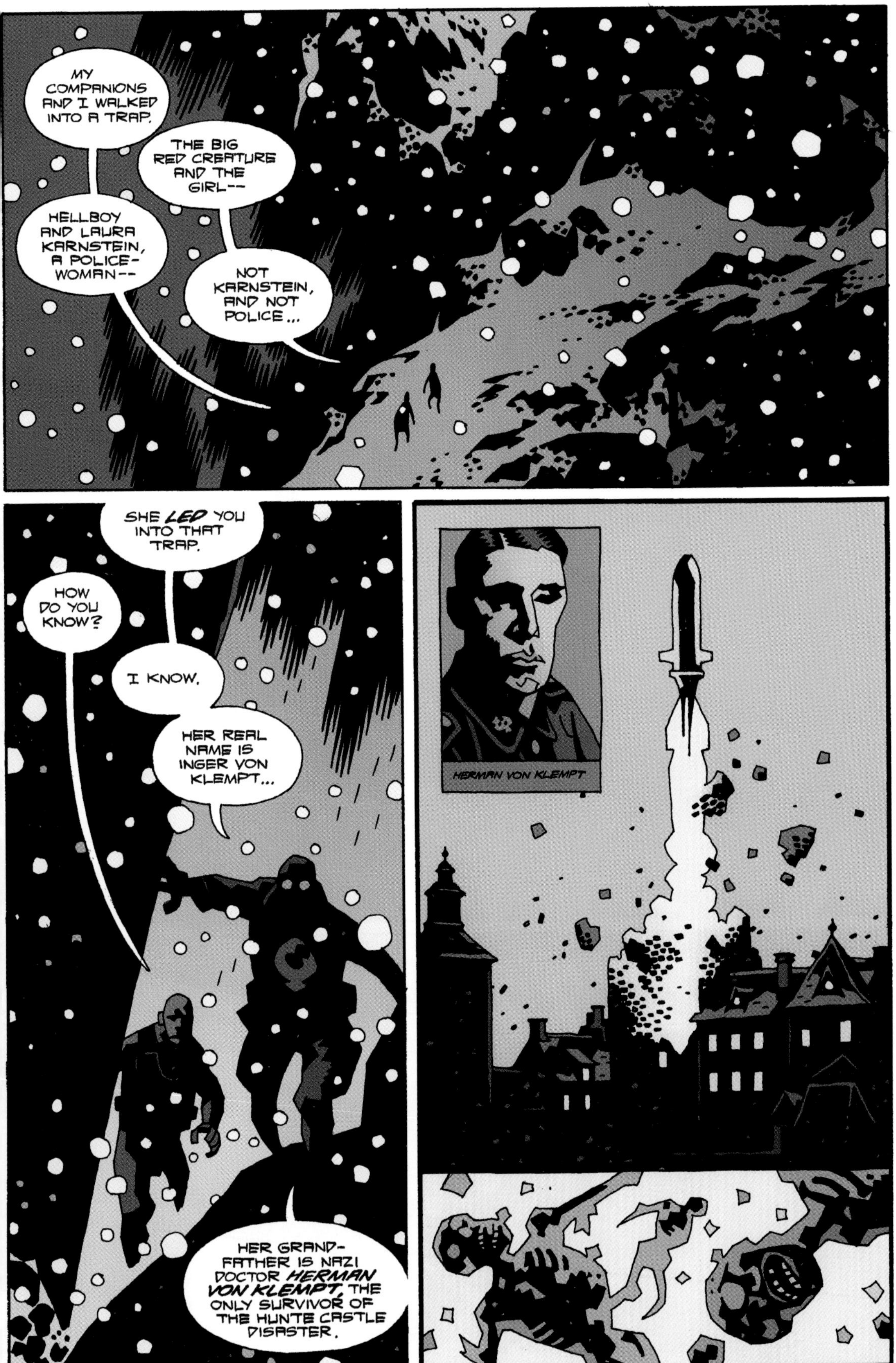
MY COMPANIONS AND I WALKED INTO A TRAP.
THE BIG RED CREATURE AND THE GIRL--
HELLBOY AND LAURA KARNSTEIN, A POLICE-WOMAN--
NOT KARNSTEIN, AND NOT POLICE...
SHE LED YOU INTO THAT TRAP.
HOW DO YOU KNOW?
I KNOW.
HER REAL NAME IS INGER VON KLEMPT...
HER GRAND-FATHER IS NAZI DOCTOR HERMAN VON KLEMPT, THE ONLY SURVIVOR OF THE HUNTE CASTLE DISASTER.
HERMAN VON KLEMPT

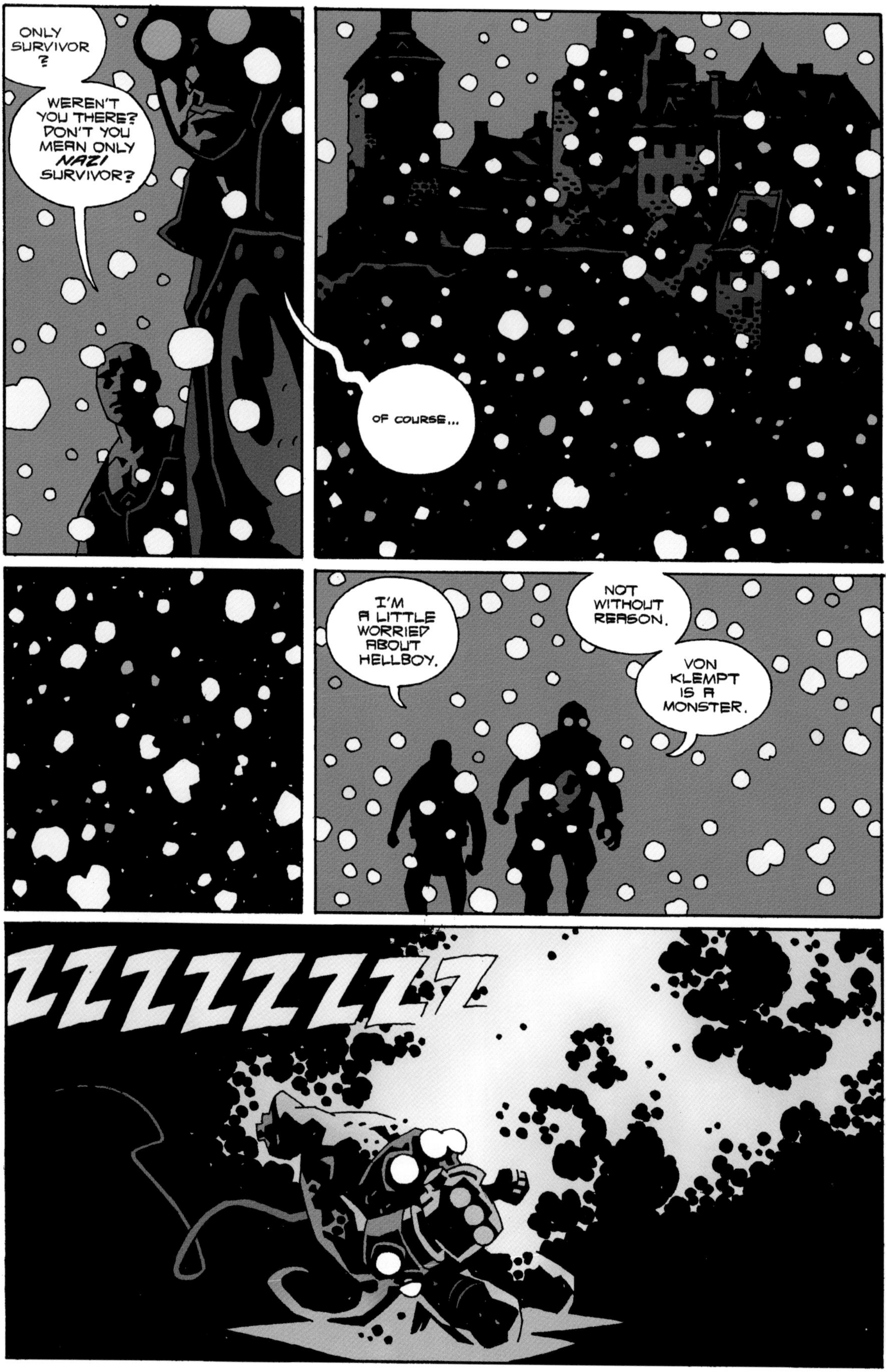
ONLY SURVIVOR ?
WEREN'T YOU THERE? DON'T YOU MEAN ONLY NAZI SURVIVOR?
OF COURSE...
I'M A LITTLE WORRIED ABOUT HELLBOY.
NOT WITHOUT REASON.
VON KLEMPT IS A MONSTER.
ZZZZZZZZZ

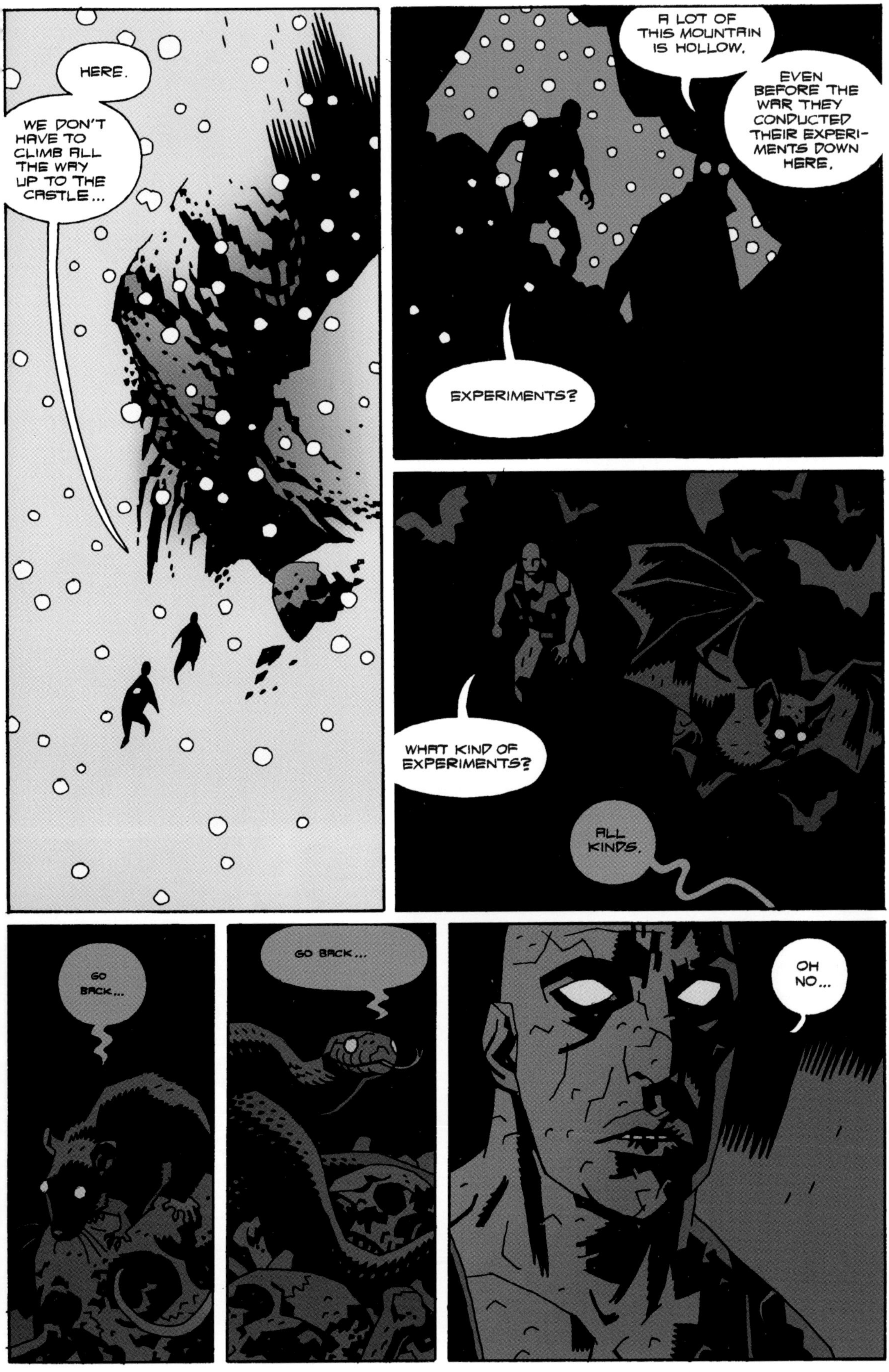
HERE.
WE DON'T HAVE TO CLIMB ALL THE WAY UP TO THE CASTLE...
A LOT OF THIS MOUNTAIN IS HOLLOW.
EVEN BEFORE THE WAR THEY CONDUCTED THEIR EXPERIMENTS DOWN HERE.
EXPERIMENTS?
WHAT KIND OF EXPERIMENTS?
ALL KINDS.
GO BACK...
GO BACK...
OH NO...

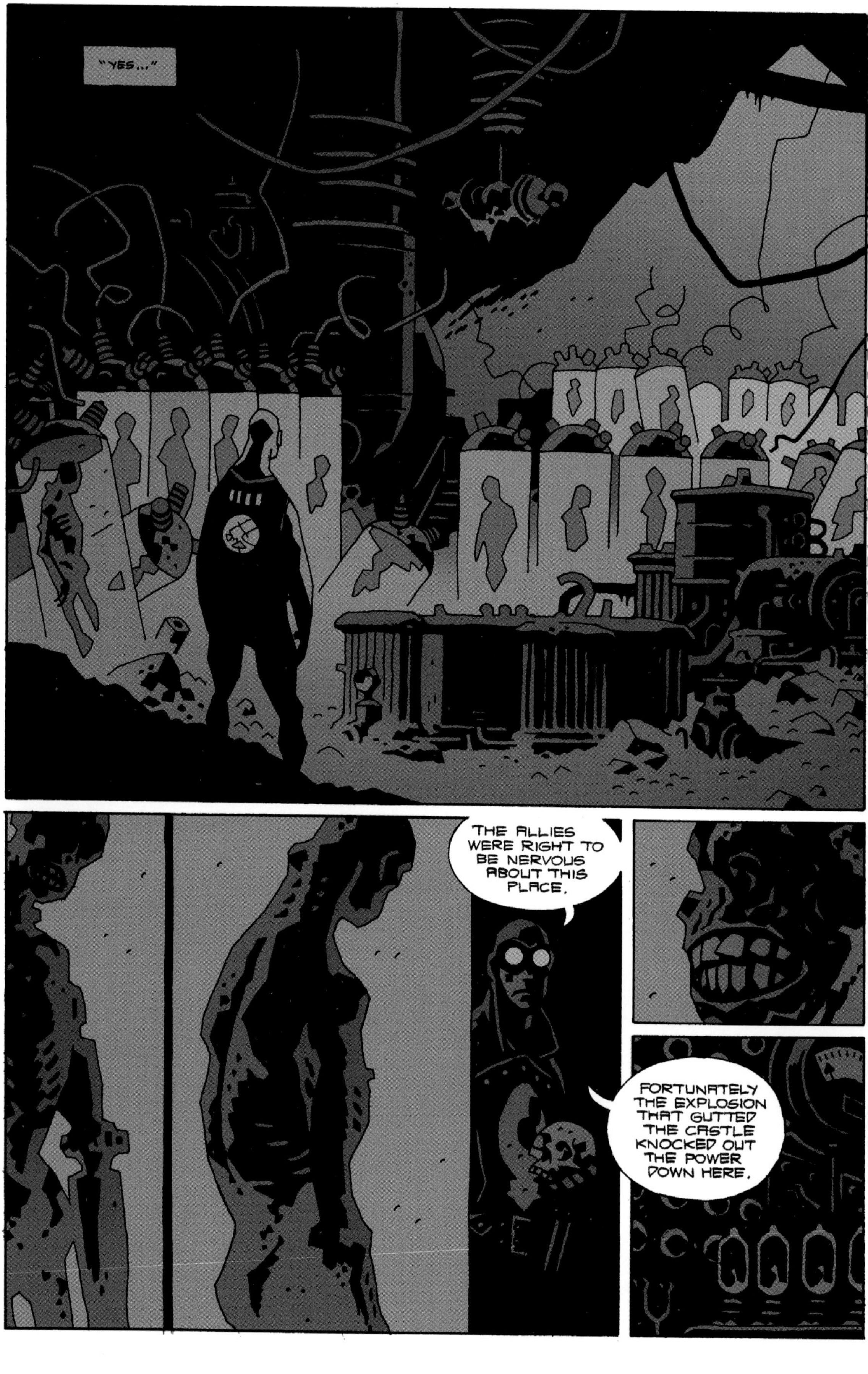
"YES..."
THE ALLIES WERE RIGHT TO BE NERVOUS ABOUT THIS PLACE.
FORTUNATELY THE EXPLOSION THAT GUTTED THE CASTLE KNOCKED OUT THE POWER DOWN HERE.

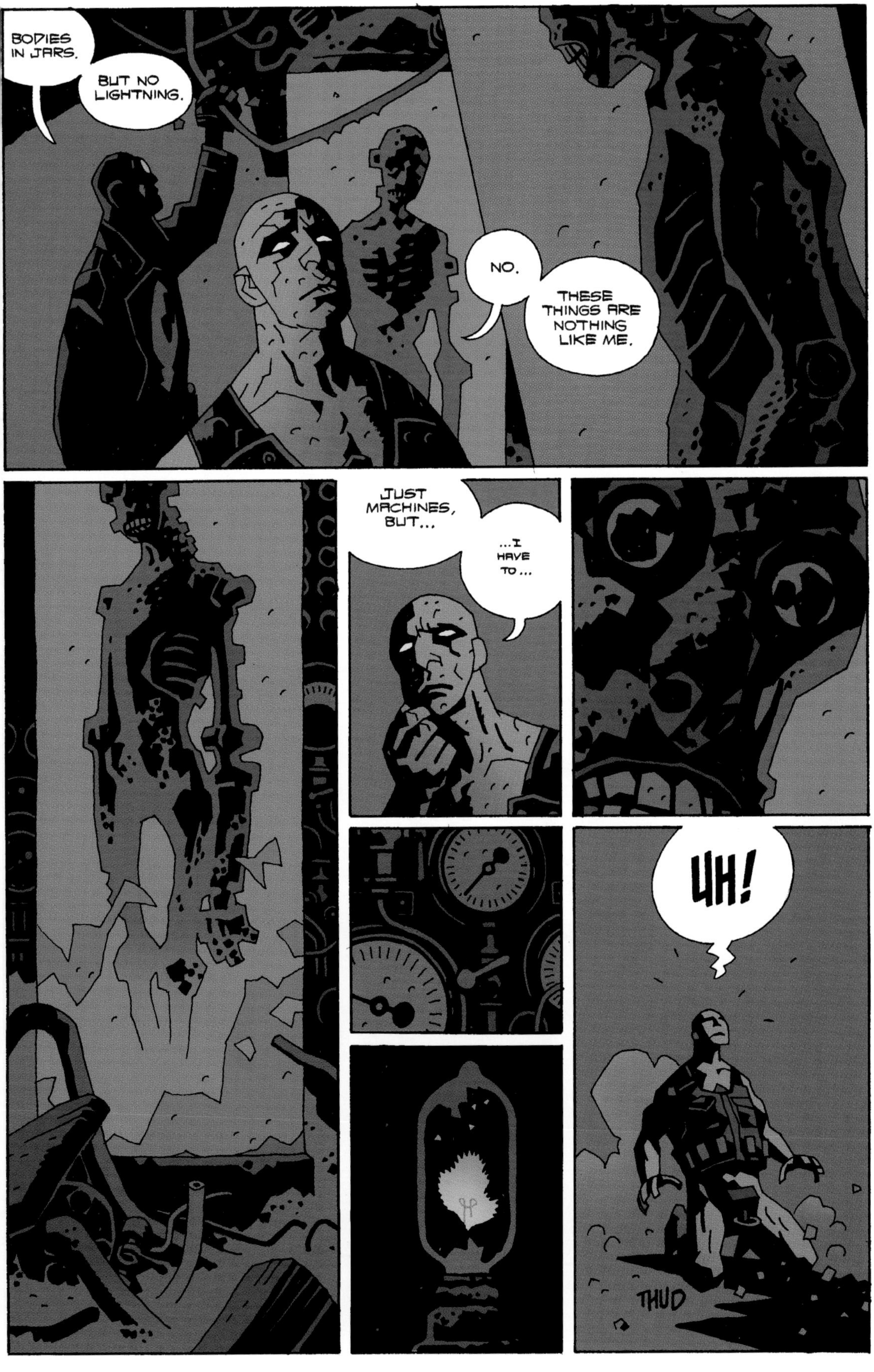
BODIES IN JARS.
BUT NO LIGHTNING.
NO.
THESE THINGS ARE NOTHING LIKE ME.
JUST MACHINES, BUT...
...I HAVE TO...
UH!
THUD

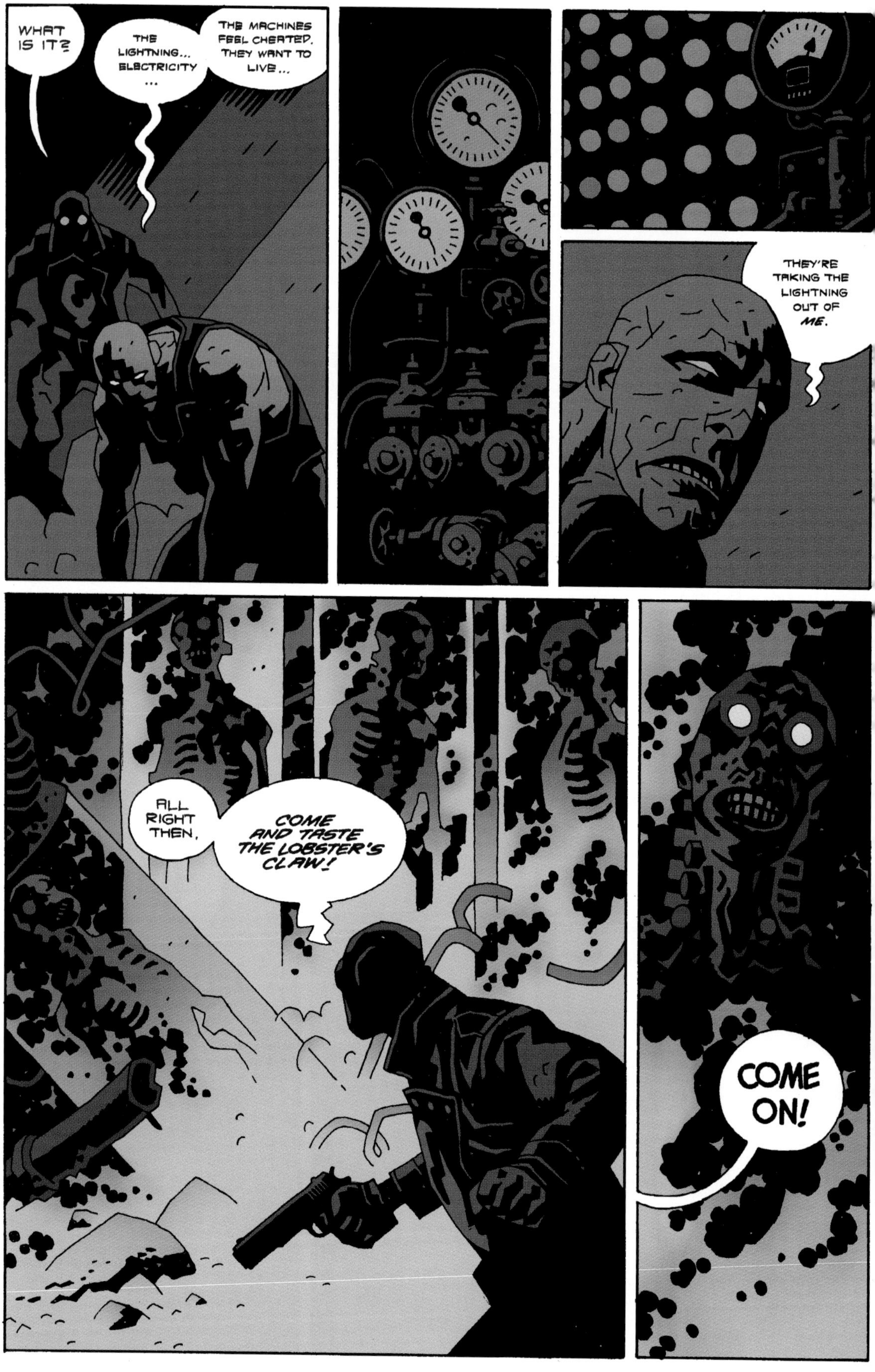
WHAT IS IT?
THE LIGHTNING... ELECTRICITY ...
THE MACHINES FEEL CHEATED. THEY WANT TO LIVE...
THEY'RE TAKING THE LIGHTNING OUT OF *ME*.
ALL RIGHT THEN.
COME AND TASTE THE LOBSTER'S CLAW!
COME ON!

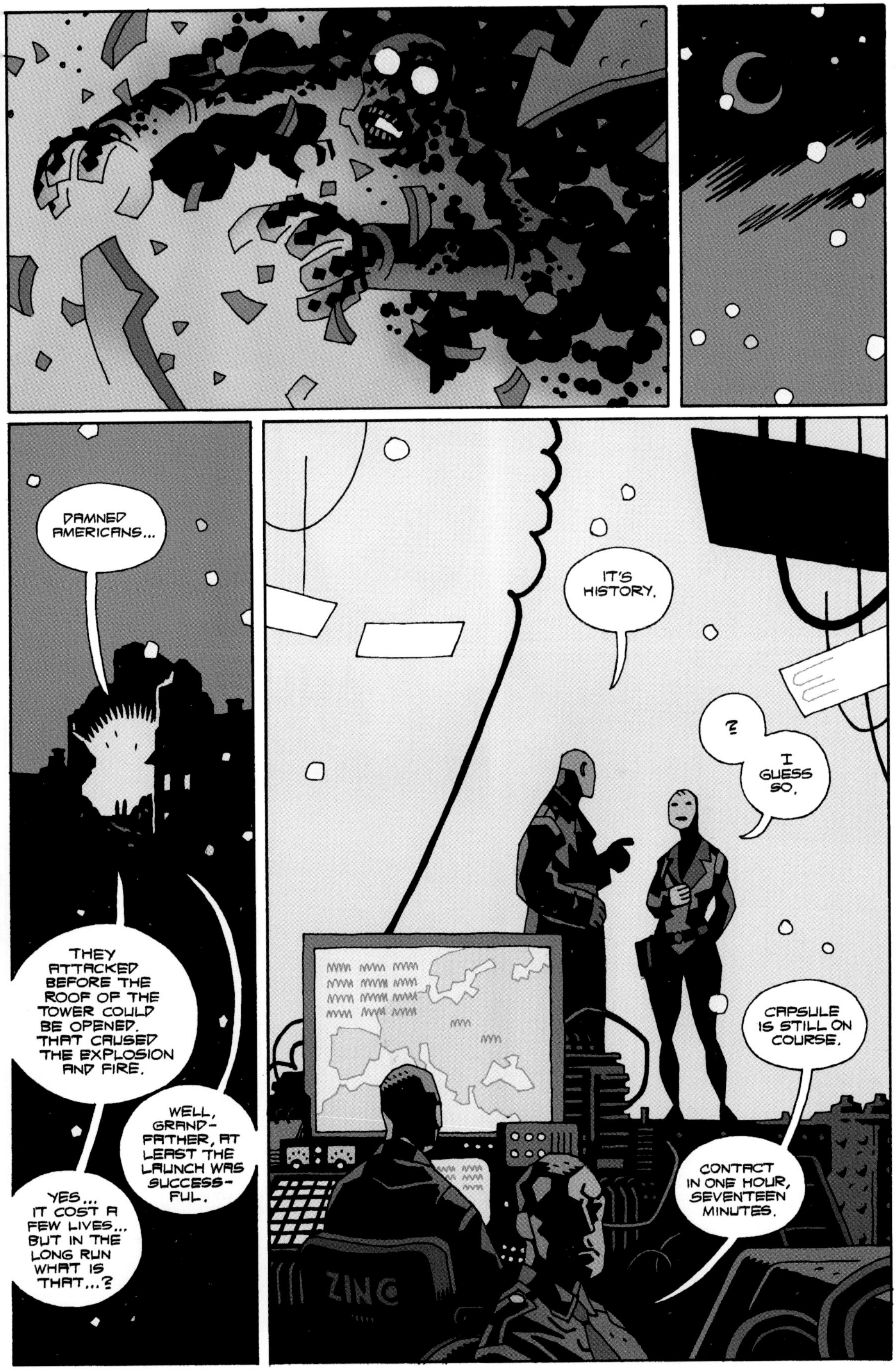
DAMNED AMERICANS...
THEY ATTACKED BEFORE THE ROOF OF THE TOWER COULD BE OPENED. THAT CAUSED THE EXPLOSION AND FIRE.
WELL, GRAND-FATHER, AT LEAST THE LAUNCH WAS SUCCESS-FUL.
YES... IT COST A FEW LIVES... BUT IN THE LONG RUN WHAT IS THAT...?
IT'S HISTORY.
?
I GUESS SO.
CAPSULE IS STILL ON COURSE.
CONTACT IN ONE HOUR, SEVENTEEN MINUTES.
ZINC

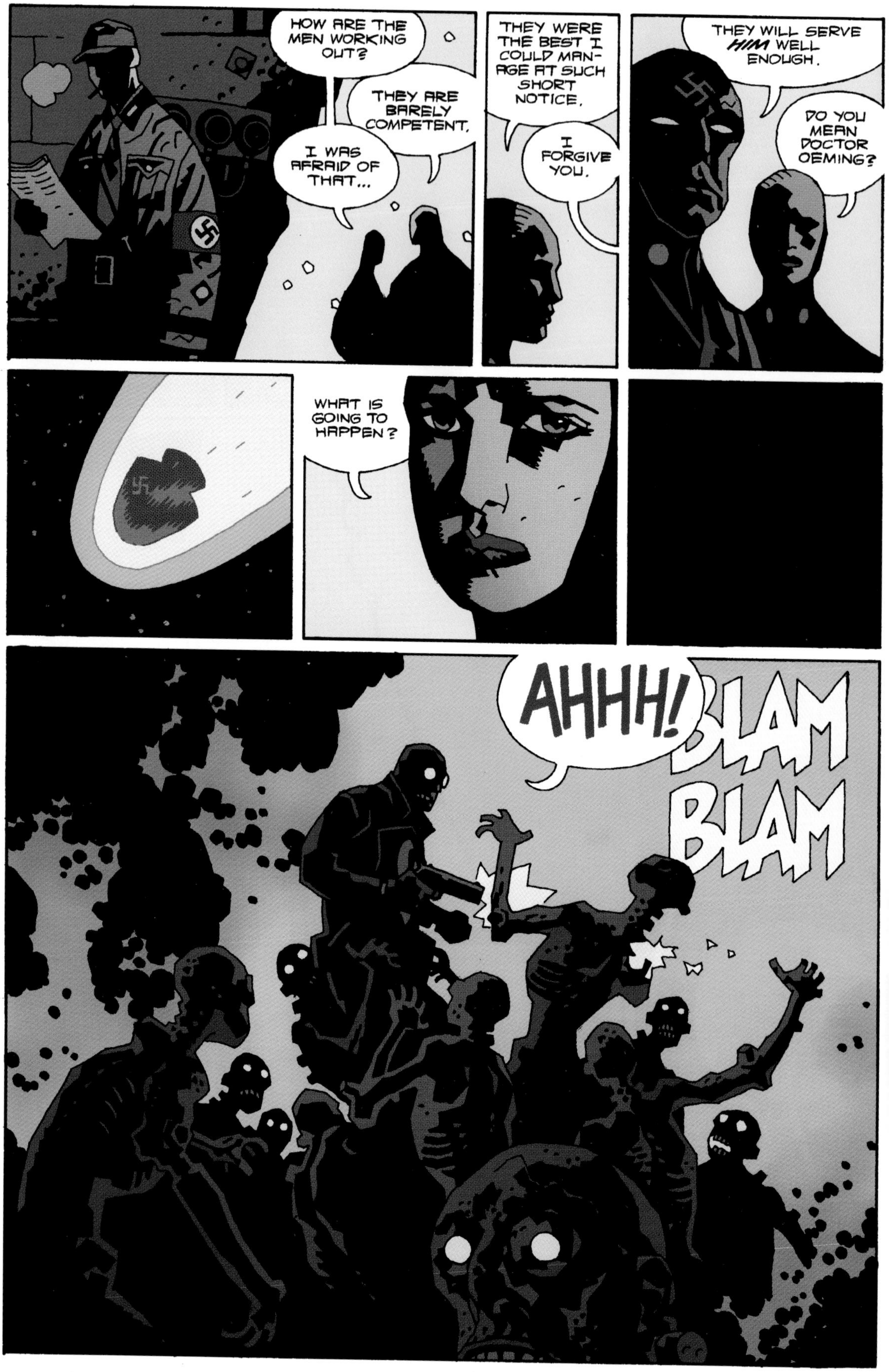

HOW ARE THE MEN WORKING OUT?
THEY ARE BARELY COMPETENT.
I WAS AFRAID OF THAT...
THEY WERE THE BEST I COULD MAN-AGE AT SUCH SHORT NOTICE.
I FORGIVE YOU.
THEY WILL SERVE HIM WELL ENOUGH.
DO YOU MEAN DOCTOR OEMING?
WHAT IS GOING TO HAPPEN?
AHHH!
BLAM
BLAM

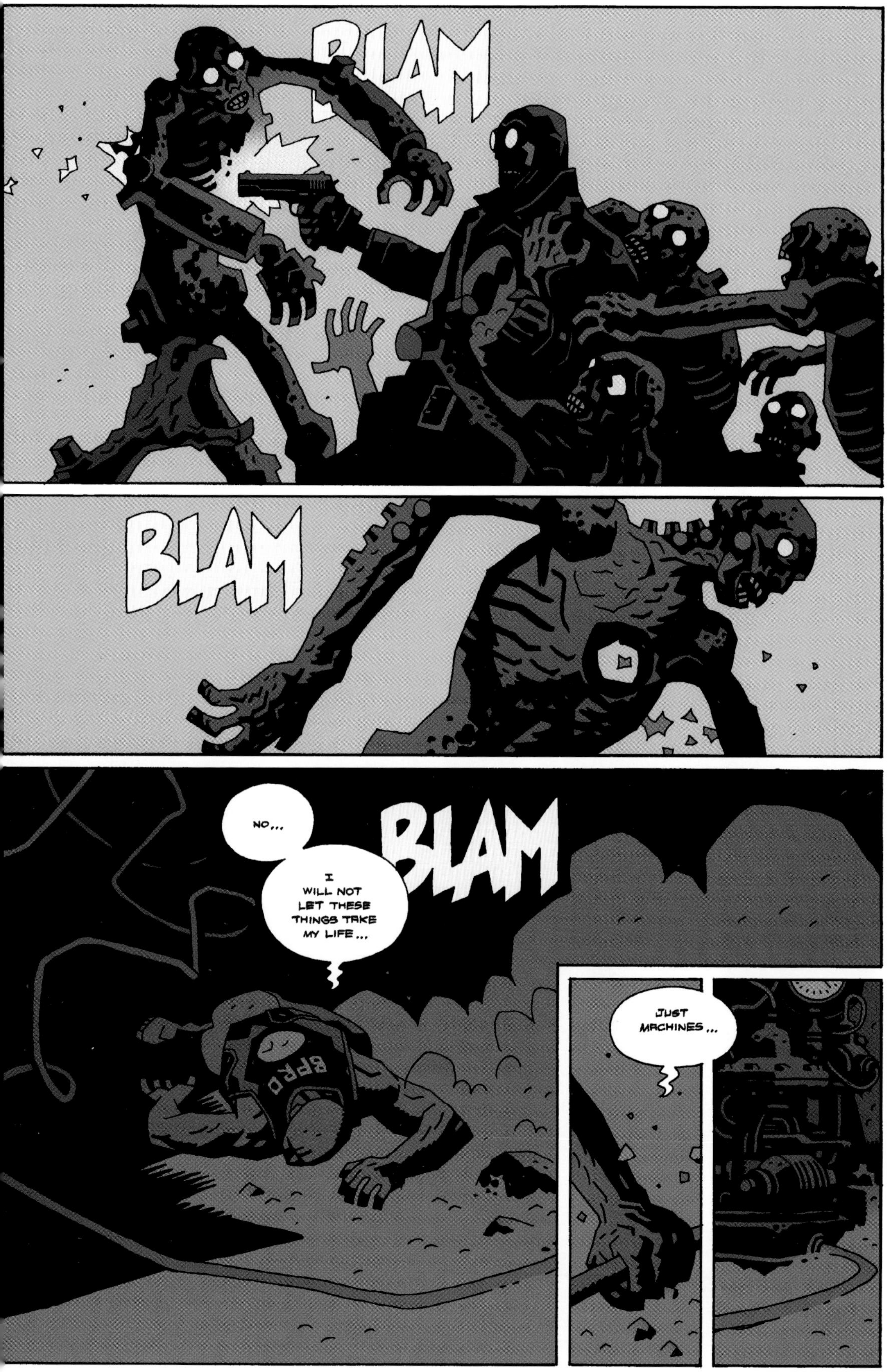
BLAM
BLAM
NO...
BLAM
I WILL NOT LET THESE THINGS TAKE MY LIFE...
BFRD
JUST MACHINES...

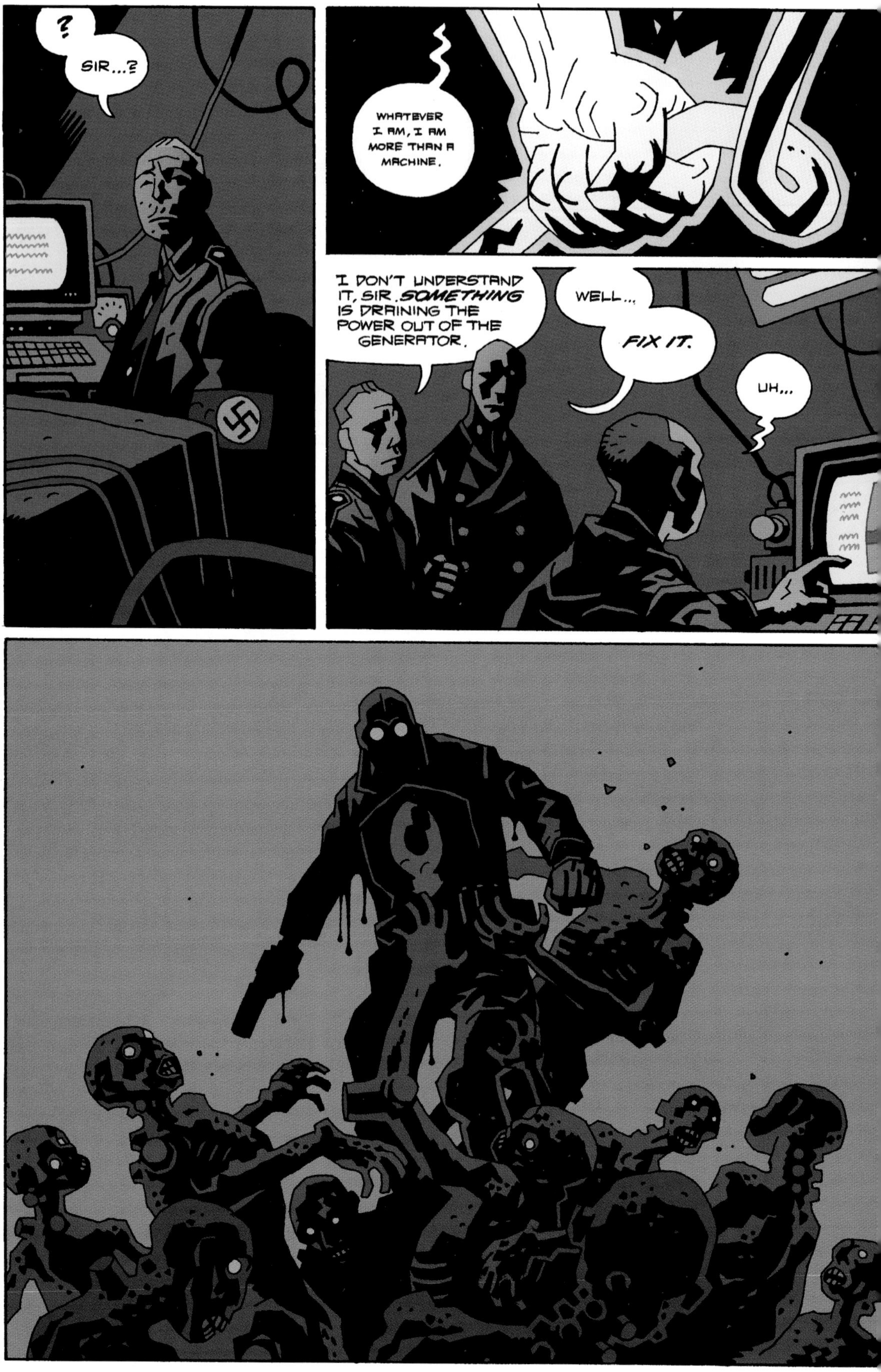
?
SIR...?
WHATEVER I AM, I AM MORE THAN A MACHINE.
I DON'T UNDERSTAND IT, SIR. SOMETHING IS DRAINING THE POWER OUT OF THE GENERATOR.
WELL...
FIX IT.
UH...

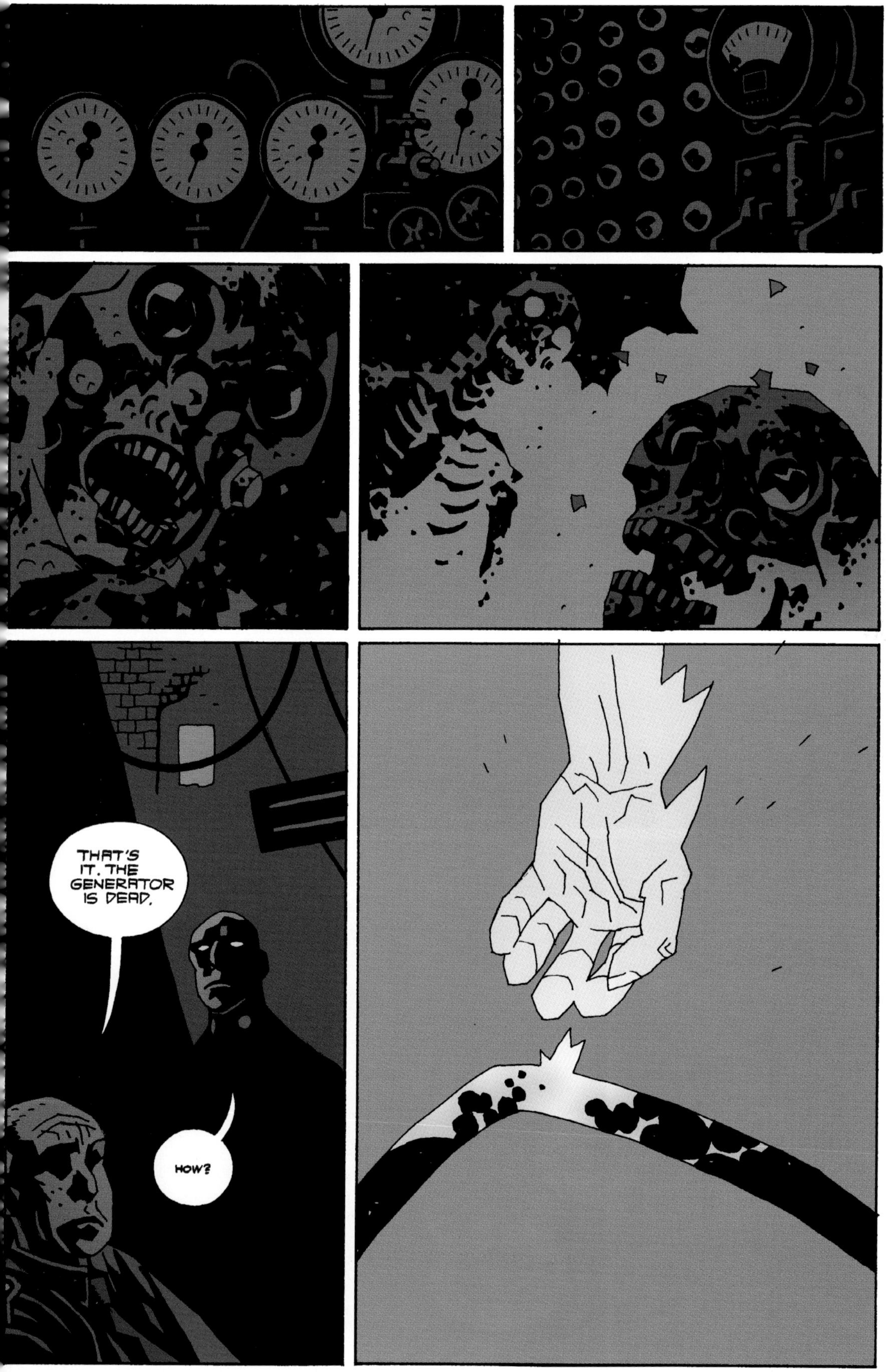
THAT'S IT. THE GENERATOR IS DEAD.
HOW?

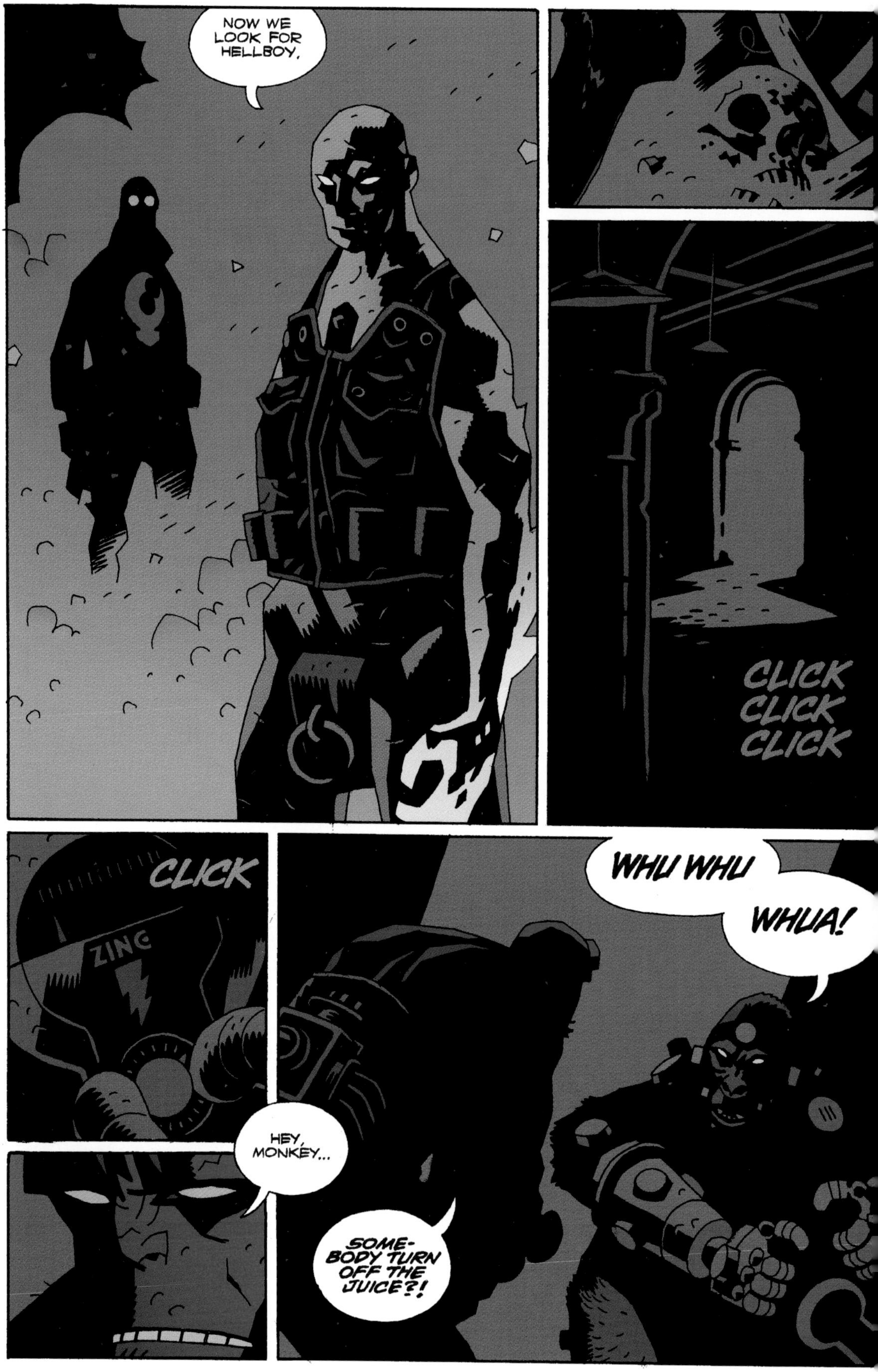
NOW WE LOOK FOR HELLBOY.
CLICK CLICK CLICK
CLICK
ZING
WHU WHU
WHUA!
HEY, MONKEY...
SOME-BODY TURN OFF THE JUICE?!

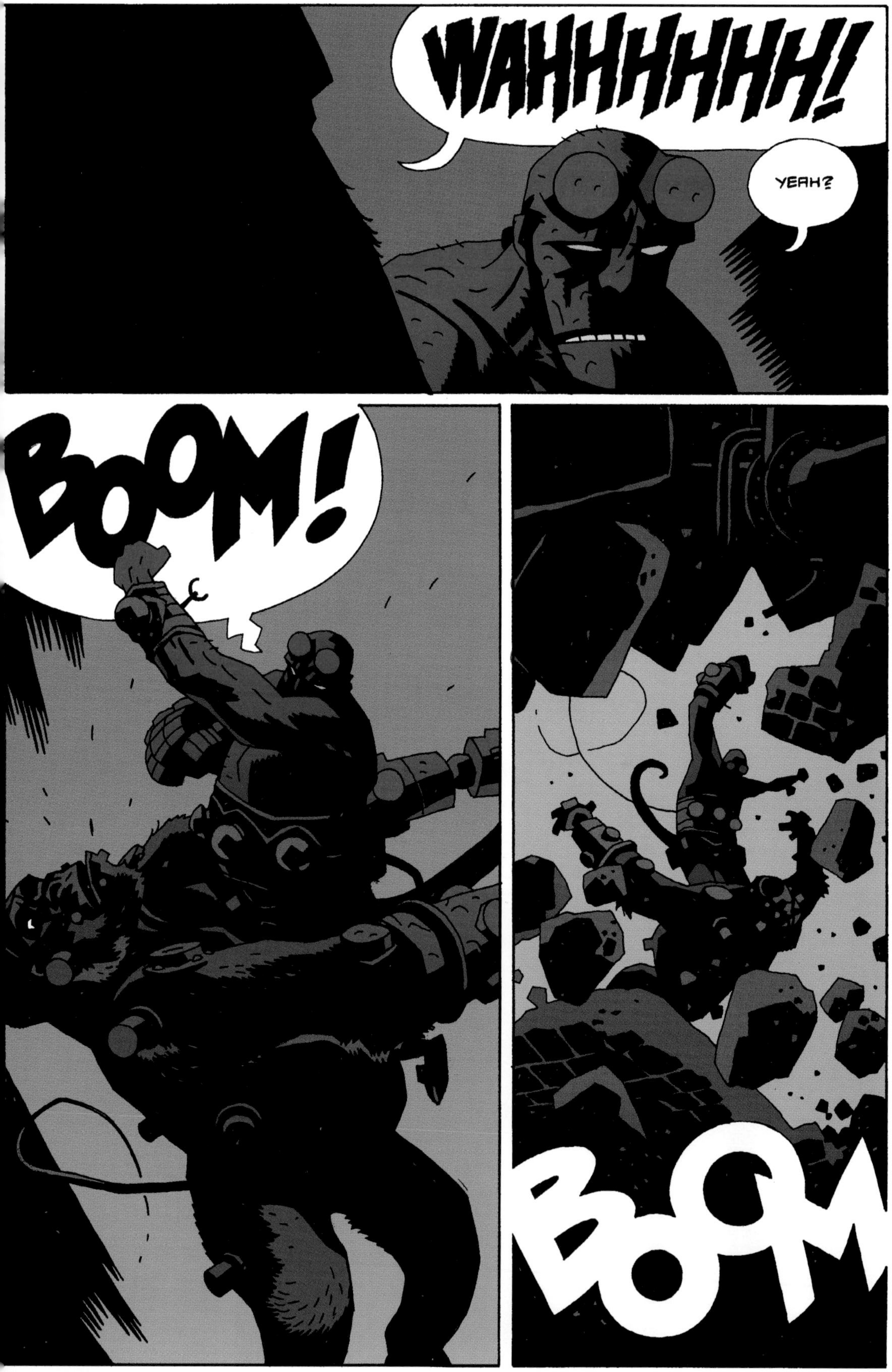
WAHHHHHH!
YEAH?
BOOM!
BOOM

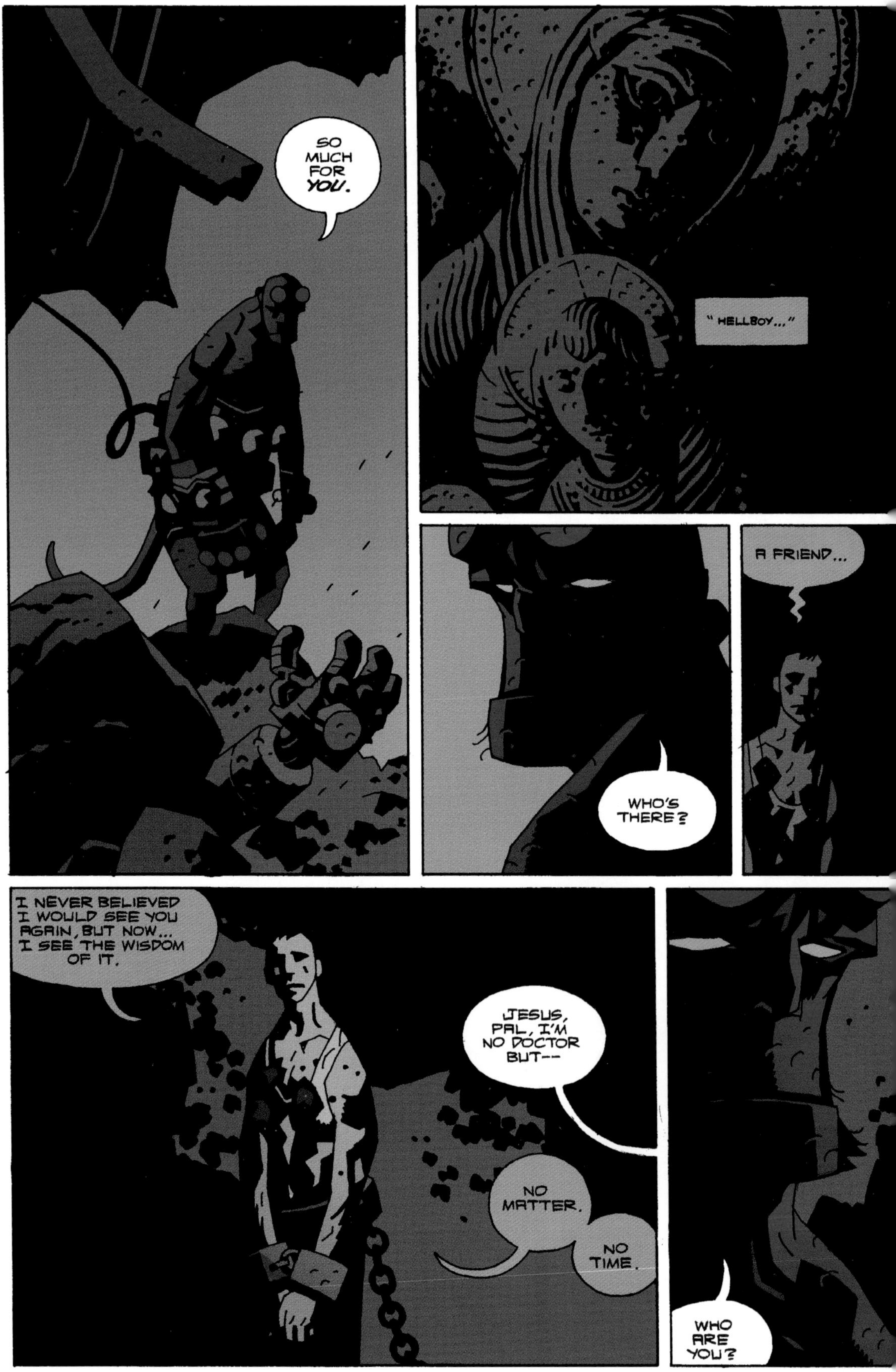
SO MUCH FOR YOU.
" HELLBOY..."
WHO'S THERE?
A FRIEND...
I NEVER BELIEVED I WOULD SEE YOU AGAIN, BUT NOW... I SEE THE WISDOM OF IT.
JESUS, PAL, I'M NO DOCTOR BUT--
NO MATTER.
NO TIME.
WHO ARE YOU?

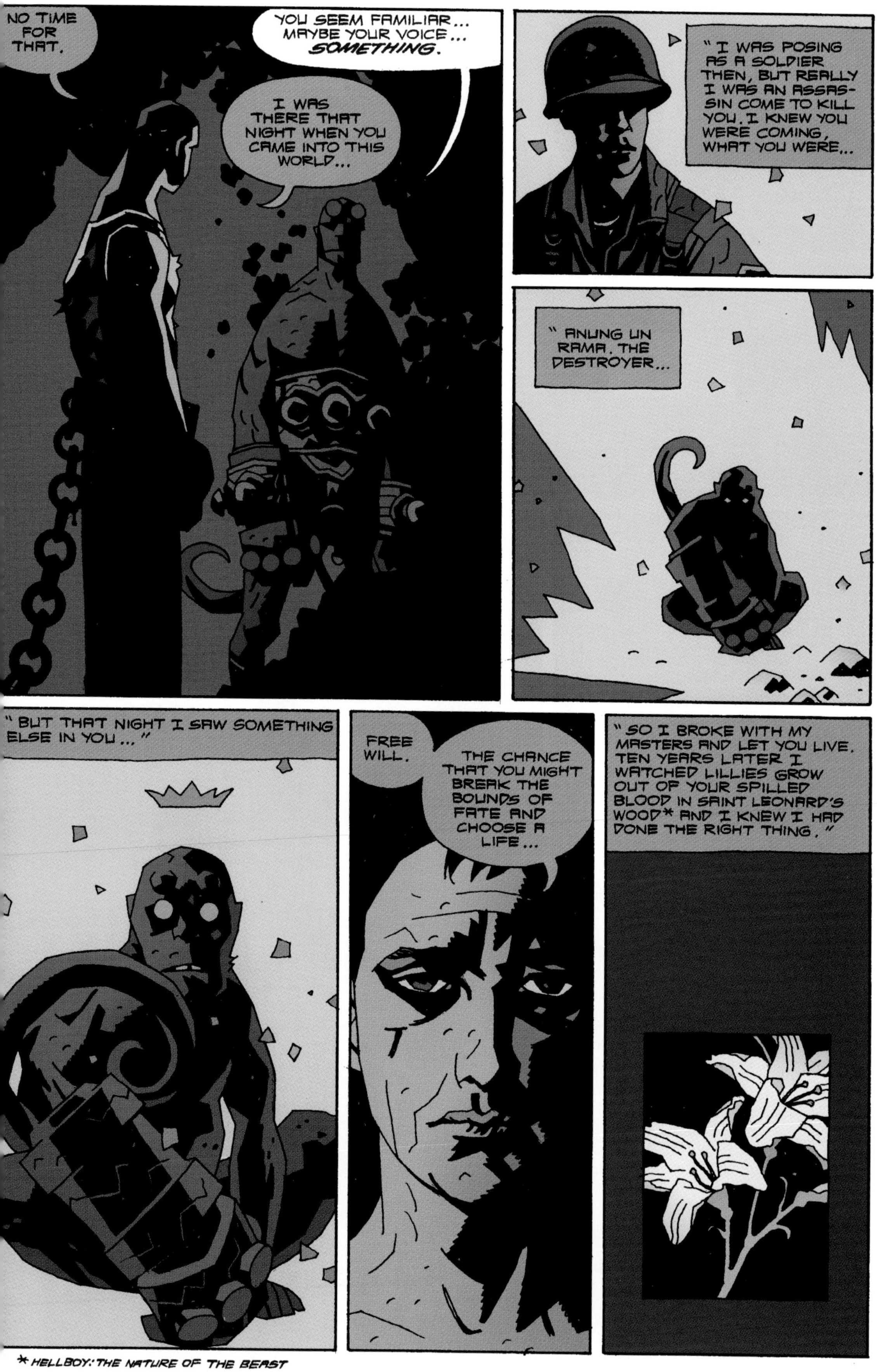
NO TIME FOR THAT.
YOU SEEM FAMILIAR... MAYBE YOUR VOICE... SOMETHING.
I WAS THERE THAT NIGHT WHEN YOU CAME INTO THIS WORLD...
"I WAS POSING AS A SOLDIER THEN, BUT REALLY I WAS AN ASSASSIN COME TO KILL YOU. I KNEW YOU WERE COMING, WHAT YOU WERE...
"ANUNG UN RAMA, THE DESTROYER...
"BUT THAT NIGHT I SAW SOMETHING ELSE IN YOU..."
FREE WILL.
THE CHANCE THAT YOU MIGHT BREAK THE BOUNDS OF FATE AND CHOOSE A LIFE...
"SO I BROKE WITH MY MASTERS AND LET YOU LIVE. TEN YEARS LATER I WATCHED LILLIES GROW OUT OF YOUR SPILLED BLOOD IN SAINT LEONARD'S WOOD* AND I KNEW I HAD DONE THE RIGHT THING."

* HELLBOY: THE NATURE OF THE BEAST

WHO *ARE* YOU?

I'M NOT IMPORTANT, BUT THE THING COMING HERE *MUST* BE STOPPED.

THE TRUTH IS THAT THERE ARE LIVING BEINGS IN SPACE, INVISIBLE TO YOUR *SCIENTISTS*, UNDETECTABLE BY MAN-MADE DEVICES. THEY ARE OLDER THAN THIS PLANET, AND IF THEY EVER HAD PHYSICAL BODIES THEY ARE RID OF THEM NOW...

"THEY SIMPLY DRIFT..., AND WAIT."

"WAIT FOR WHAT?"

"THEY WAIT TO CELEBRATE THE DOWNFALL OF MAN. IF THEY CAN, THEY WILL *CAUSE* IT, THEY LONG TO DEVOUR ALL LIGHT AND LIFE, TO MAKE EVERYTHING AS COLD AND EMPTY AS THEY ARE THEMSELVES. WHO CAN UNDERSTAND A THING LIKE THAT...?"

"BUT THEY HAVE ALWAYS CALLED OUT TO MAN. IN THE PAST THERE WERE HUMANS WHO COULD *HEAR* THEM, WHO COULD COMMUNICATE WITH THEM, BUT THESE WERE HUMANS OF A RARE SENSITIVITY OF MIND."

"HOW THE DULL, EVIL MEN OF THIS PLACE MANAGED TO DO THE SAME I DON'T KNOW..."

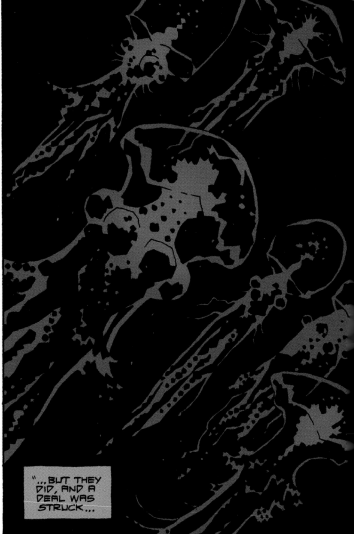

"...BUT THEY DID, AND A DEAL WAS STRUCK..."

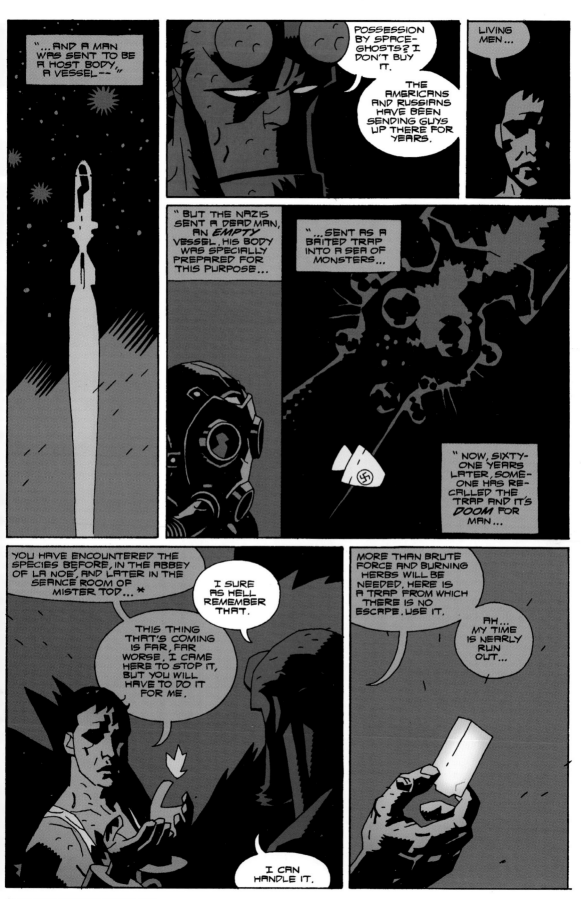

"...AND A MAN WAS SENT TO BE A HOST BODY, A VESSEL--"

POSSESSION BY SPACE-GHOSTS? I DON'T BUY IT.

THE AMERICANS AND RUSSIANS HAVE BEEN SENDING GUYS UP THERE FOR YEARS.

LIVING MEN...

"BUT THE NAZIS SENT A DEAD MAN, AN EMPTY VESSEL. HIS BODY WAS SPECIALLY PREPARED FOR THIS PURPOSE...

"...SENT AS A BAITED TRAP INTO A SEA OF MONSTERS...

"NOW, SIXTY-ONE YEARS LATER, SOMEONE HAS RE-CALLED THE TRAP AND IT'S DOOM FOR MAN...

YOU HAVE ENCOUNTERED THE SPECIES BEFORE, IN THE ABBEY OF LA NOE, AND LATER IN THE SEANCE ROOM OF MISTER TOD... *

I SURE AS HELL REMEMBER THAT.

THIS THING THAT'S COMING IS FAR, FAR WORSE. I CAME HERE TO STOP IT, BUT YOU WILL HAVE TO DO IT FOR ME.

I CAN HANDLE IT.

MORE THAN BRUTE FORCE AND BURNING HERBS WILL BE NEEDED. HERE IS A TRAP FROM WHICH THERE IS NO ESCAPE. USE IT.

AH... MY TIME IS NEARLY RUN OUT...

* HELLBOY: GOODBYE MISTER TOD

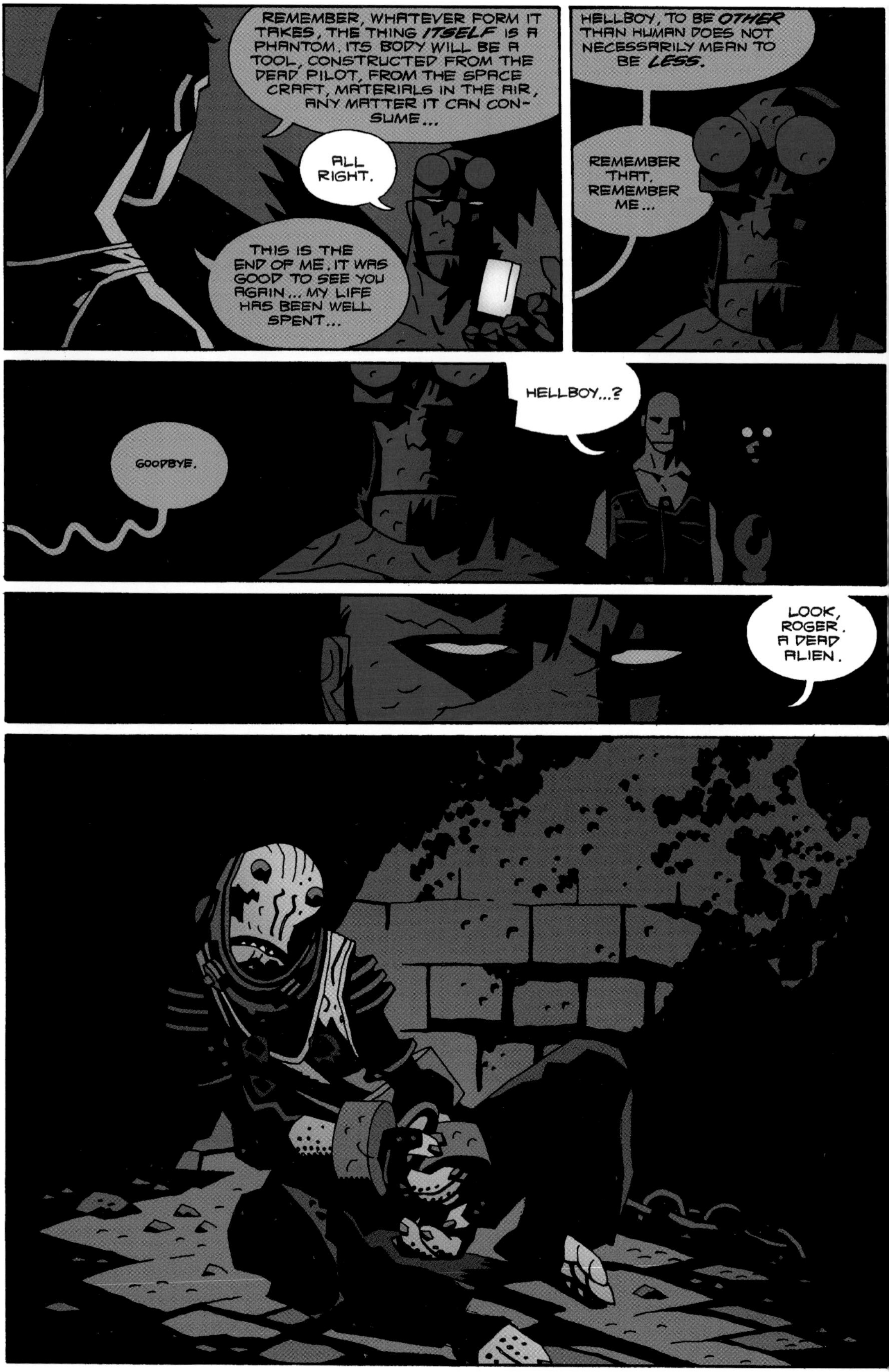
REMEMBER, WHATEVER FORM IT TAKES, THE THING ITSELF IS A PHANTOM. ITS BODY WILL BE A TOOL, CONSTRUCTED FROM THE DEAD PILOT, FROM THE SPACE CRAFT, MATERIALS IN THE AIR, ANY MATTER IT CAN CONSUME...
ALL RIGHT.
THIS IS THE END OF ME. IT WAS GOOD TO SEE YOU AGAIN... MY LIFE HAS BEEN WELL SPENT...
HELLBOY, TO BE OTHER THAN HUMAN DOES NOT NECESSARILY MEAN TO BE LESS.
REMEMBER THAT. REMEMBER ME...
GOODBYE.
HELLBOY...?
LOOK, ROGER. A DEAD ALIEN.

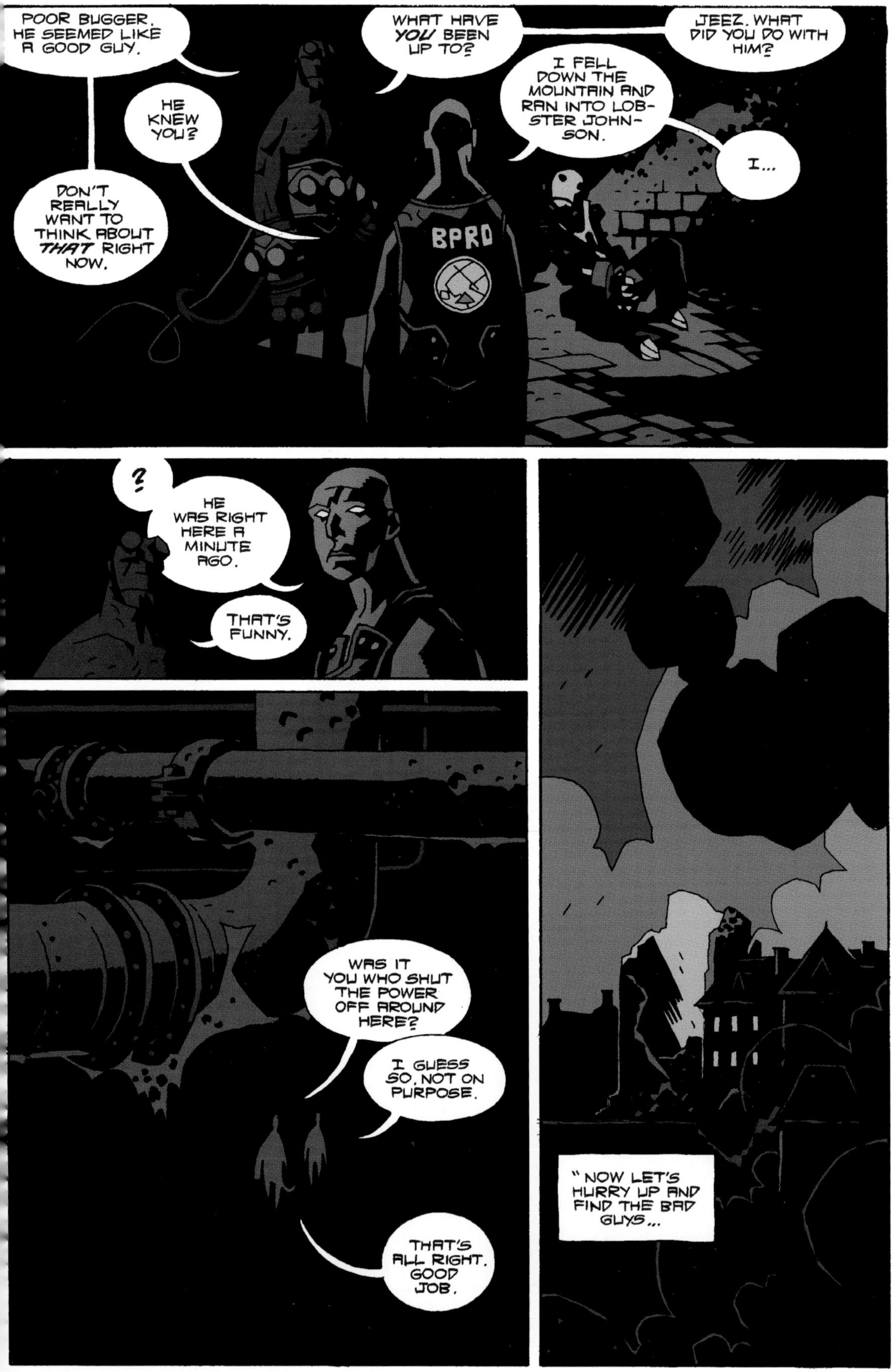
POOR BUGGER. HE SEEMED LIKE A GOOD GUY.
HE KNEW YOU?
DON'T REALLY WANT TO THINK ABOUT *THAT* RIGHT NOW.
WHAT HAVE *YOU* BEEN UP TO?
I FELL DOWN THE MOUNTAIN AND RAN INTO LOB-STER JOHN-SON.
JEEZ. WHAT DID YOU DO WITH HIM?
I...
?
HE WAS RIGHT HERE A MINUTE AGO.
THAT'S FUNNY.
WAS IT YOU WHO SHUT THE POWER OFF AROUND HERE?
I GUESS SO. NOT ON PURPOSE.
THAT'S ALL RIGHT. GOOD JOB.
"NOW LET'S HURRY UP AND FIND THE BAD GUYS...

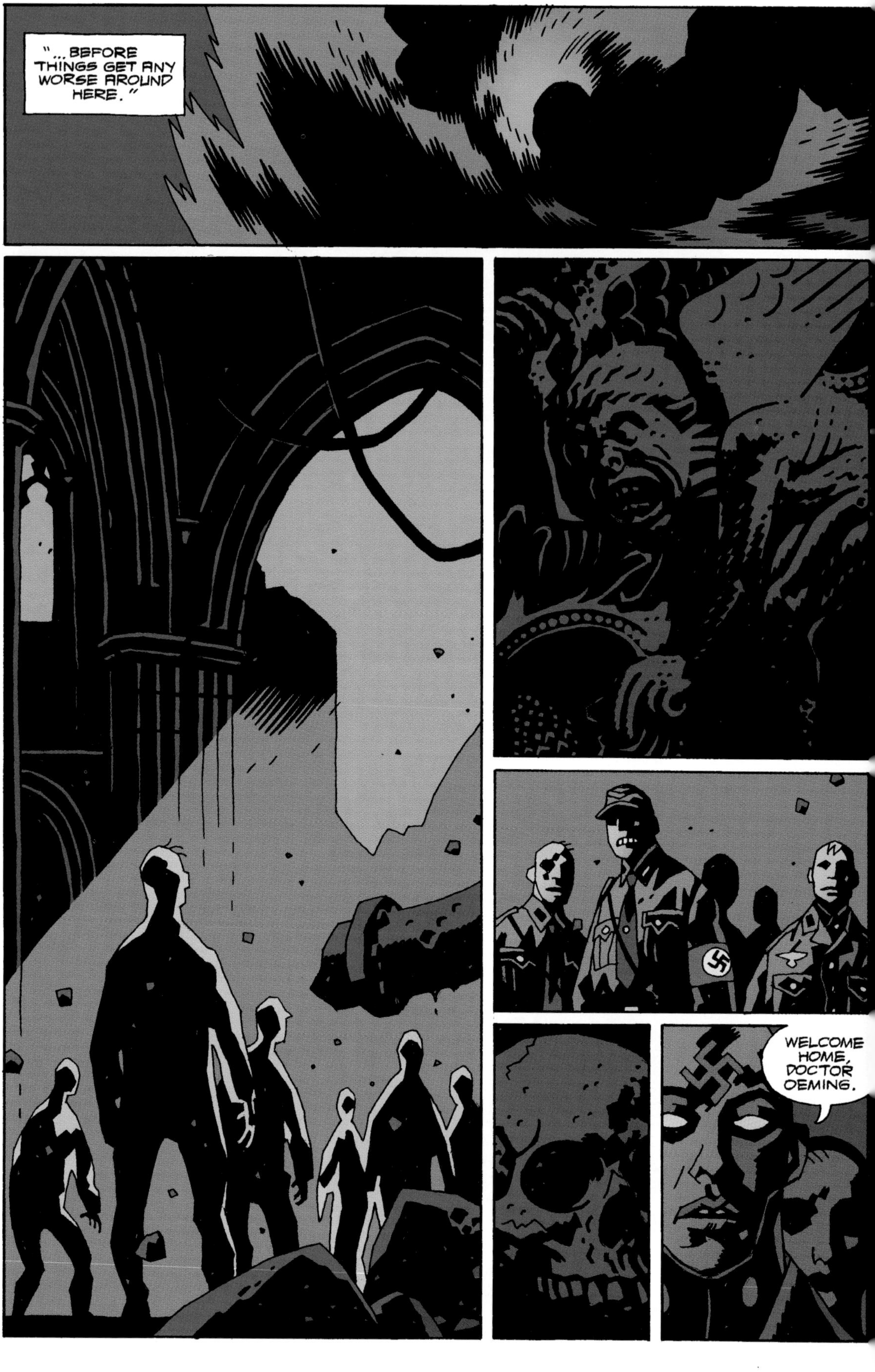
"... BEFORE THINGS GET ANY WORSE AROUND HERE."
WELCOME HOME, DOCTOR OEMING.

Chapter Three

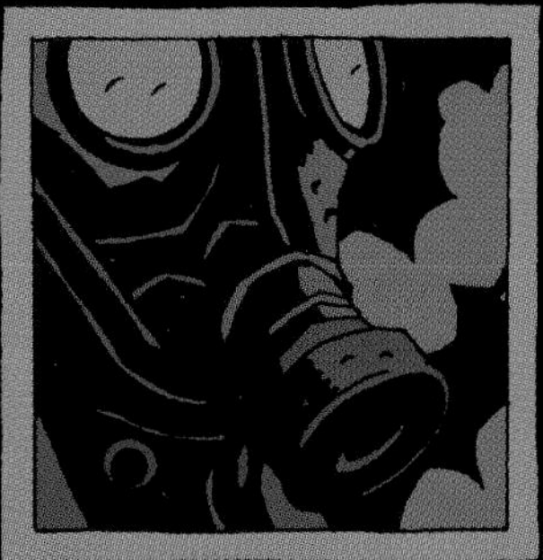

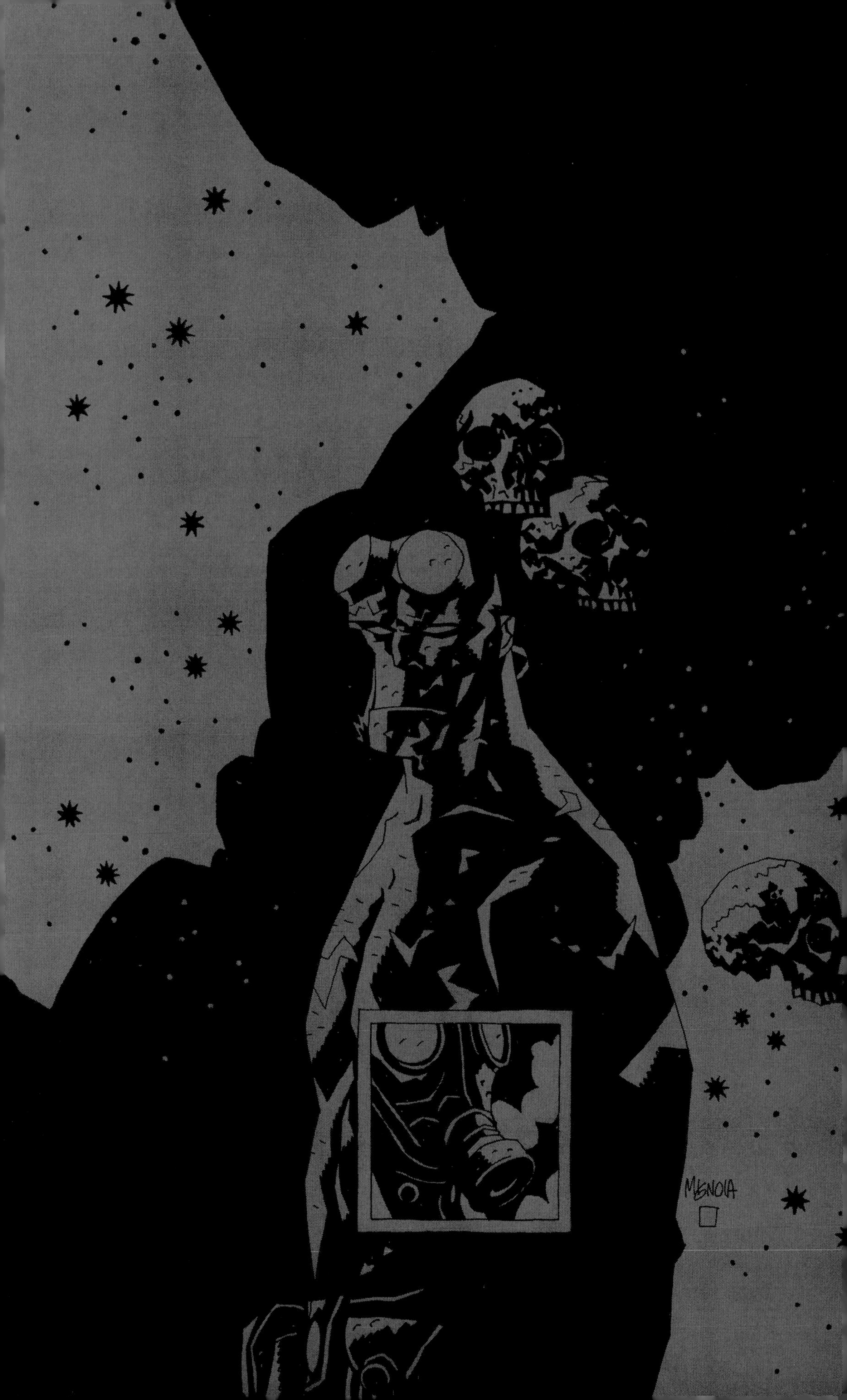
MIGNOLA

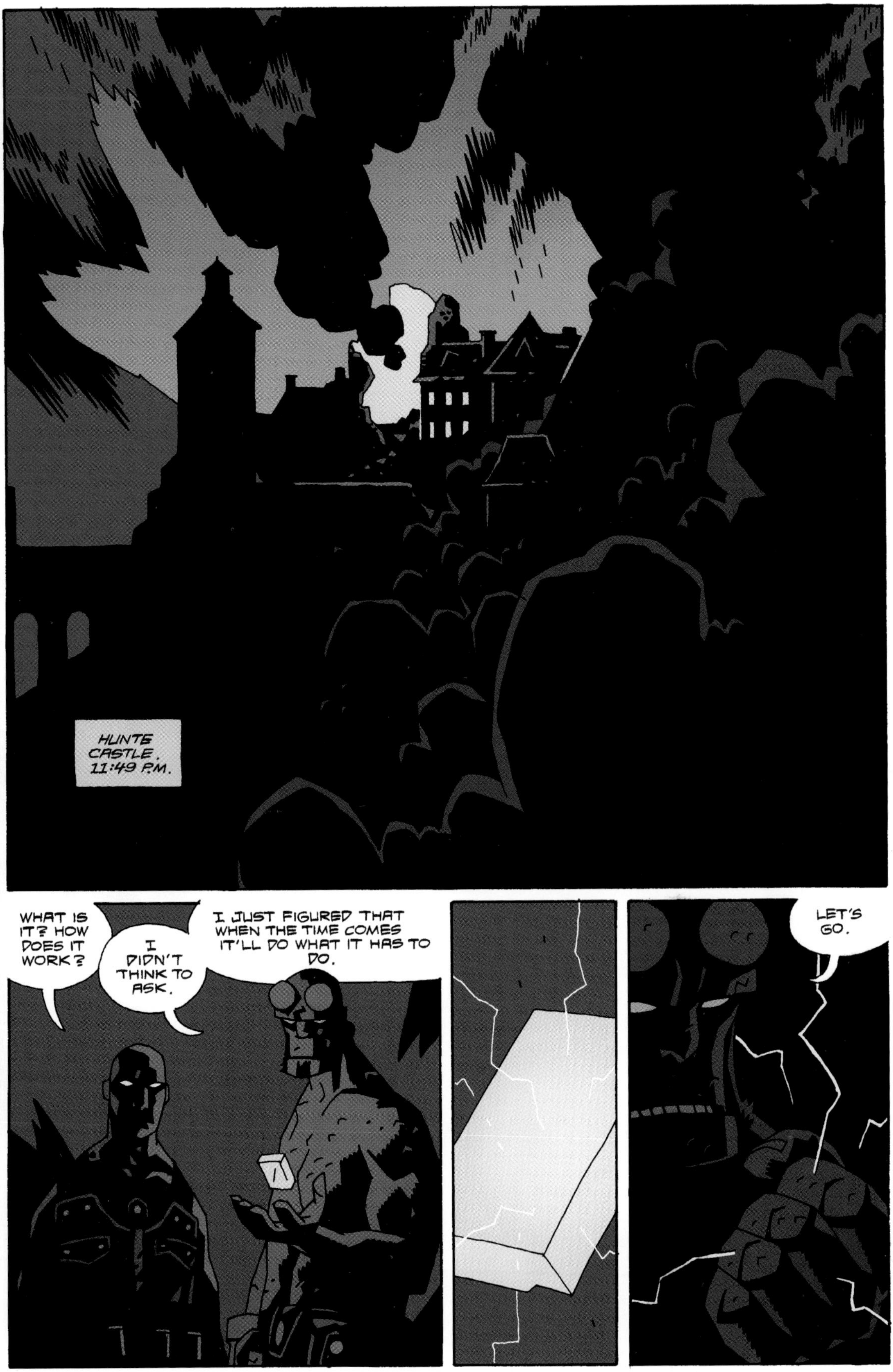
HUNTE CASTLE. 11:49 P.M.
WHAT IS IT? HOW DOES IT WORK?
I DIDN'T THINK TO ASK.
I JUST FIGURED THAT WHEN THE TIME COMES IT'LL DO WHAT IT HAS TO DO.
LET'S GO.

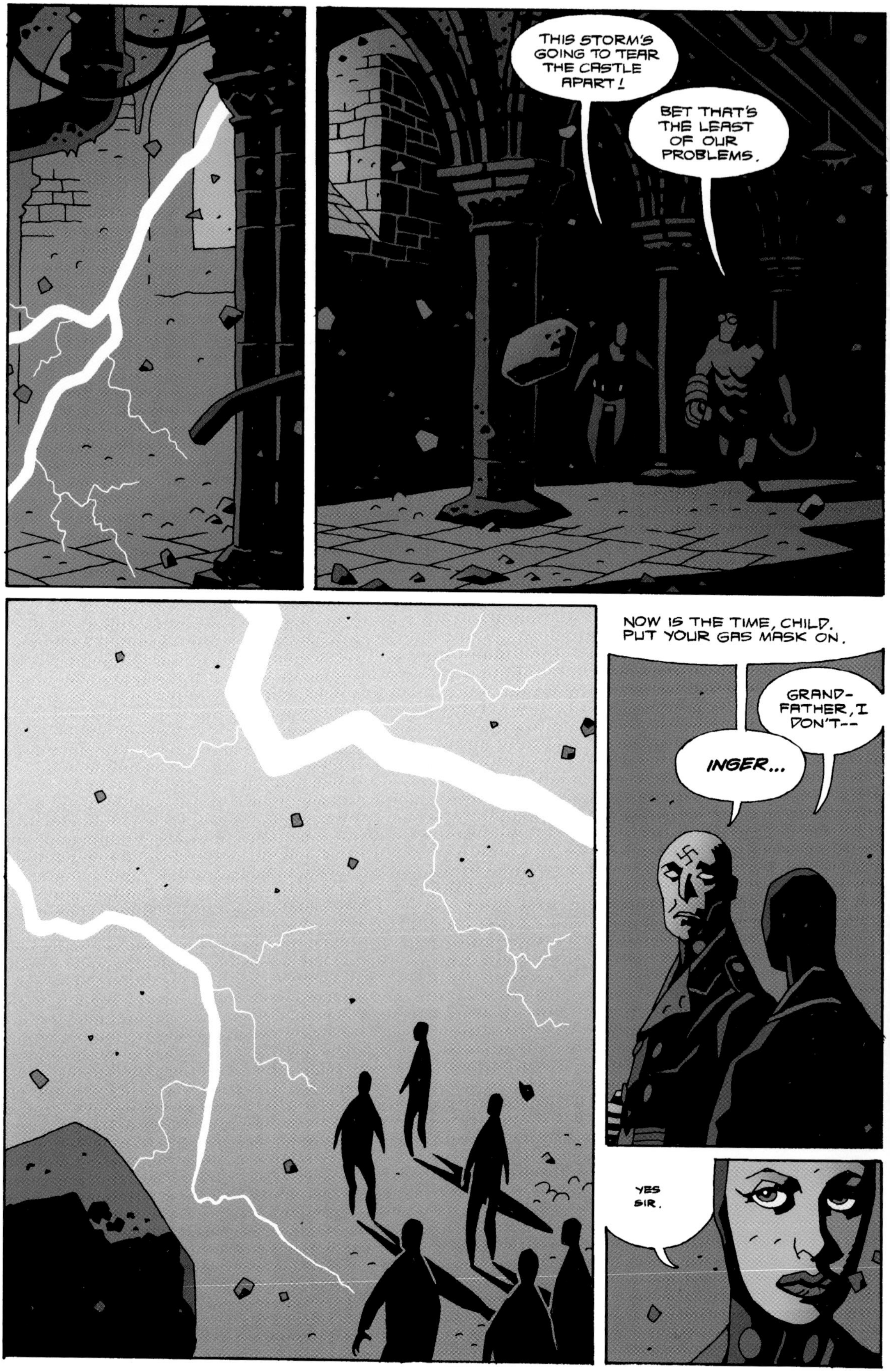
THIS STORM'S GOING TO TEAR THE CASTLE APART!
BET THAT'S THE LEAST OF OUR PROBLEMS.
NOW IS THE TIME, CHILD. PUT YOUR GAS MASK ON.
INGER...
GRAND-FATHER, I DON'T--
YES SIR.

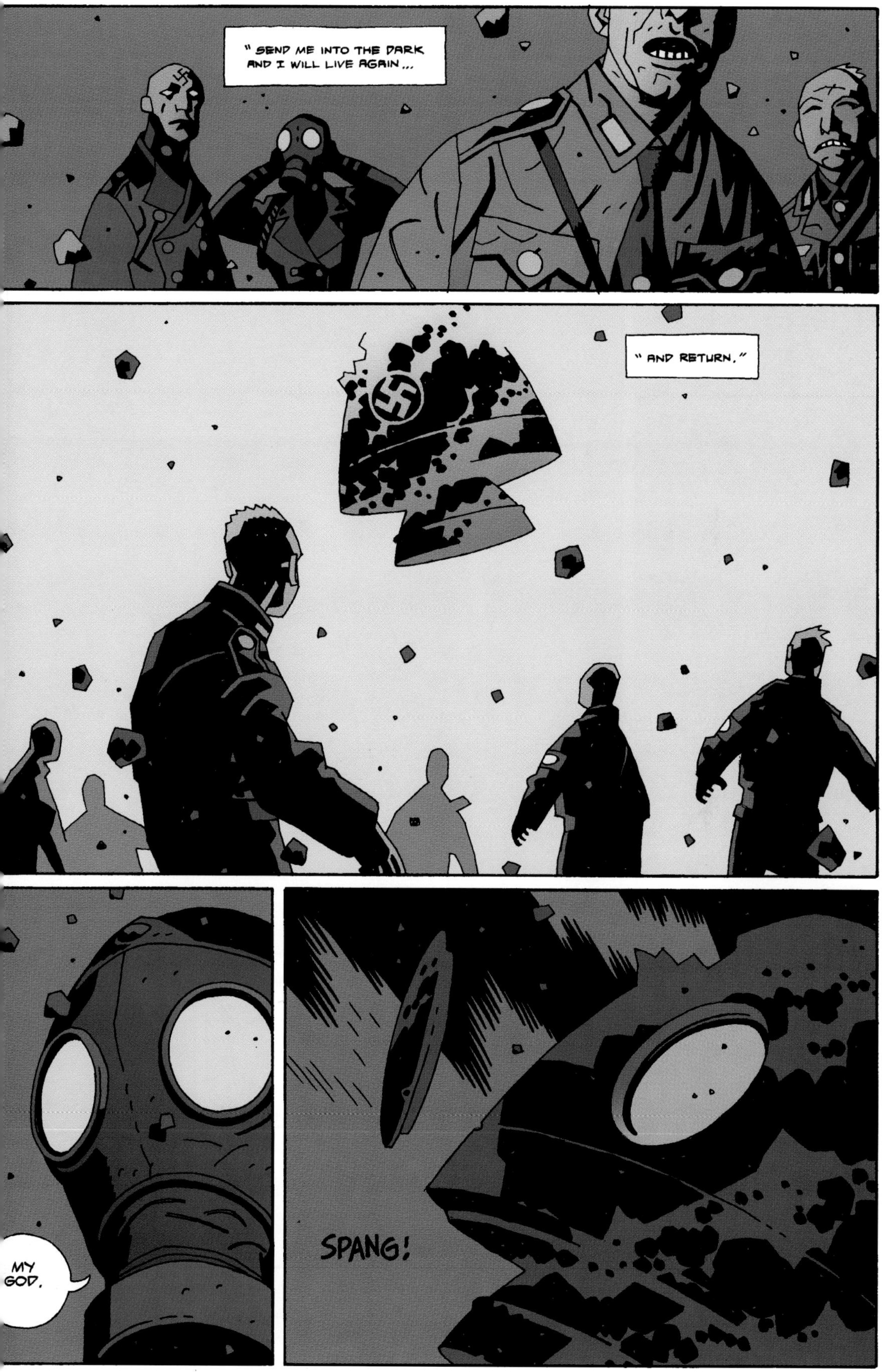
"SEND ME INTO THE DARK AND I WILL LIVE AGAIN...
"AND RETURN."
MY GOD.
SPANG!

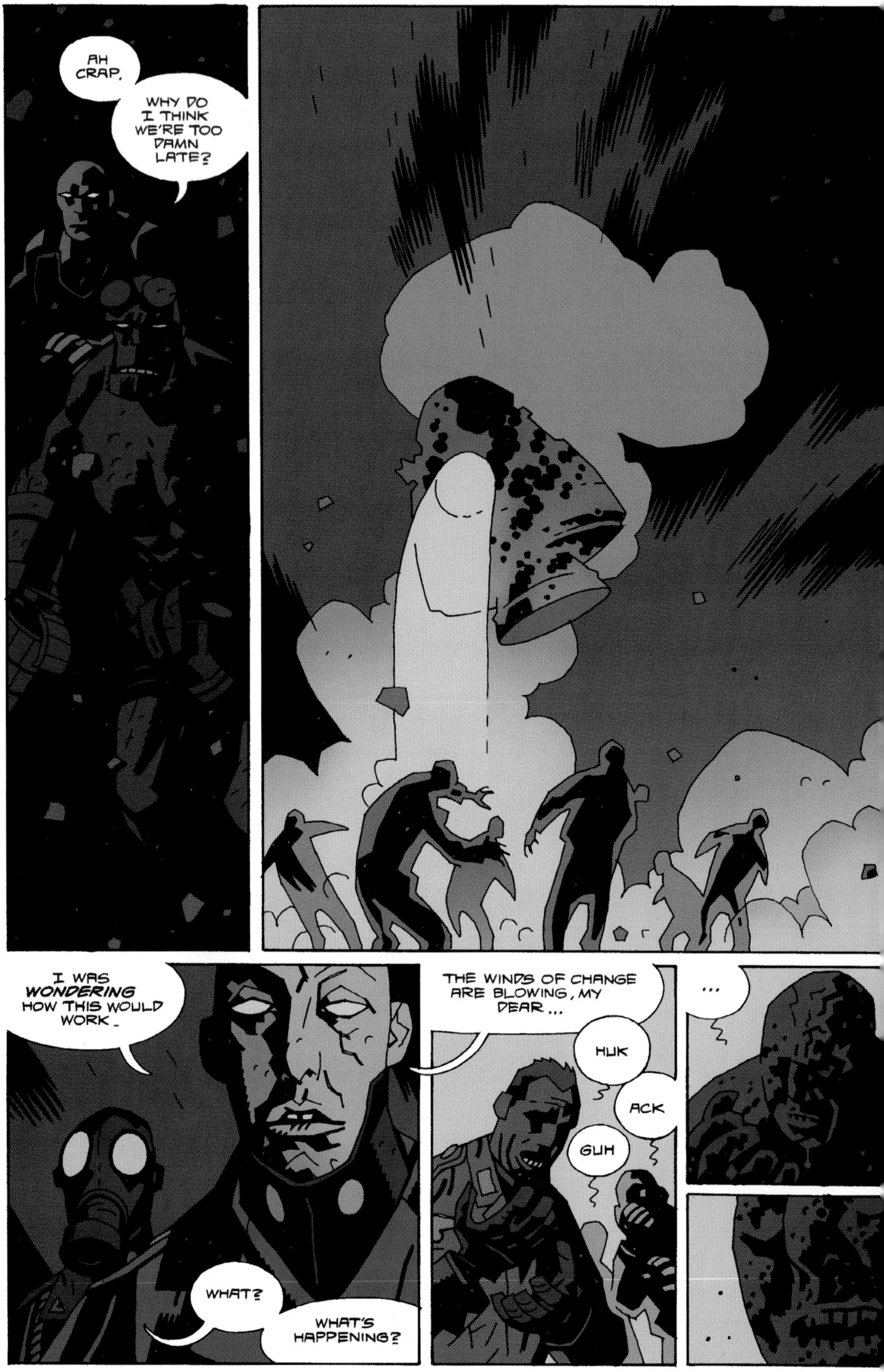

AH CRAP.
WHY DO I THINK WE'RE TOO DAMN LATE?
I WAS *WONDERING* HOW THIS WOULD WORK.
WHAT?
WHAT'S HAPPENING?
THE WINDS OF CHANGE ARE BLOWING, MY DEAR...
HUK
ACK
GUH
...

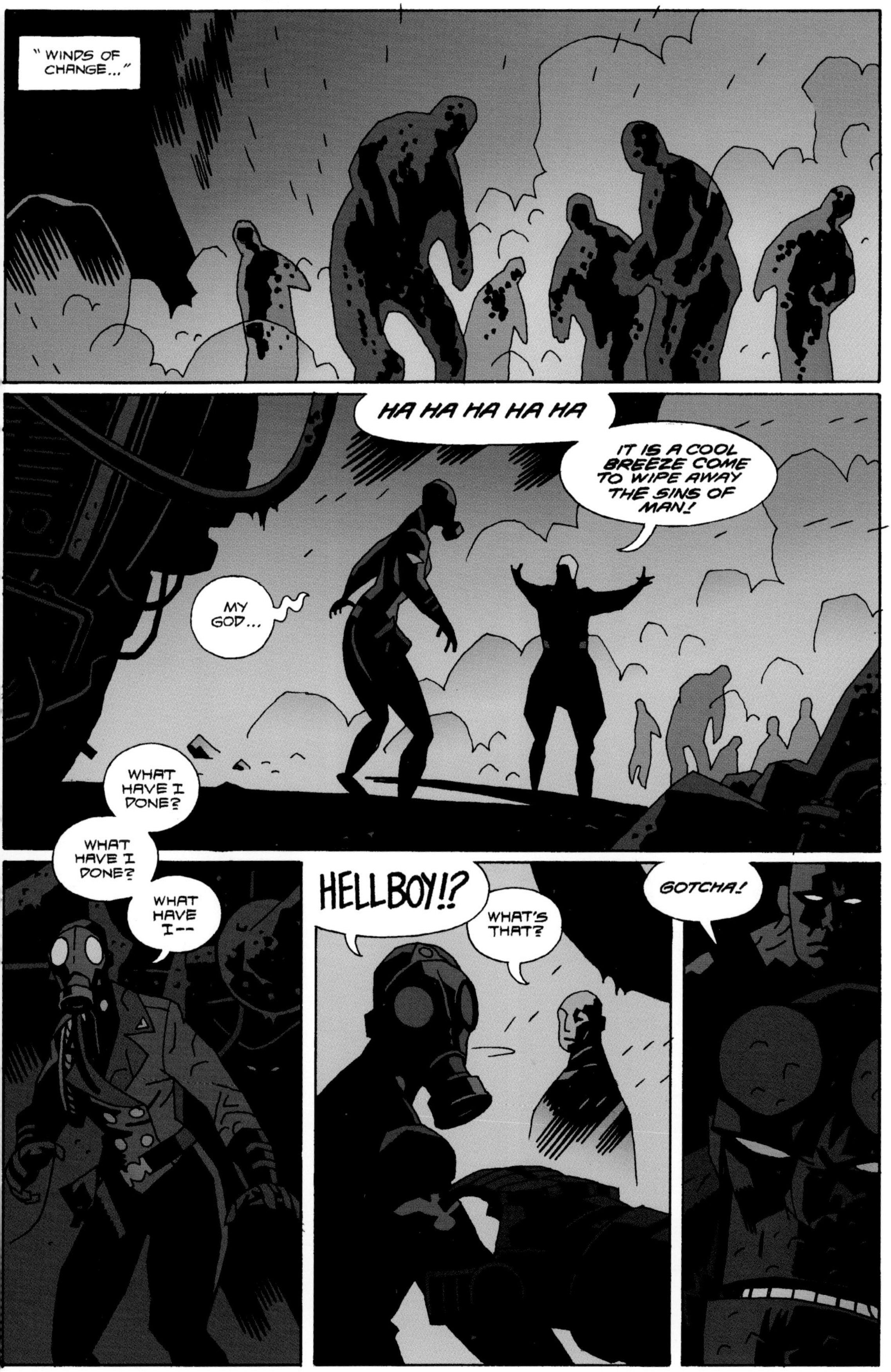
"WINDS OF CHANGE..."
HA HA HA HA HA
IT IS A COOL BREEZE COME TO WIPE AWAY THE SINS OF MAN!
MY GOD...
WHAT HAVE I DONE?
WHAT HAVE I DONE?
WHAT HAVE I--
HELLBOY!?
WHAT'S THAT?
GOTCHA!

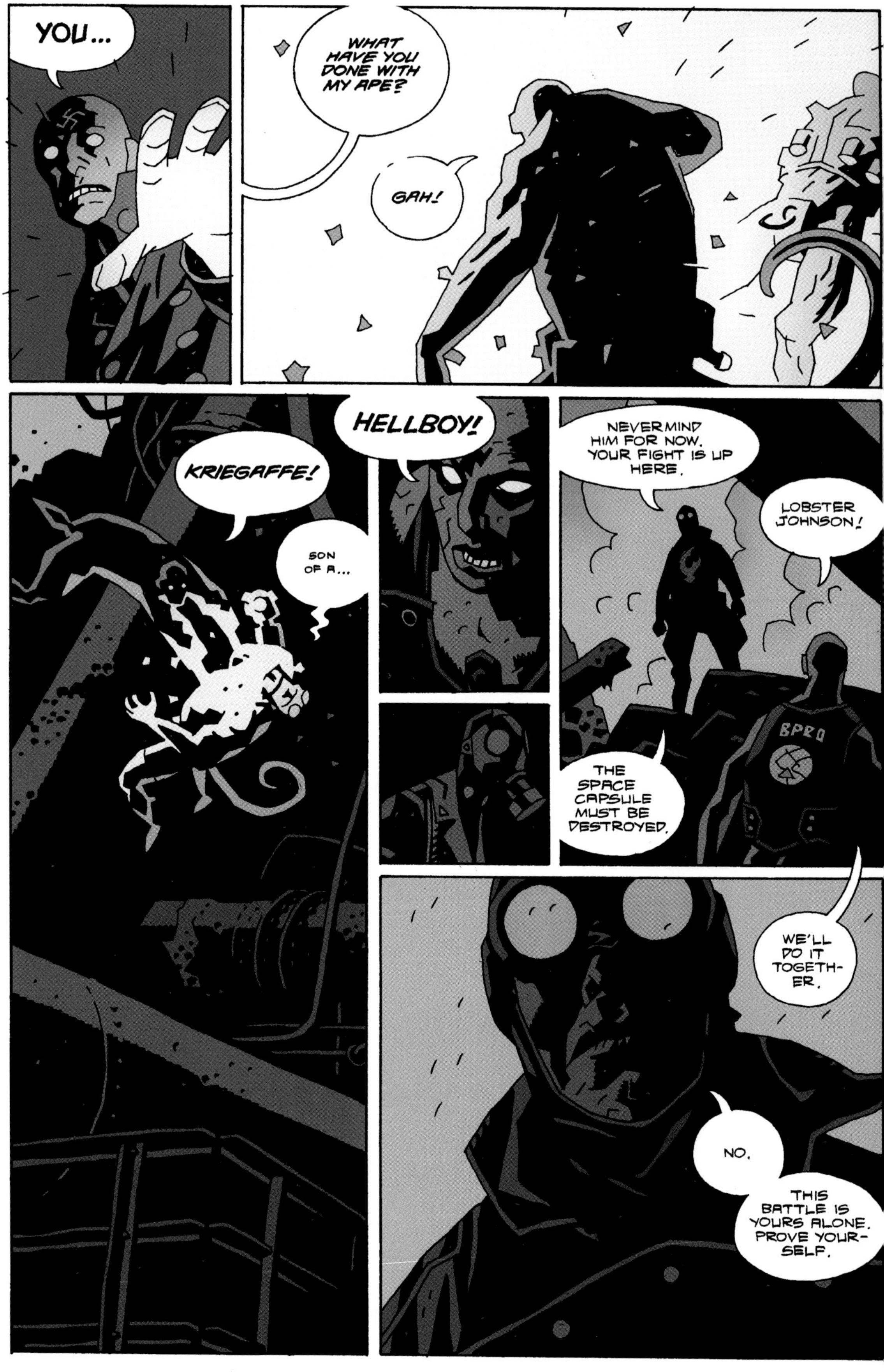
YOU...
WHAT HAVE YOU DONE WITH MY APE?
GAH!
KRIEGAFFE!
SON OF A...
HELLBOY!
NEVERMIND HIM FOR NOW. YOUR FIGHT IS UP HERE.
LOBSTER JOHNSON!
BPRD
THE SPACE CAPSULE MUST BE DESTROYED.
WE'LL DO IT TOGETH-ER.
NO.
THIS BATTLE IS YOURS ALONE. PROVE YOUR-SELF.

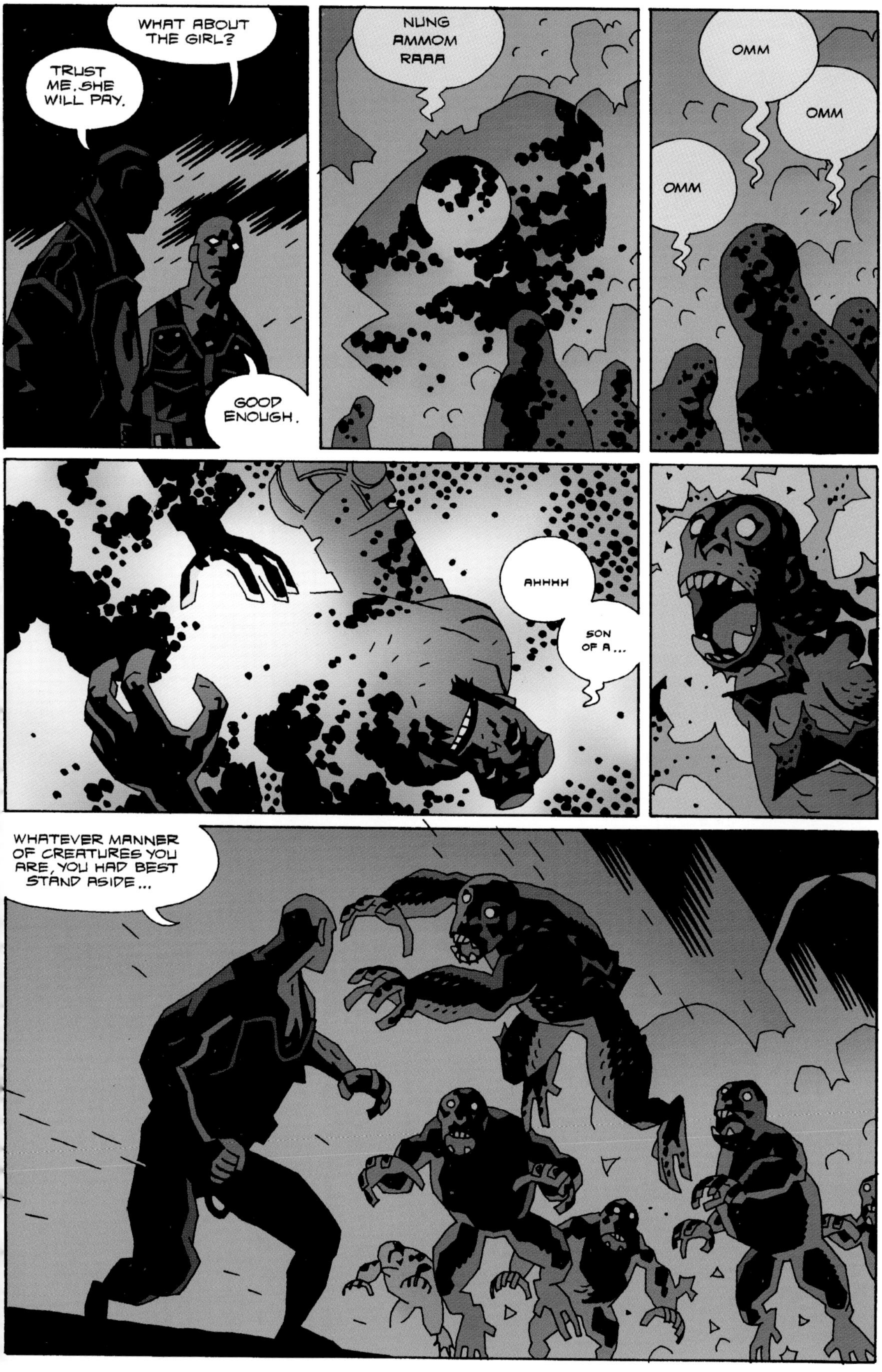
WHAT ABOUT THE GIRL?
TRUST ME, SHE WILL PAY.
GOOD ENOUGH.
NUNG AMMOM RAAA
OMM
OMM
OMM
AHHHH
SON OF A...
WHATEVER MANNER OF CREATURES YOU ARE, YOU HAD BEST STAND ASIDE...

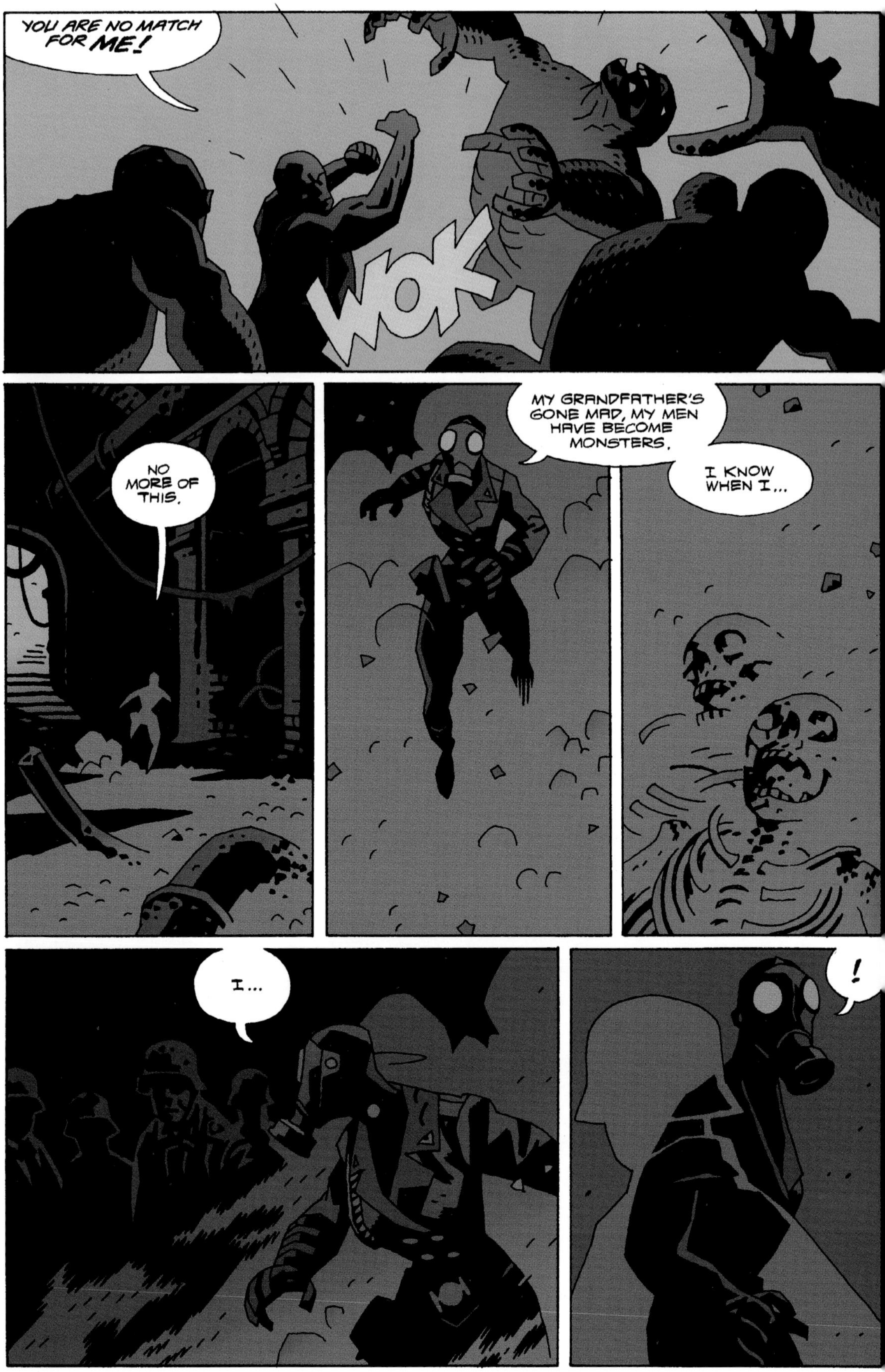
YOU ARE NO MATCH FOR ME!
WOK
NO MORE OF THIS.
MY GRANDFATHER'S GONE MAD, MY MEN HAVE BECOME MONSTERS.
I KNOW WHEN I...
I...
!

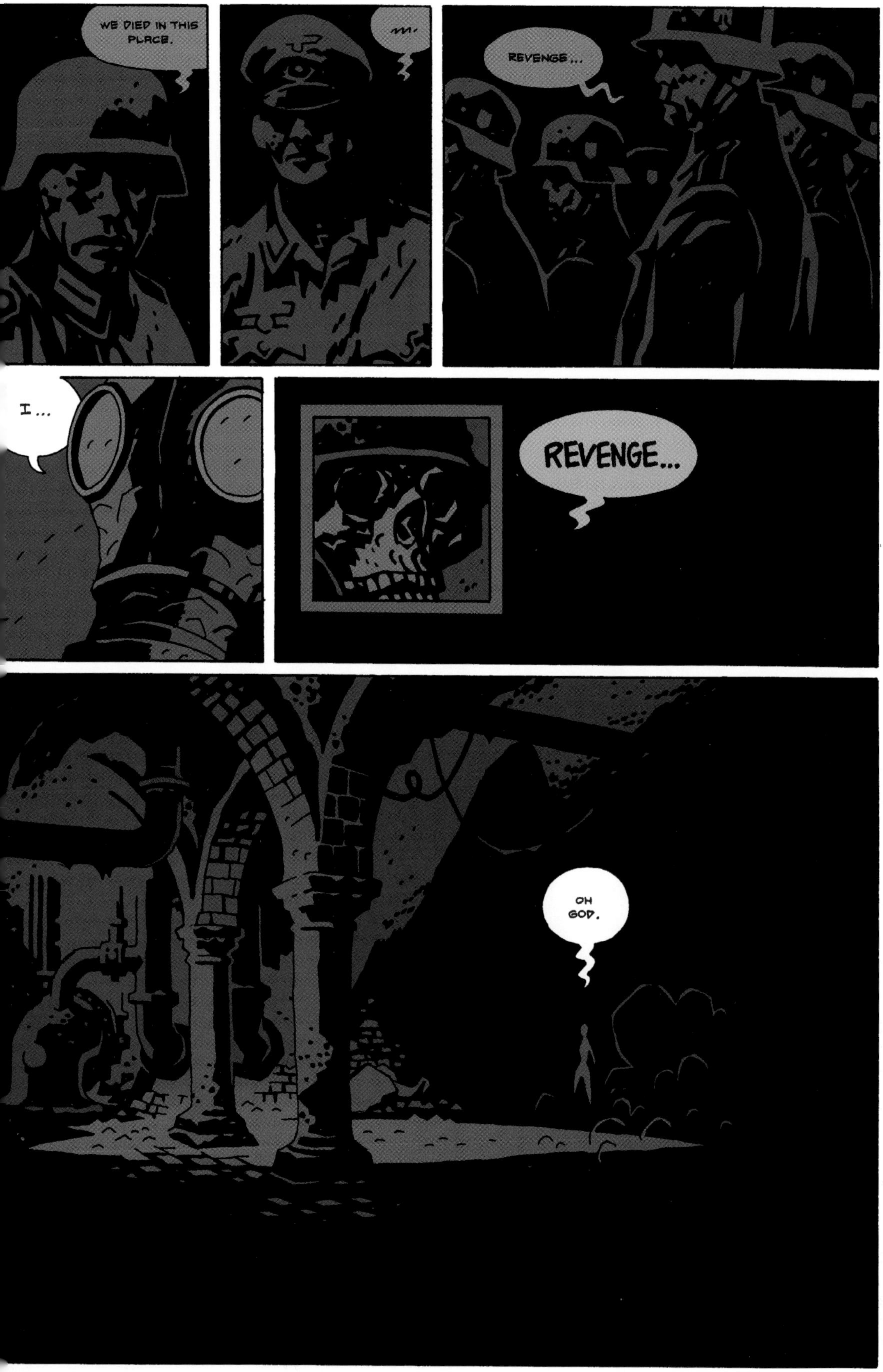
WE DIED IN THIS PLACE.
REVENGE...
I...
REVENGE...
OH GOD.

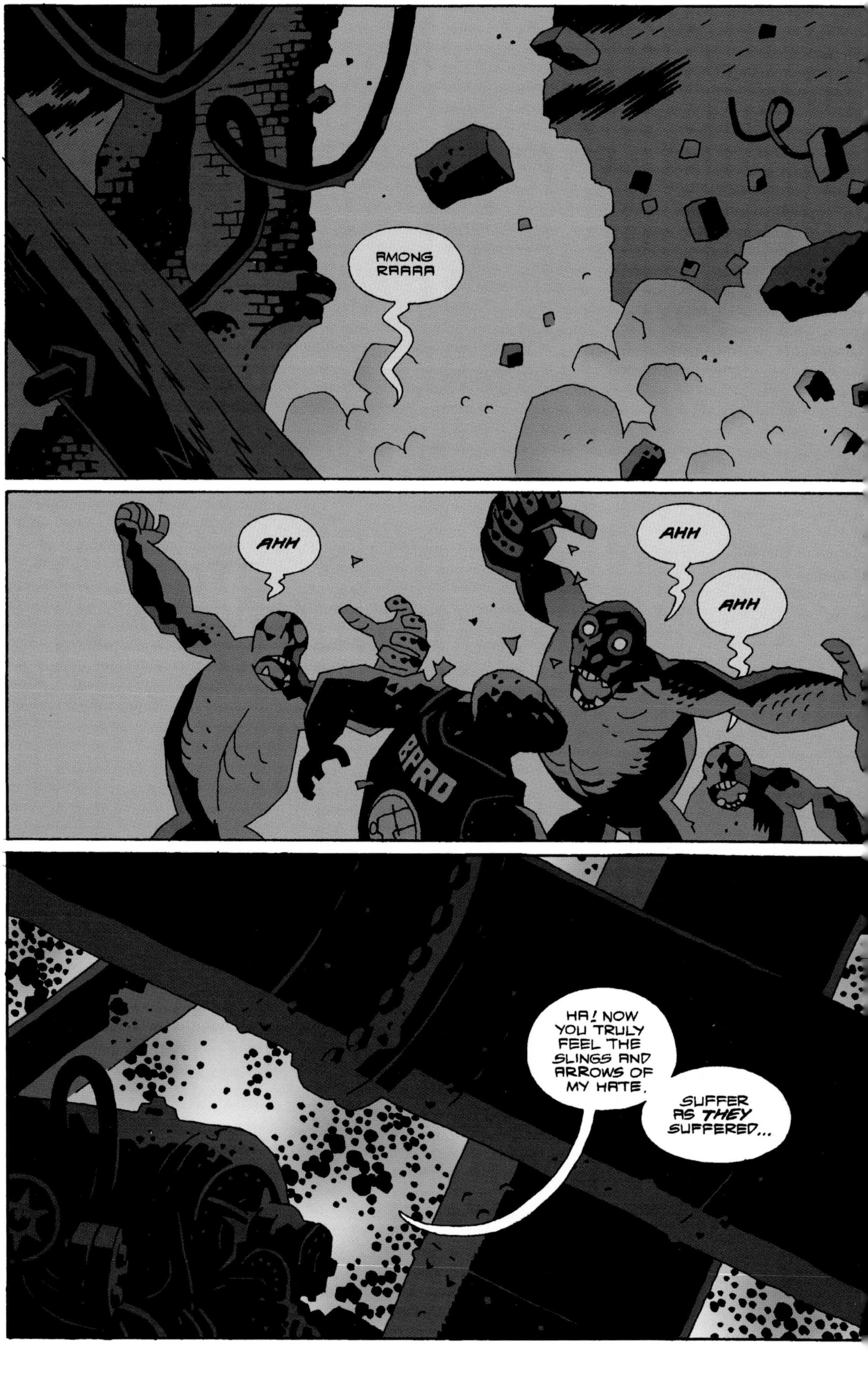
AMONG
RAAAAA
AHH
AHH
AHH
BPRD
HA! NOW YOU TRULY FEEL THE SLINGS AND ARROWS OF MY HATE.
SUFFER AS *THEY* SUFFERED...

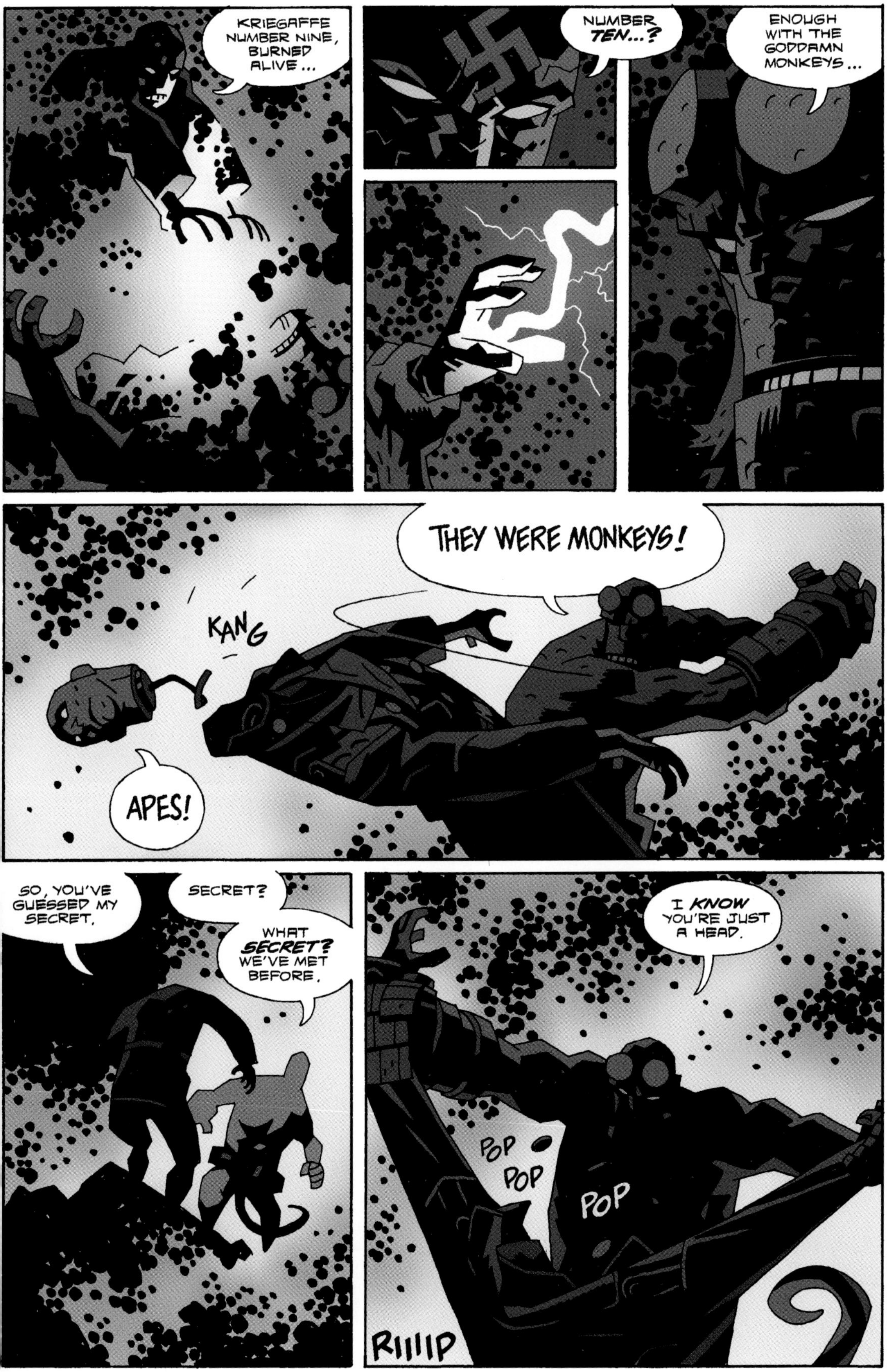
KRIEGAFFE NUMBER NINE, BURNED ALIVE...
NUMBER *TEN*...?
ENOUGH WITH THE GODDAMN MONKEYS...
THEY WERE MONKEYS!
KANG
APES!
SO, YOU'VE GUESSED MY SECRET.
SECRET?
WHAT *SECRET?* WE'VE MET BEFORE.
I *KNOW* YOU'RE JUST A HEAD.
POP
POP
POP
RIIIIP

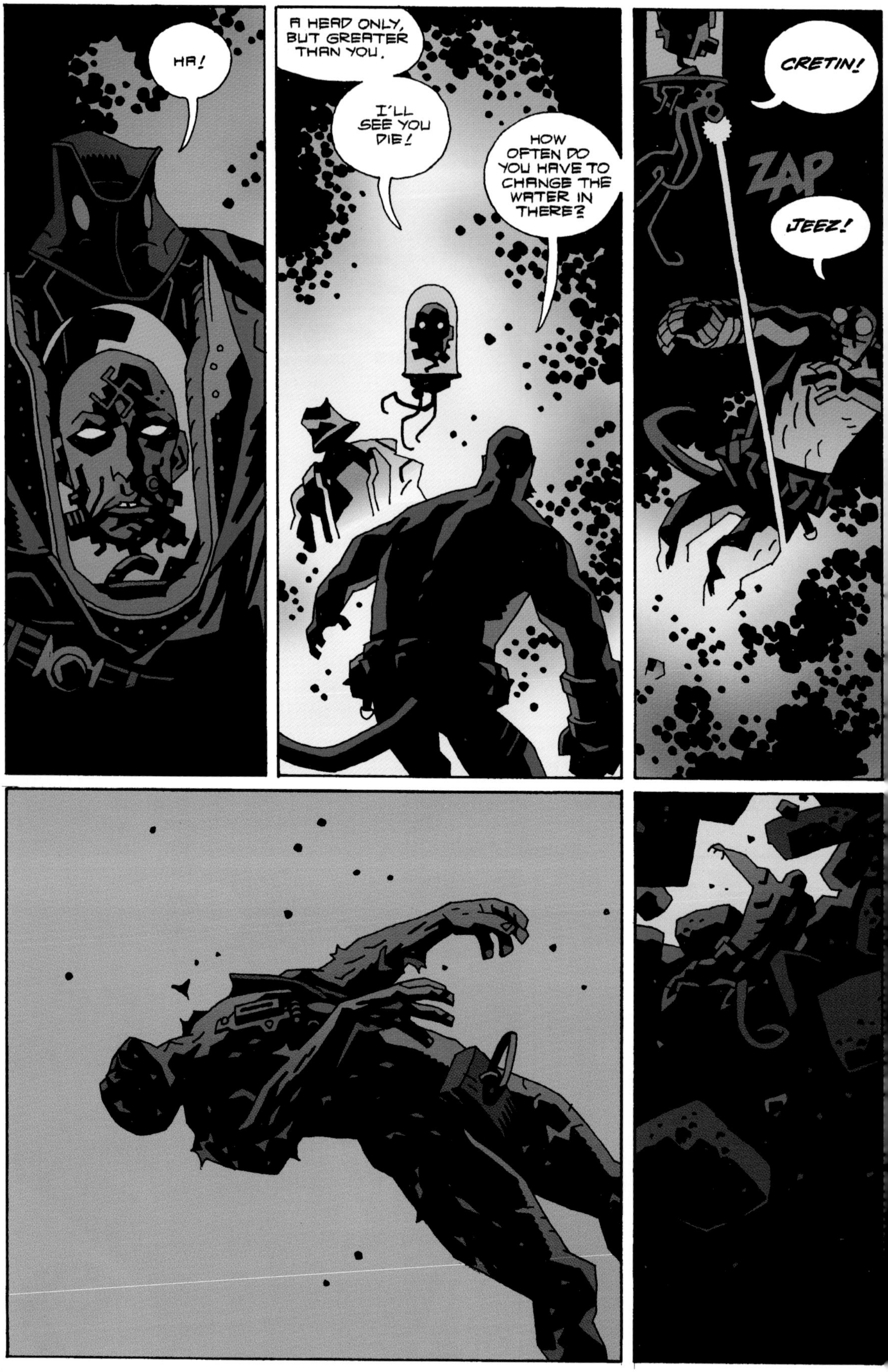
HA!
A HEAD ONLY, BUT GREATER THAN YOU.
I'LL SEE YOU DIE!
HOW OFTEN DO YOU HAVE TO CHANGE THE WATER IN THERE?
CRETIN!
ZAP
JEEZ!

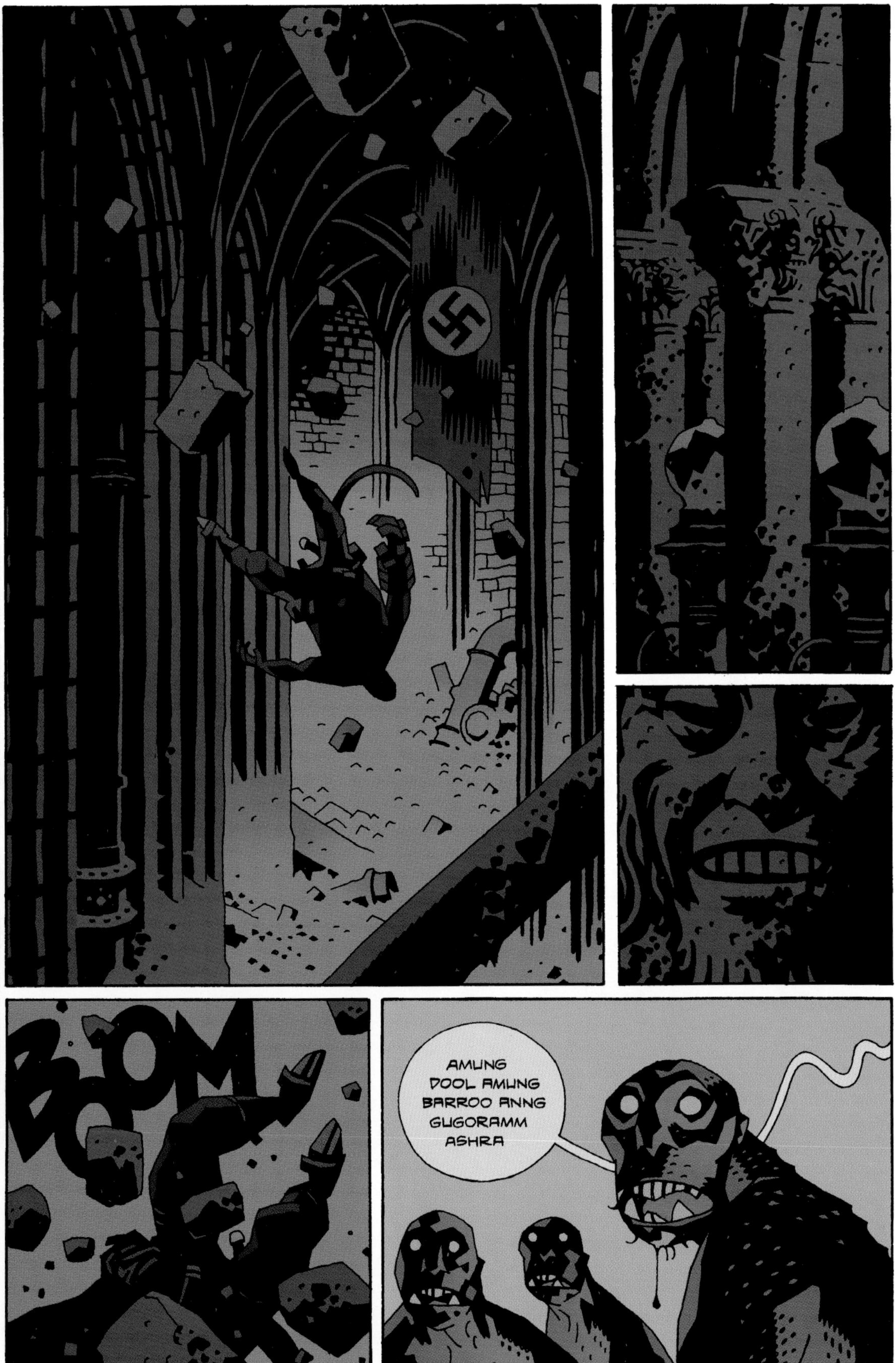
BOOM
AMUNG DOOL AMUNG BARROO ANNG GUGORAMM ASHRA

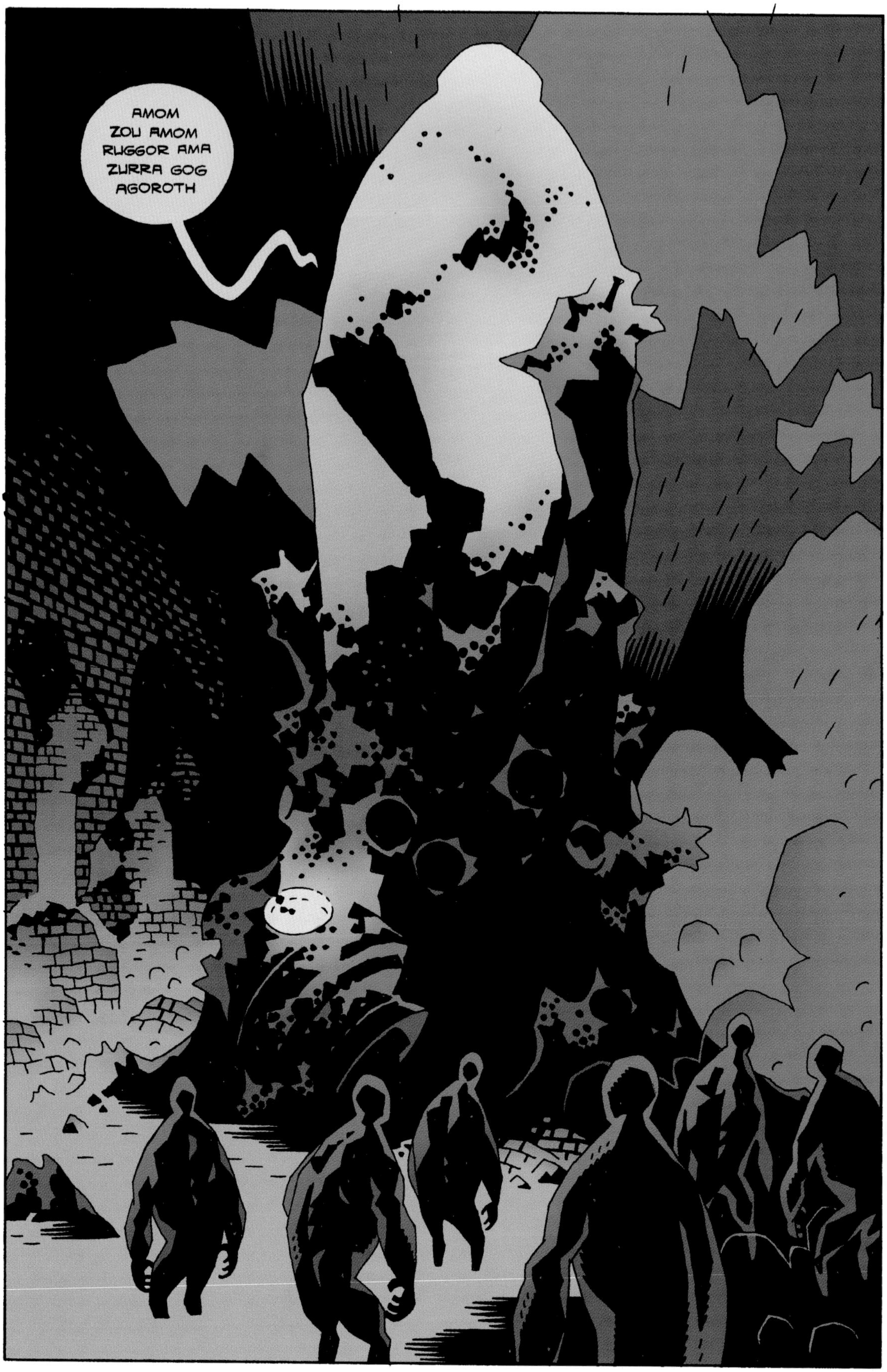
AMOM ZOU AMOM RUGGOR AMA ZURRA GOG AGOROTH

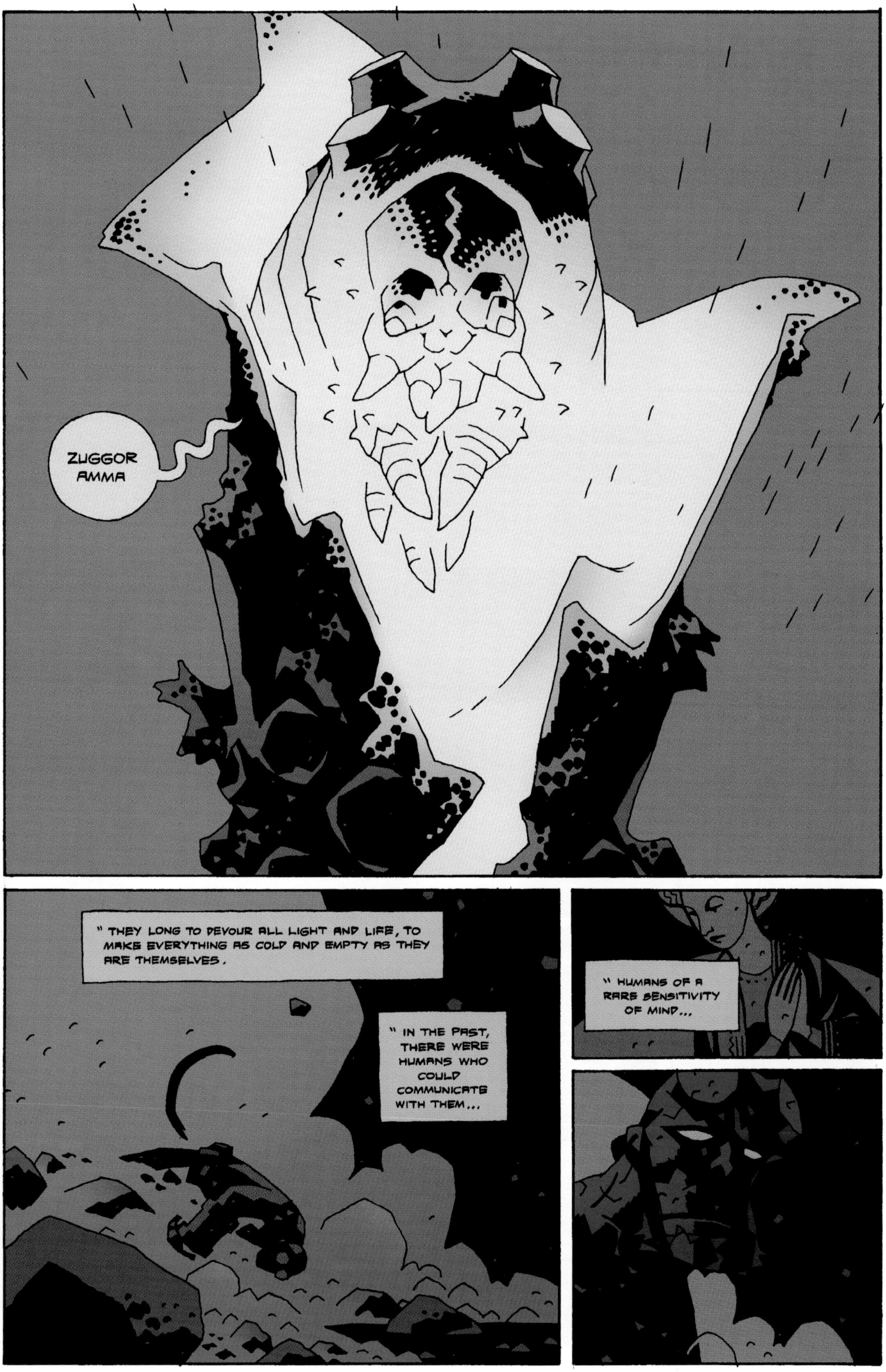
ZUGGOR AMMA
" THEY LONG TO DEVOUR ALL LIGHT AND LIFE, TO MAKE EVERYTHING AS COLD AND EMPTY AS THEY ARE THEMSELVES.
" IN THE PAST, THERE WERE HUMANS WHO COULD COMMUNICATE WITH THEM...
" HUMANS OF A RARE SENSITIVITY OF MIND...

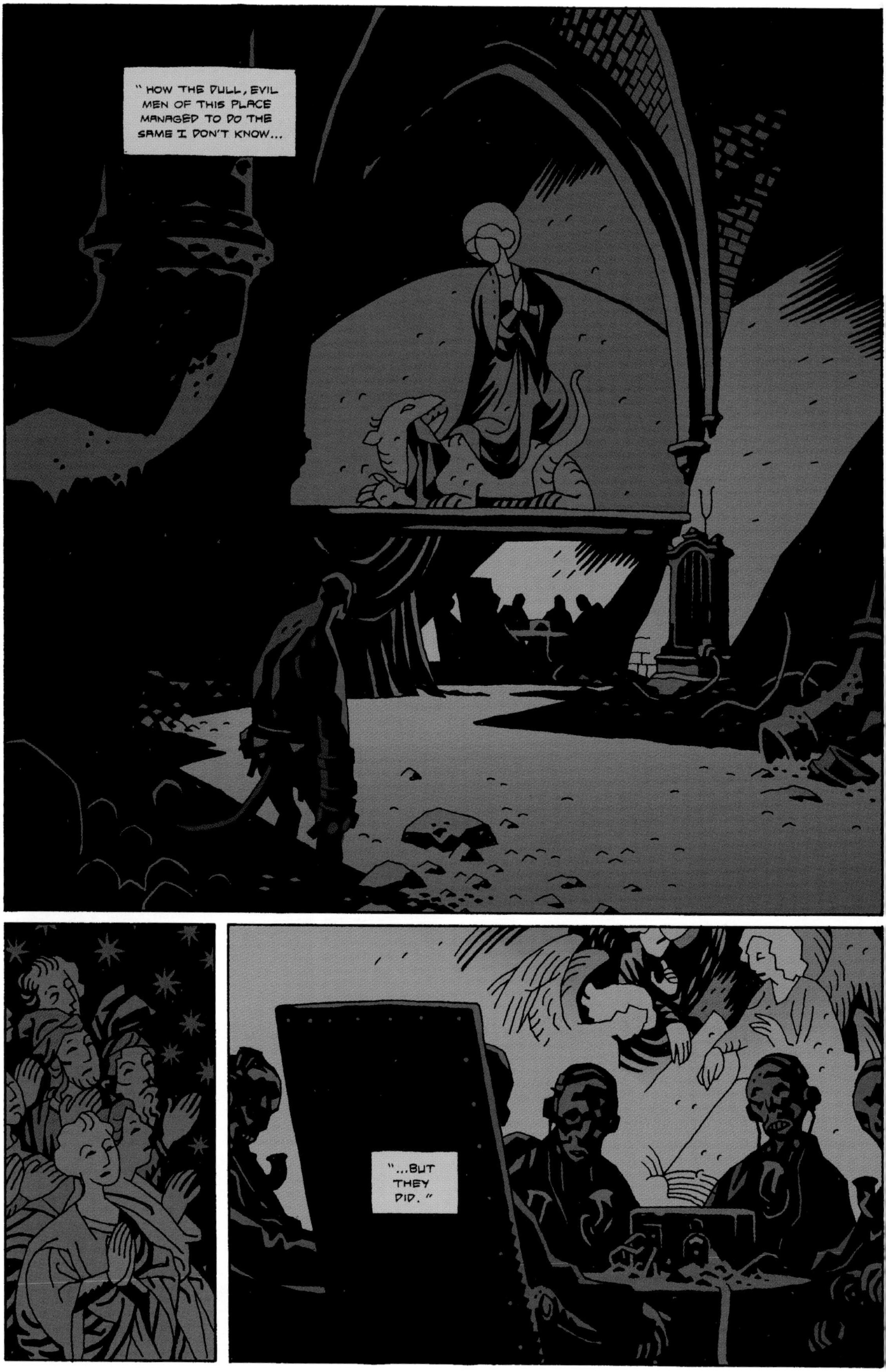
"HOW THE DULL, EVIL MEN OF THIS PLACE MANAGED TO DO THE SAME I DON'T KNOW...
"...BUT THEY DID."

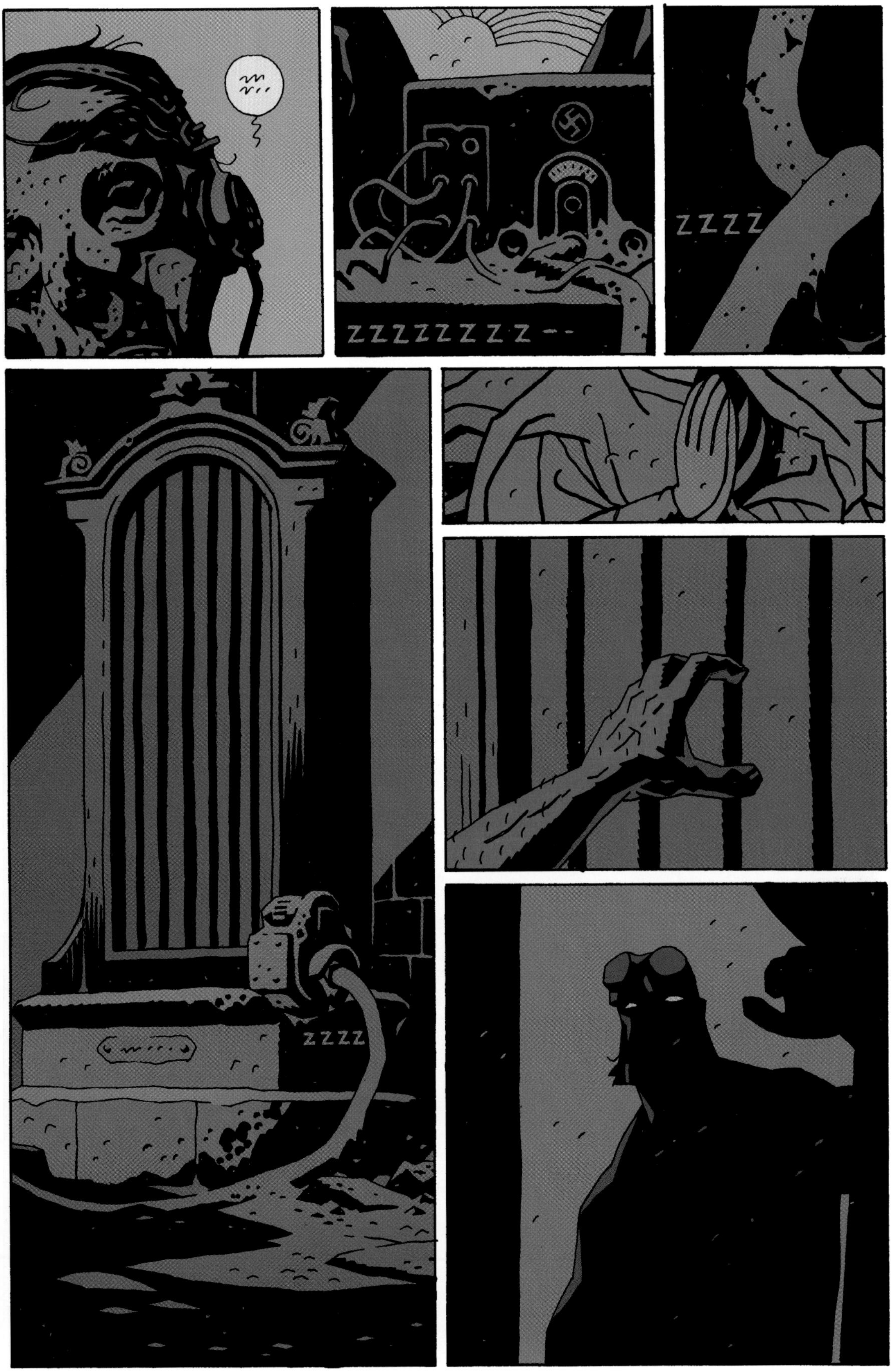
ZZZZZZZZZ--
ZZZZ
ZZZZ

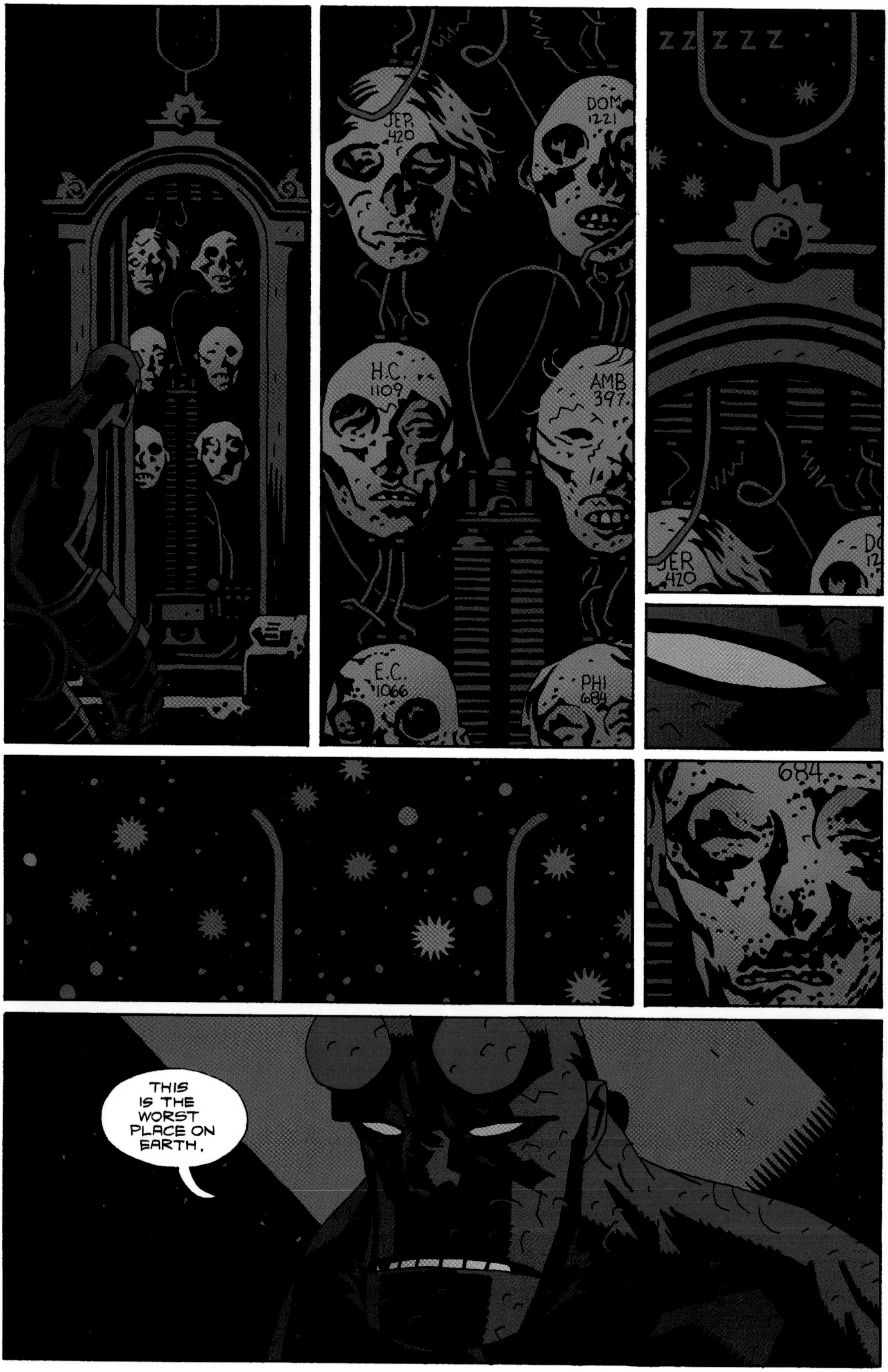

JER. 420
DOM 1221
H.C. 1109
AMB 397.
E.C. 1066
PHI 684
Z Z Z Z Z
JER 420
684
THIS IS THE WORST PLACE ON EARTH.

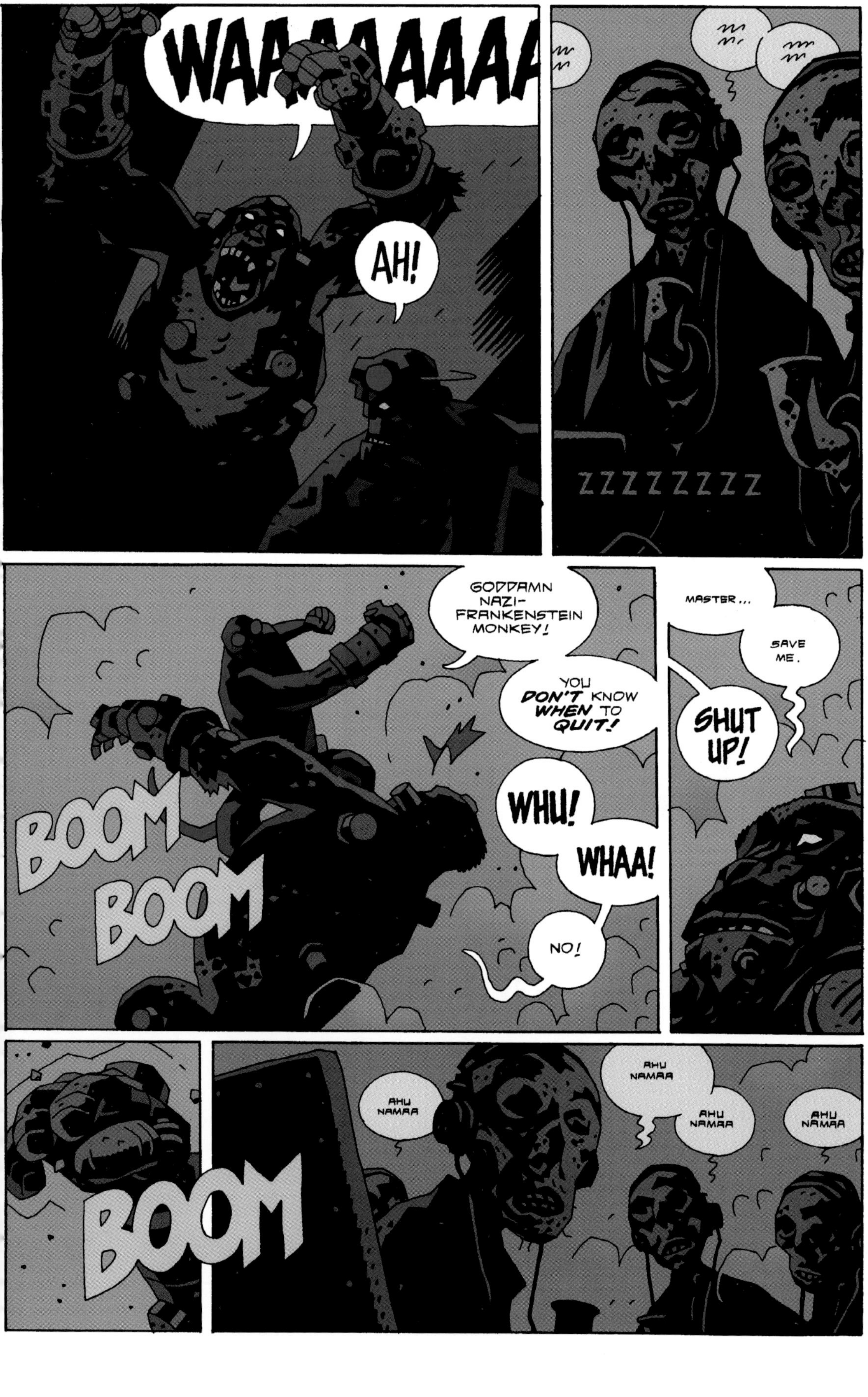
WAAAAAAAA
AH!
ZZZZZZZZ
GODDAMN NAZI-FRANKENSTEIN MONKEY!
YOU DON'T KNOW WHEN TO QUIT!
BOOM
BOOM
WHU!
WHAA!
NO!
MASTER...
SAVE ME.
SHUT UP!
BOOM
AHU NAMAA
AHU NAMAA
AHU NAMAA
AHU NAMAA

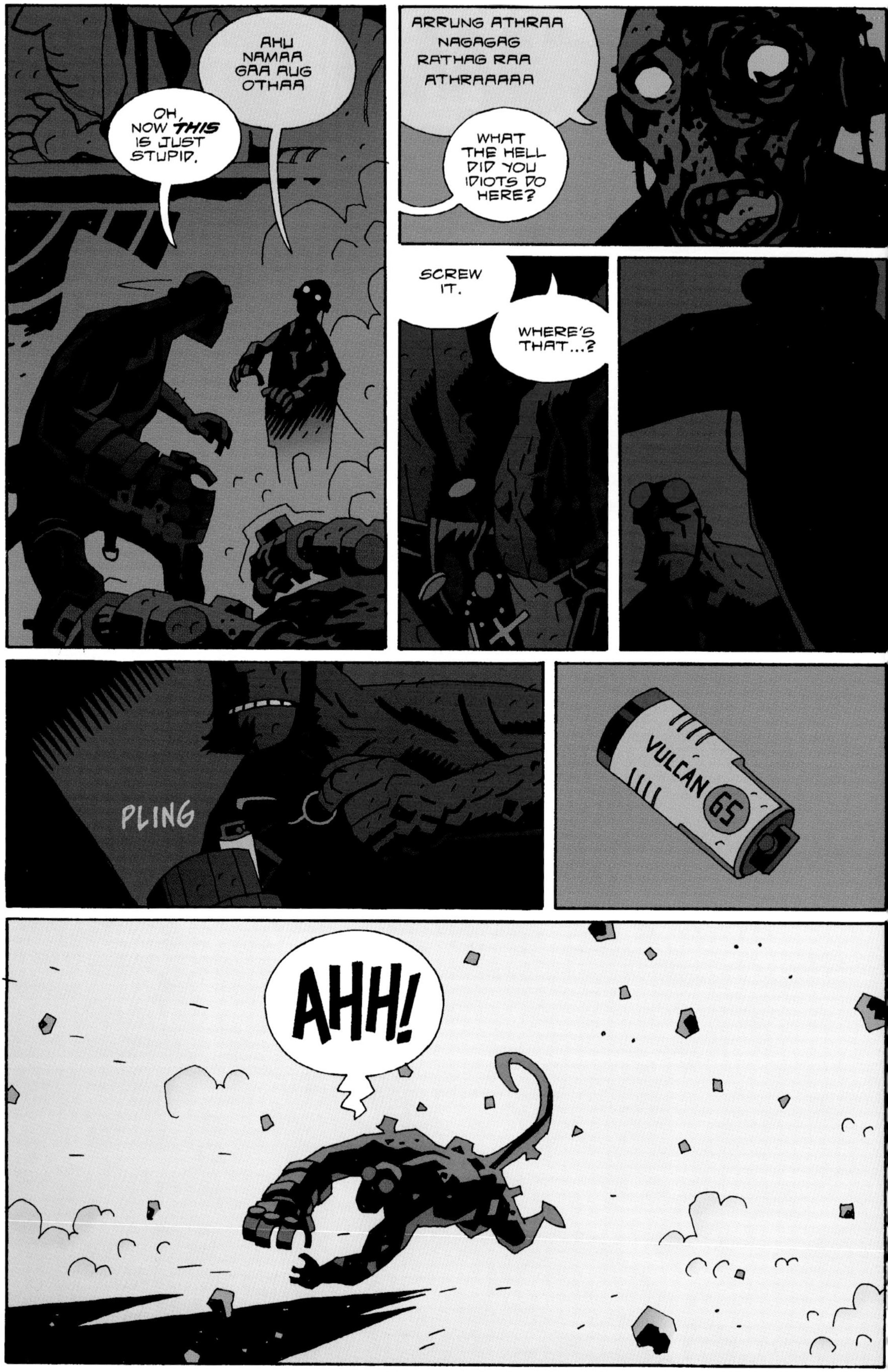

AHU NAMAA GAA AUG OTHAA
OH, NOW THIS IS JUST STUPID.
ARRUNG ATHRAA NAGAGAG RATHAG RAA ATHRAAAAA
WHAT THE HELL DID YOU IDIOTS DO HERE?
SCREW IT.
WHERE'S THAT...?
PLING
VULCAN 65
AHH!

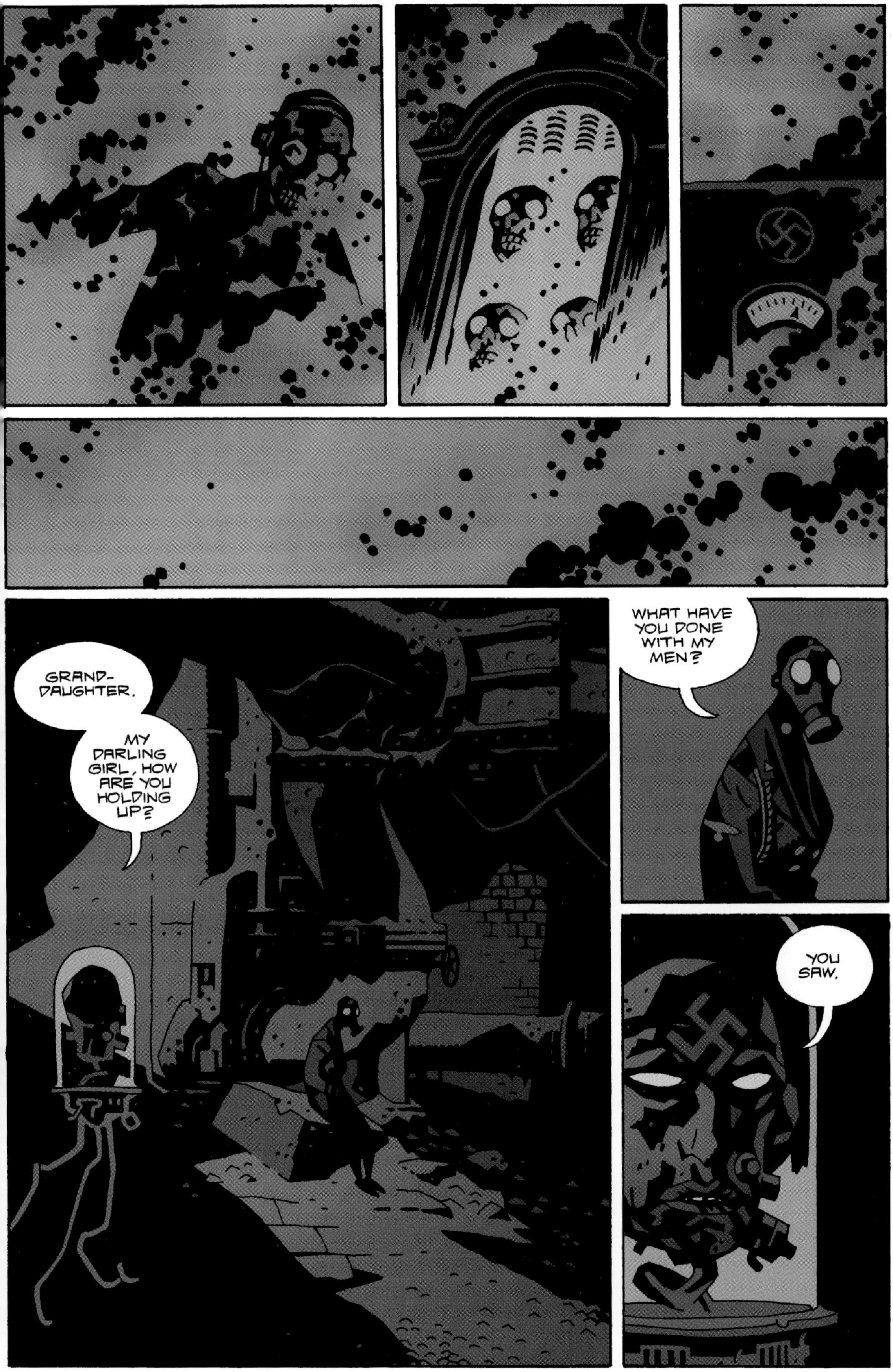
GRAND-DAUGHTER.
MY DARLING GIRL, HOW ARE YOU HOLDING UP?
WHAT HAVE YOU DONE WITH MY MEN?
YOU SAW.

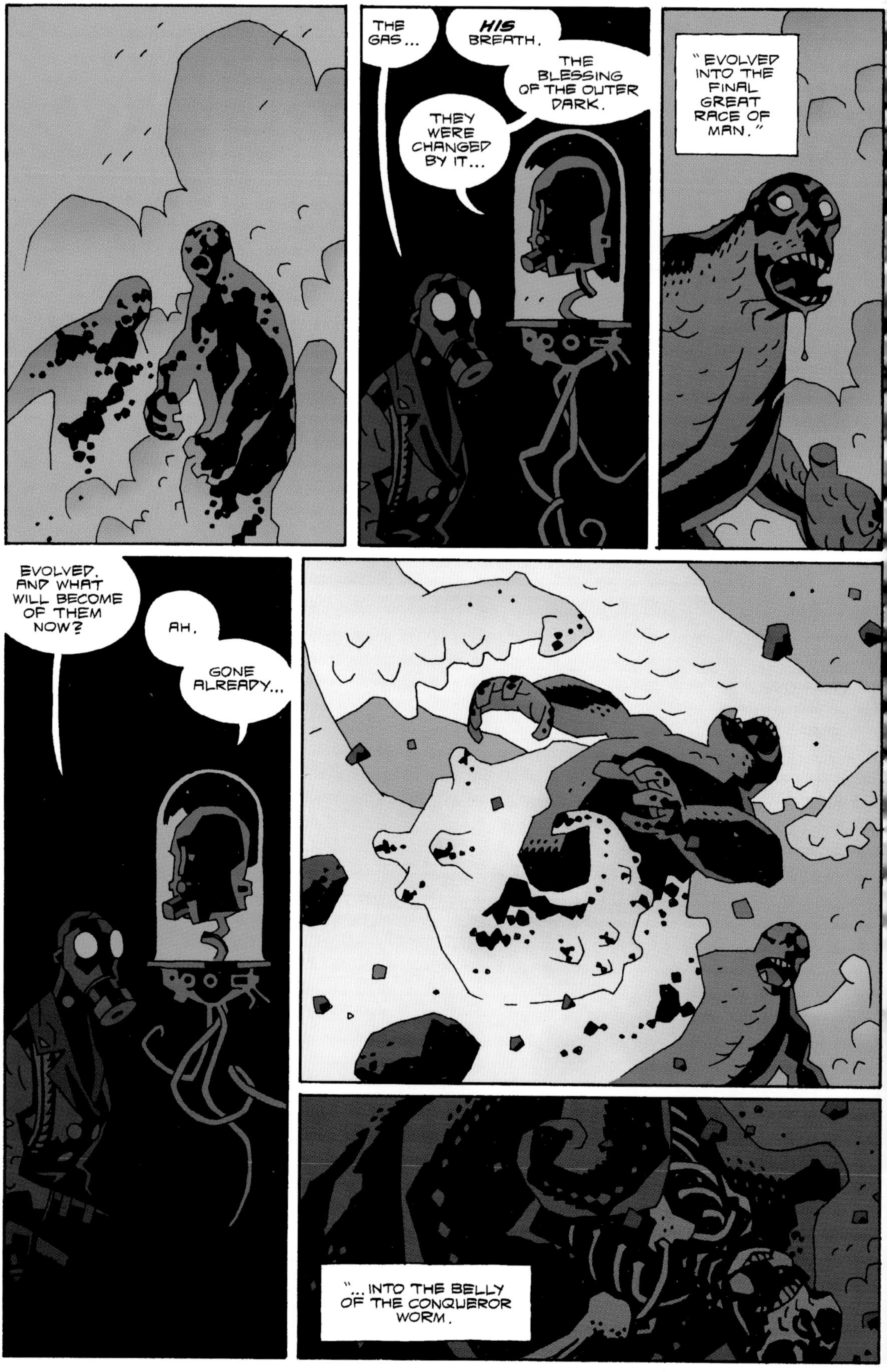
THE GAS...
HIS BREATH.
THE BLESSING OF THE OUTER DARK.
THEY WERE CHANGED BY IT...
"EVOLVED INTO THE FINAL GREAT RACE OF MAN."
EVOLVED. AND WHAT WILL BECOME OF THEM NOW?
AH.
GONE ALREADY...
"...INTO THE BELLY OF THE CONQUEROR WORM.

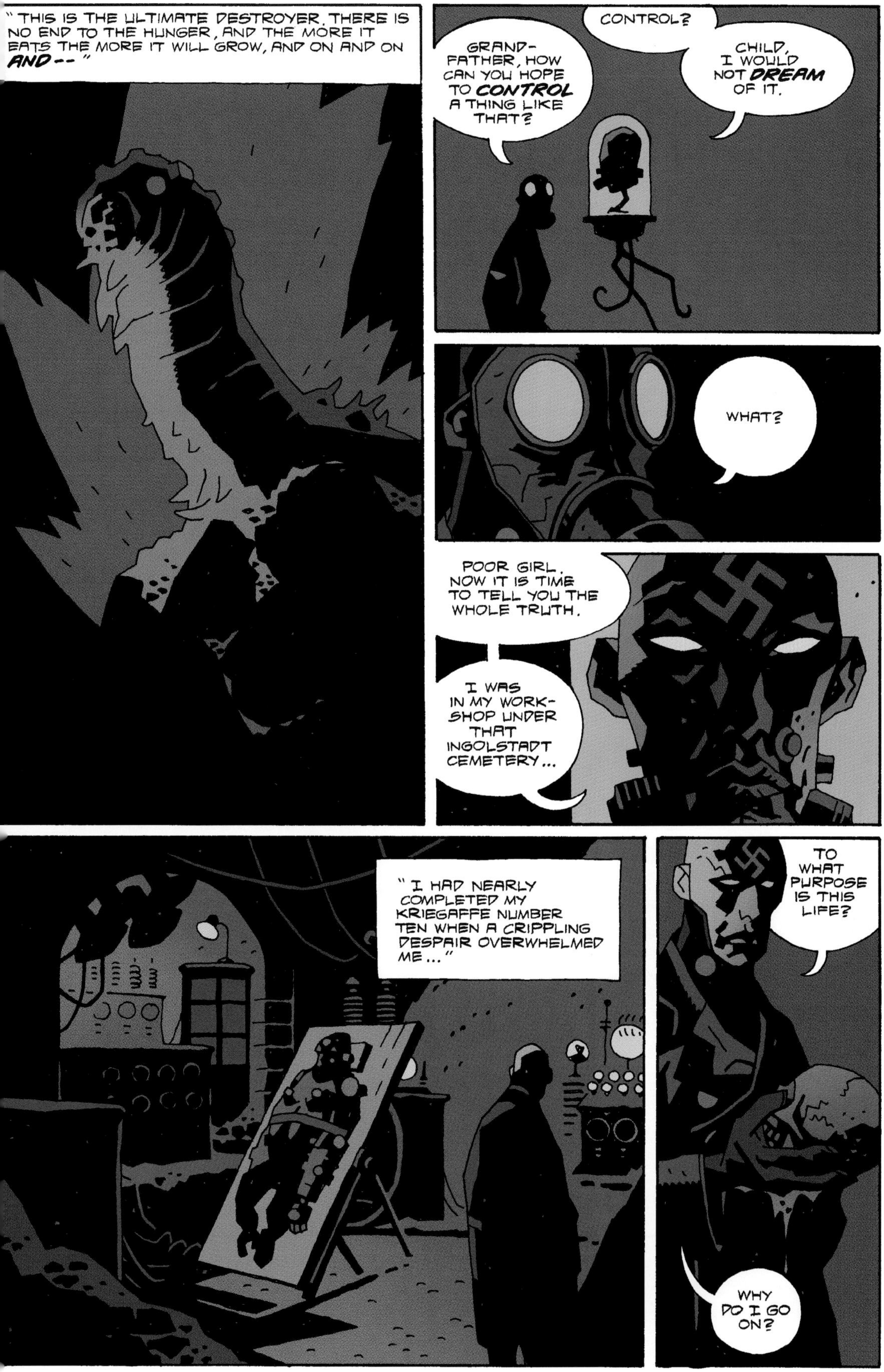
"THIS IS THE ULTIMATE DESTROYER. THERE IS NO END TO THE HUNGER, AND THE MORE IT EATS THE MORE IT WILL GROW, AND ON AND ON AND--"
GRAND-FATHER, HOW CAN YOU HOPE TO CONTROL A THING LIKE THAT?
CONTROL?
CHILD, I WOULD NOT DREAM OF IT.
WHAT?
POOR GIRL. NOW IT IS TIME TO TELL YOU THE WHOLE TRUTH.
I WAS IN MY WORK-SHOP UNDER THAT INGOLSTADT CEMETERY...
"I HAD NEARLY COMPLETED MY KRIEGAFFE NUMBER TEN WHEN A CRIPPLING DESPAIR OVERWHELMED ME..."
TO WHAT PURPOSE IS THIS LIFE?
WHY DO I GO ON?

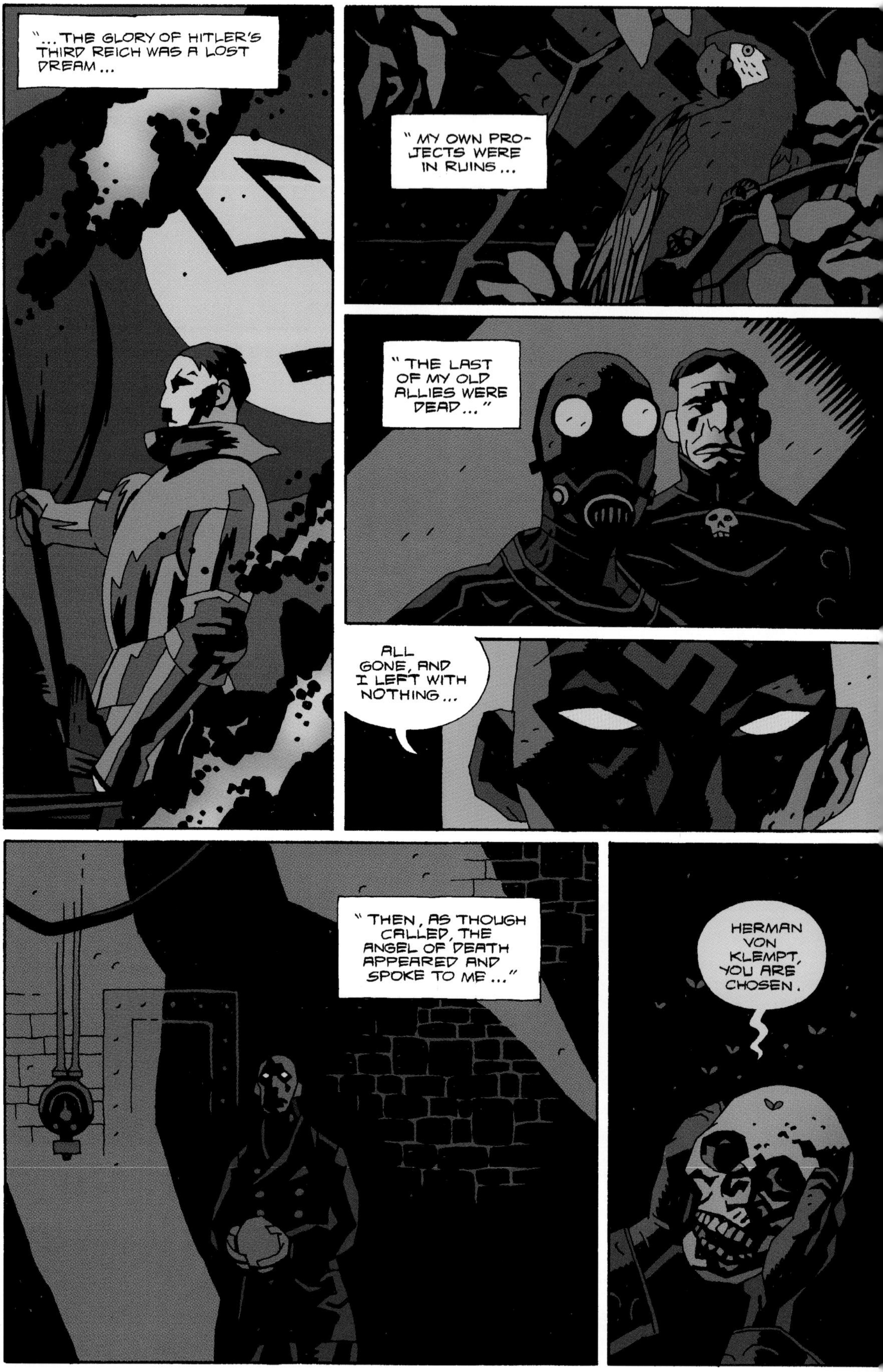
"...THE GLORY OF HITLER'S THIRD REICH WAS A LOST DREAM...
"MY OWN PRO-JECTS WERE IN RUINS...
"THE LAST OF MY OLD ALLIES WERE DEAD..."
ALL GONE, AND I LEFT WITH NOTHING...
"THEN, AS THOUGH CALLED, THE ANGEL OF DEATH APPEARED AND SPOKE TO ME..."
HERMAN VON KLEMPT, YOU ARE CHOSEN.

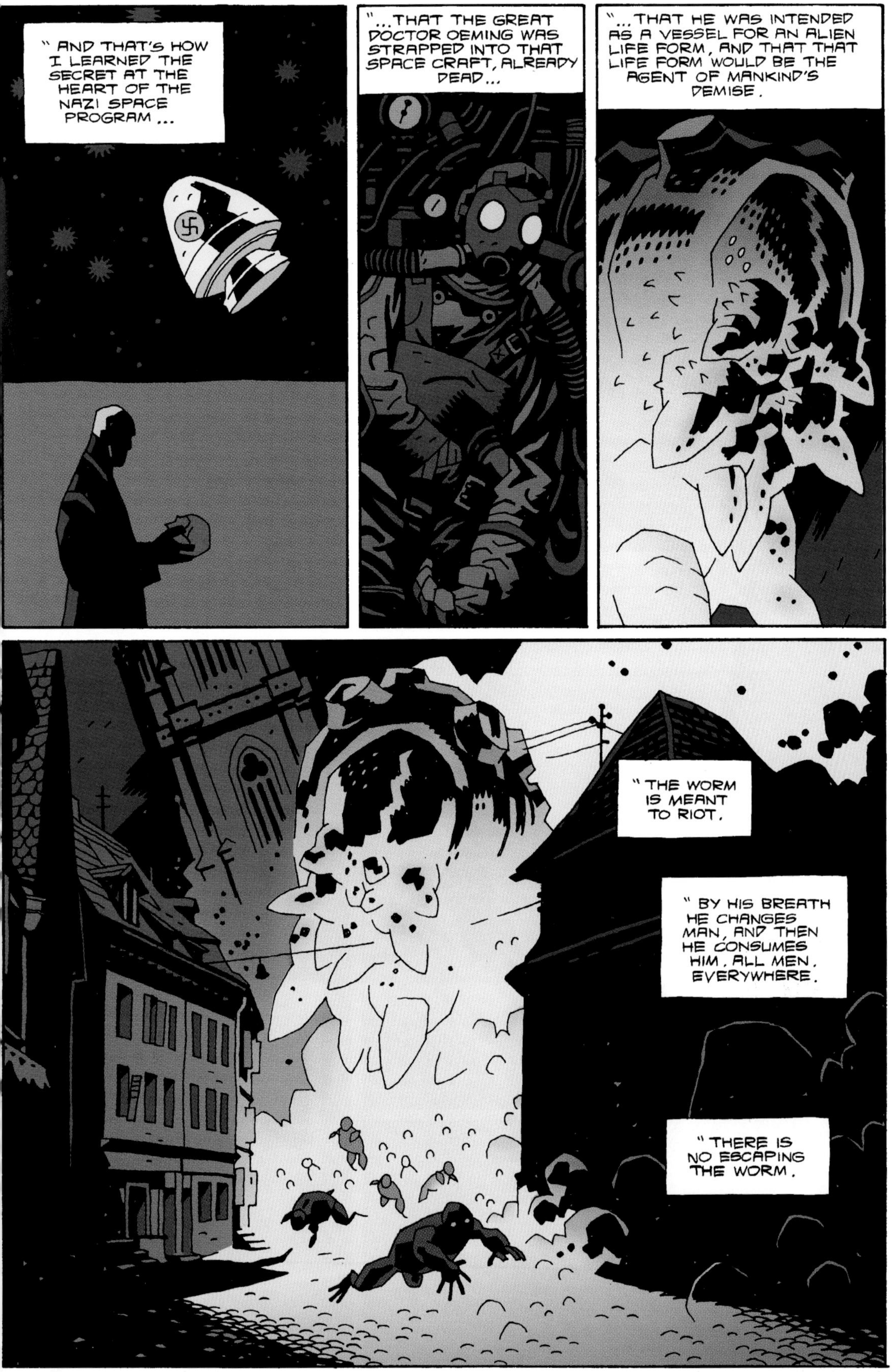
"AND THAT'S HOW I LEARNED THE SECRET AT THE HEART OF THE NAZI SPACE PROGRAM ...
"...THAT THE GREAT DOCTOR OEMING WAS STRAPPED INTO THAT SPACE CRAFT, ALREADY DEAD...
"...THAT HE WAS INTENDED AS A VESSEL FOR AN ALIEN LIFE FORM, AND THAT THAT LIFE FORM WOULD BE THE AGENT OF MANKIND'S DEMISE.
"THE WORM IS MEANT TO RIOT.
"BY HIS BREATH HE CHANGES MAN, AND THEN HE CONSUMES HIM. ALL MEN. EVERYWHERE.
"THERE IS NO ESCAPING THE WORM.

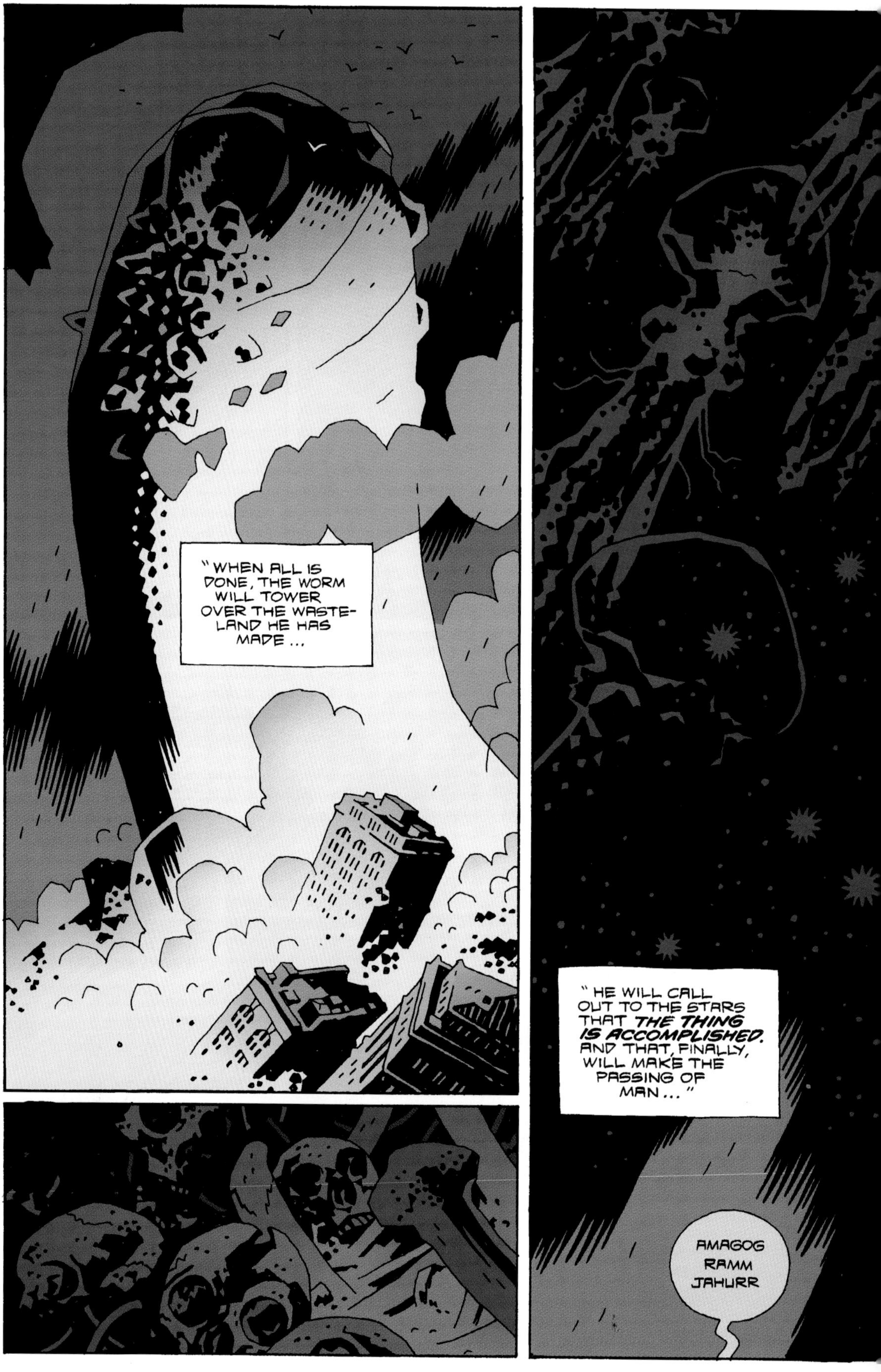
"WHEN ALL IS DONE, THE WORM WILL TOWER OVER THE WASTE-LAND HE HAS MADE ...
" HE WILL CALL OUT TO THE STARS THAT **THE THING IS ACCOMPLISHED.** AND THAT, FINALLY, WILL MAKE THE PASSING OF MAN ... "
AMAGOG RAMM JAHURR

" THEN THE THREE HUNDRED AND SIXTY-NINE CHILDREN OF THE OGDRU JAHAD WILL WAKE AND COME UP OUT OF THEIR PRISONS IN THE EARTH AND IN THE SEA.

" THEN THE OGDRU JAHAD WILL WAKE. THE SEVEN WHO ARE ONE, THE SERPENT...

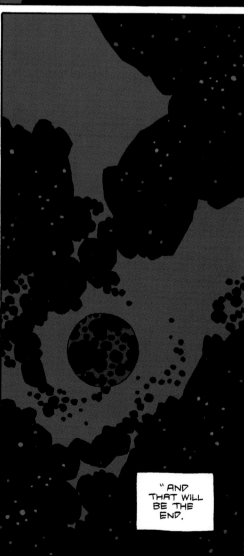

" THEY WILL CAST OFF THEIR CHAINS, COME OUT OF THEIR PRISONS, AND BURN THE EARTH ...

" MAKE OF IT A BLACKENED CINDER ...

" AND THAT WILL BE THE END.

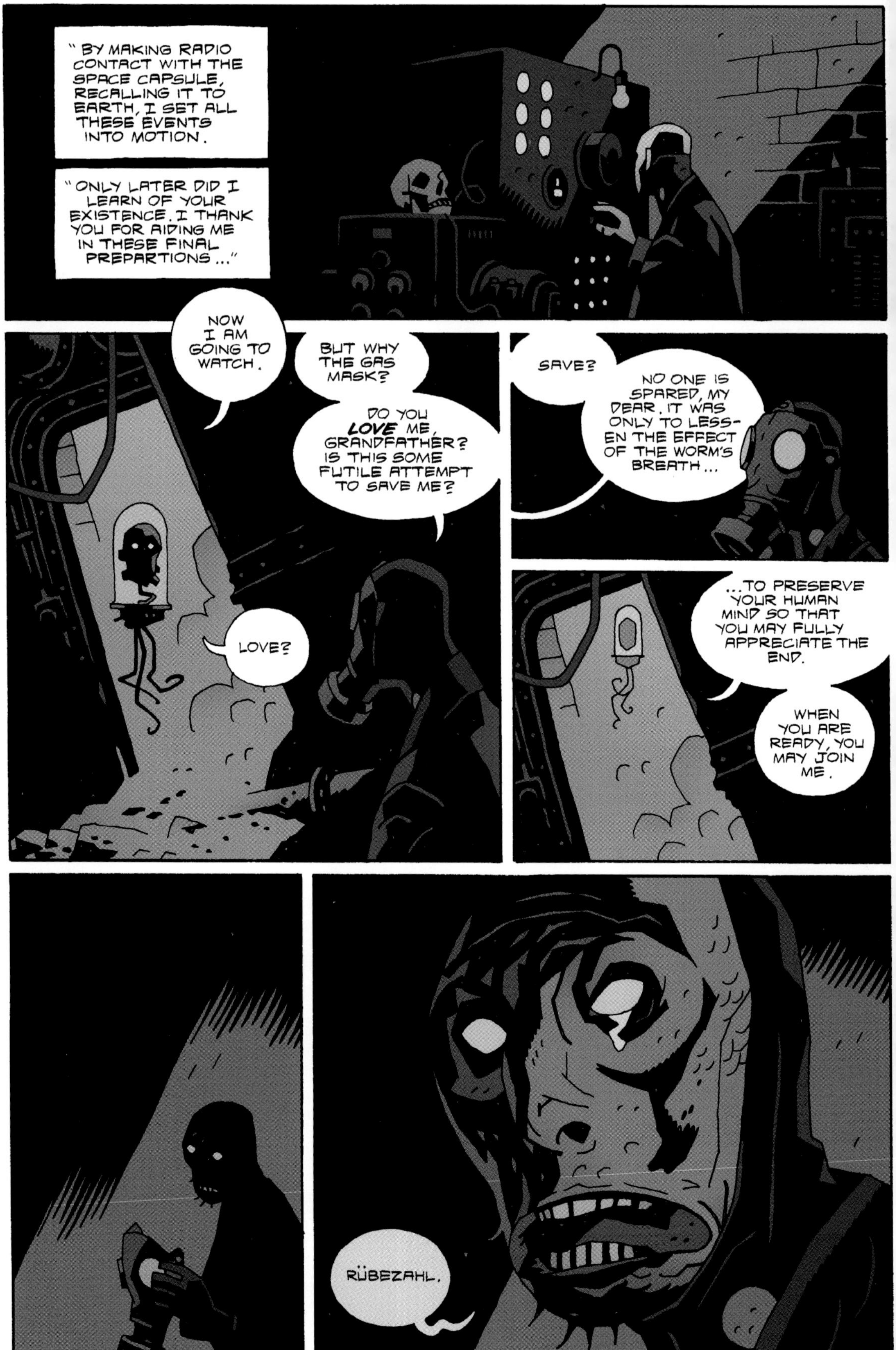
"BY MAKING RADIO CONTACT WITH THE SPACE CAPSULE, RECALLING IT TO EARTH, I SET ALL THESE EVENTS INTO MOTION.
"ONLY LATER DID I LEARN OF YOUR EXISTENCE. I THANK YOU FOR AIDING ME IN THESE FINAL PREPARTIONS..."
NOW I AM GOING TO WATCH.
BUT WHY THE GAS MASK?
DO YOU LOVE ME, GRANDFATHER? IS THIS SOME FUTILE ATTEMPT TO SAVE ME?
LOVE?
SAVE?
NO ONE IS SPARED, MY DEAR. IT WAS ONLY TO LESS-EN THE EFFECT OF THE WORM'S BREATH...
...TO PRESERVE YOUR HUMAN MIND SO THAT YOU MAY FULLY APPRECIATE THE END.
WHEN YOU ARE READY, YOU MAY JOIN ME.
RÜBEZAHL.

CHAPTER FOUR

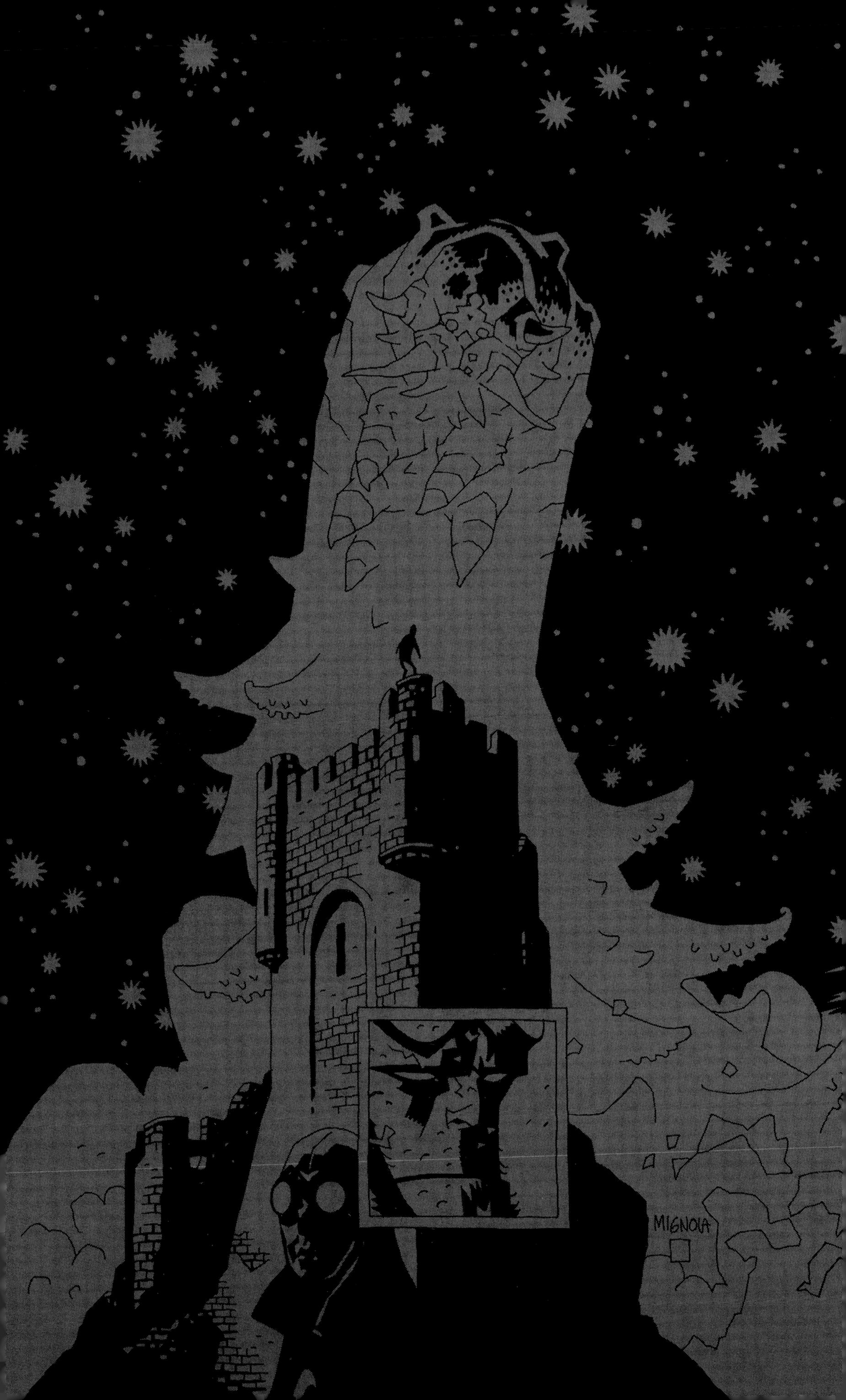
MIGNOLA

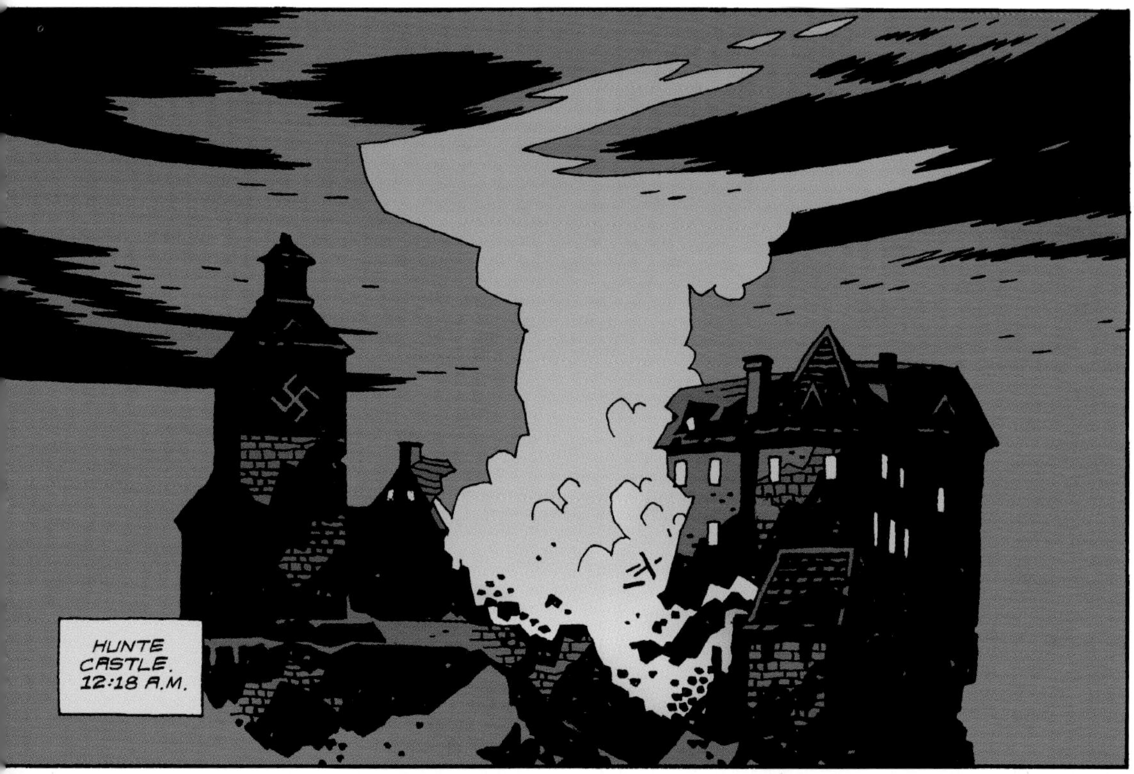
HUNTE CASTLE. 12:18 A.M.

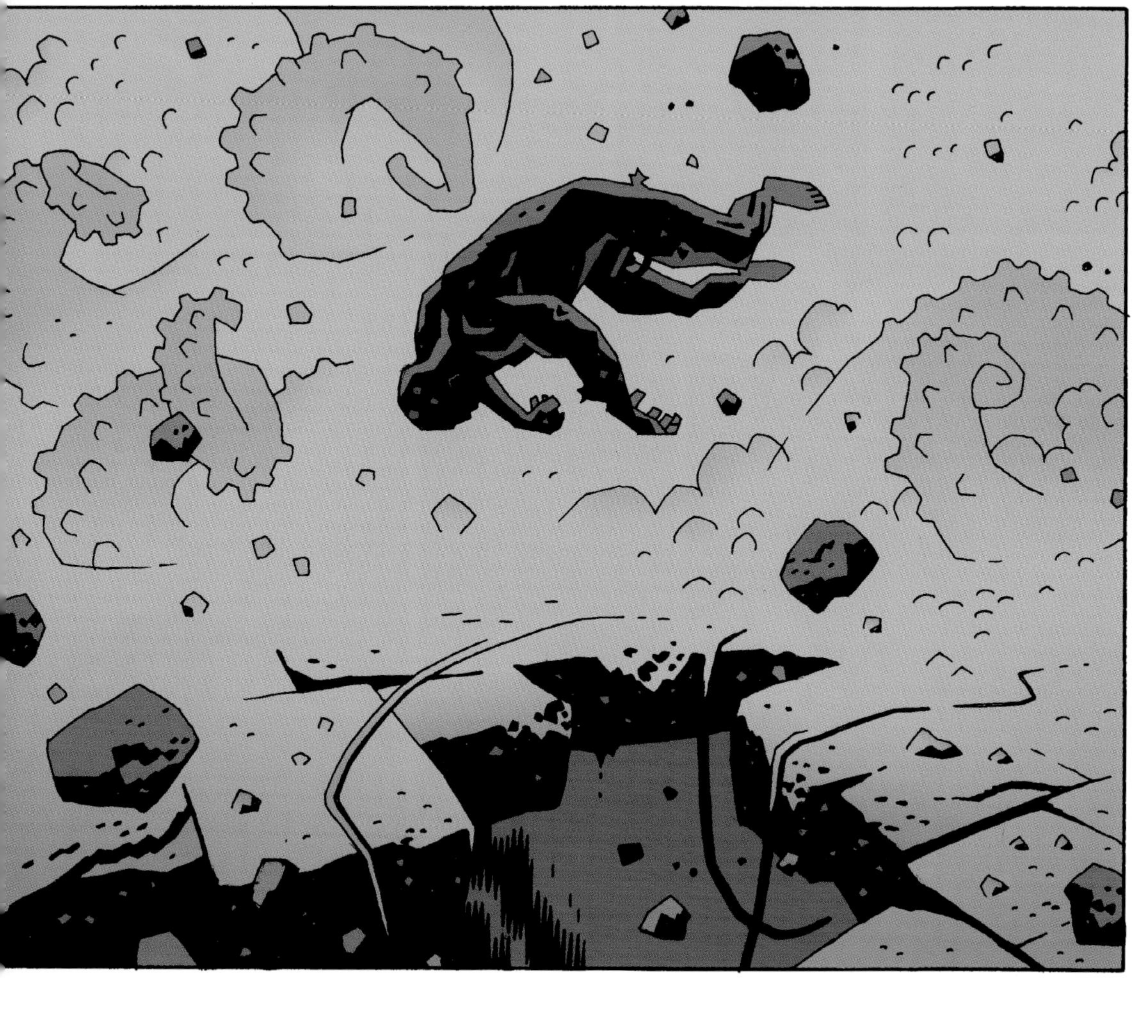

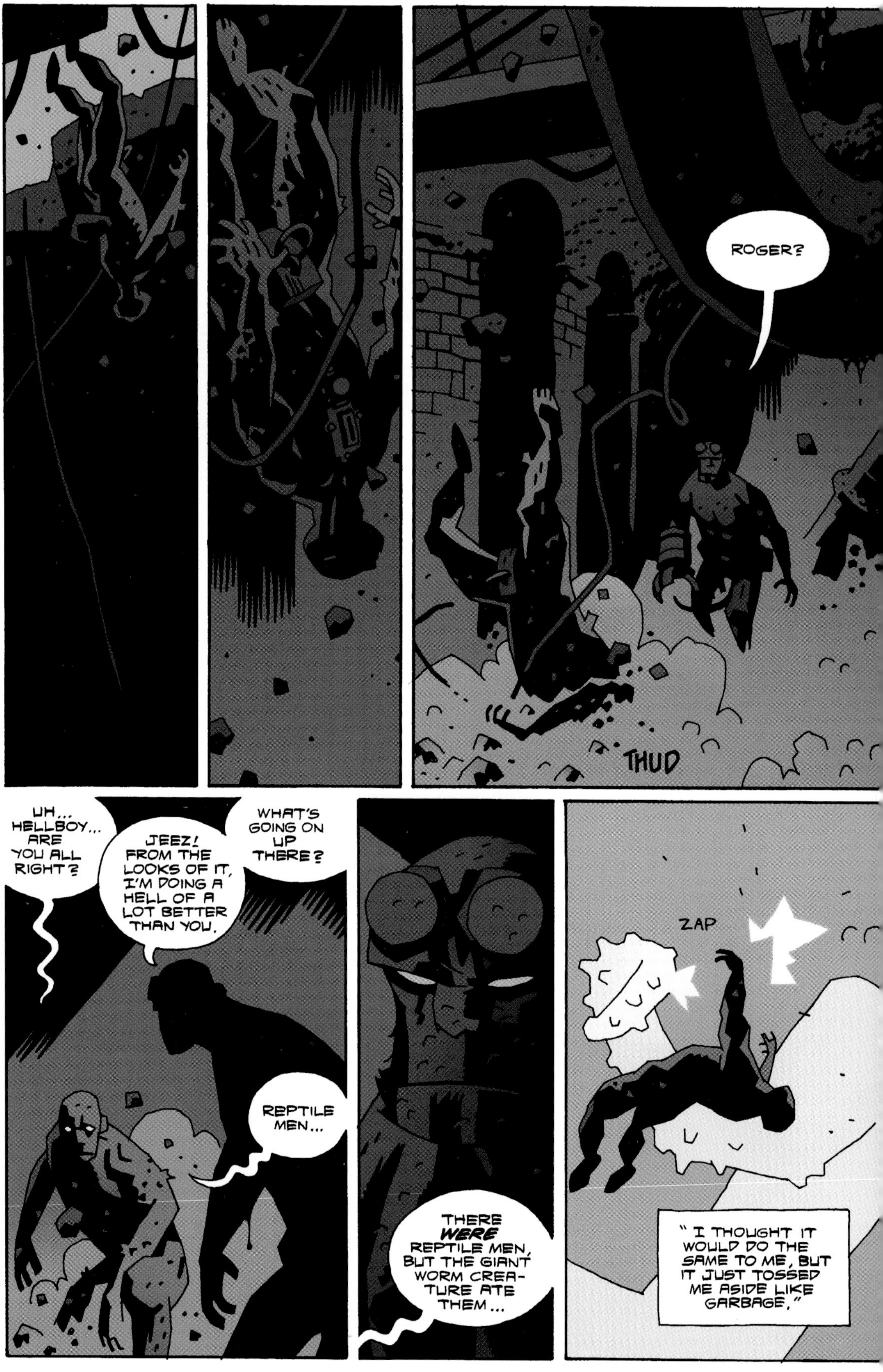
ROGER?
THUD
UH... HELLBOY... ARE YOU ALL RIGHT?
JEEZ! FROM THE LOOKS OF IT, I'M DOING A HELL OF A LOT BETTER THAN YOU.
WHAT'S GOING ON UP THERE?
REPTILE MEN...
THERE WERE REPTILE MEN, BUT THE GIANT WORM CREATURE ATE THEM...
ZAP
" I THOUGHT IT WOULD DO THE SAME TO ME, BUT IT JUST TOSSED ME ASIDE LIKE GARBAGE."

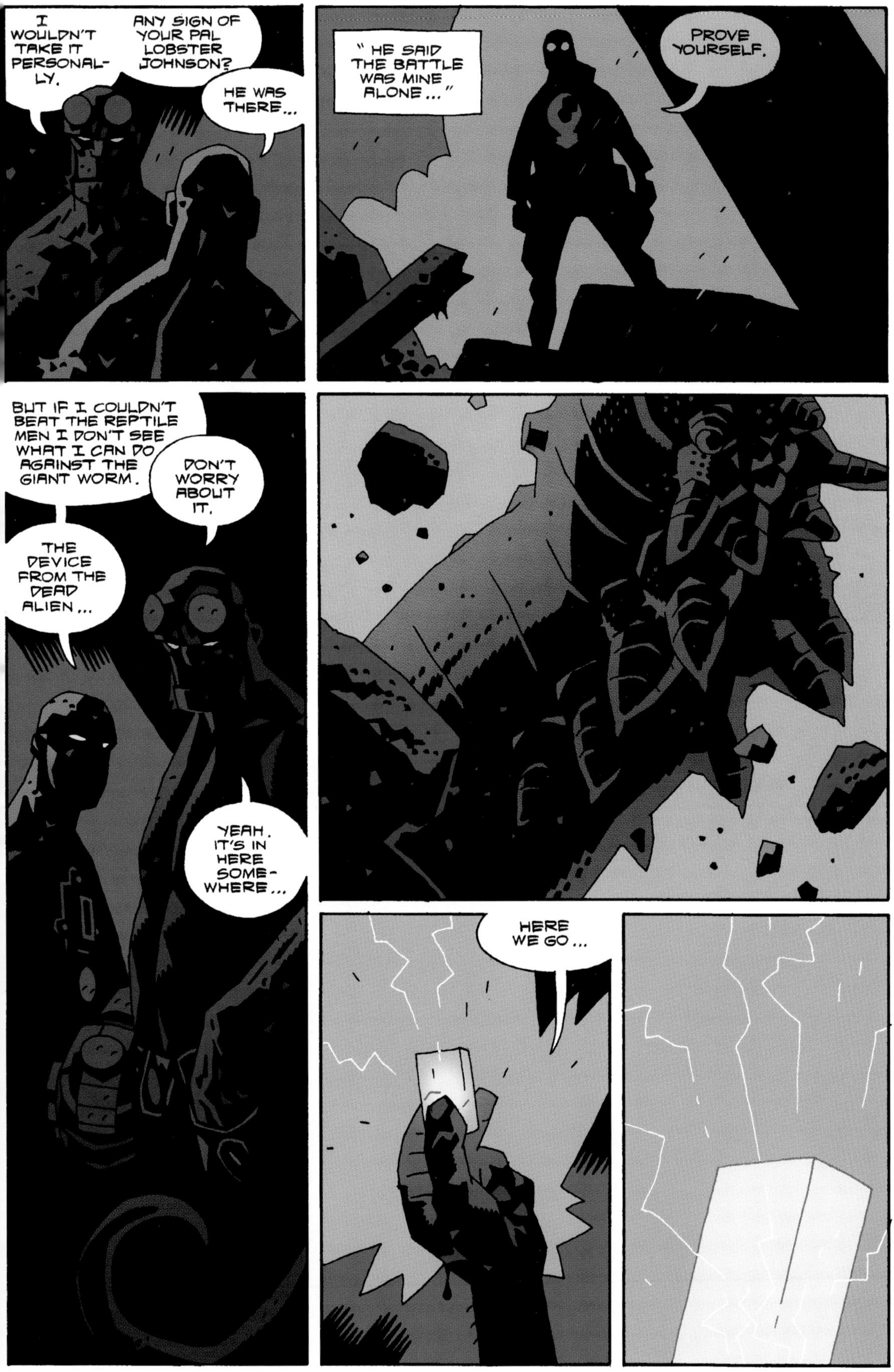
I WOULDN'T TAKE IT PERSONAL-LY.
ANY SIGN OF YOUR PAL LOBSTER JOHNSON?
HE WAS THERE...
" HE SAID THE BATTLE WAS MINE ALONE..."
PROVE YOURSELF.
BUT IF I COULDN'T BEAT THE REPTILE MEN I DON'T SEE WHAT I CAN DO AGAINST THE GIANT WORM.
DON'T WORRY ABOUT IT.
THE DEVICE FROM THE DEAD ALIEN...
YEAH. IT'S IN HERE SOME-WHERE...
HERE WE GO...

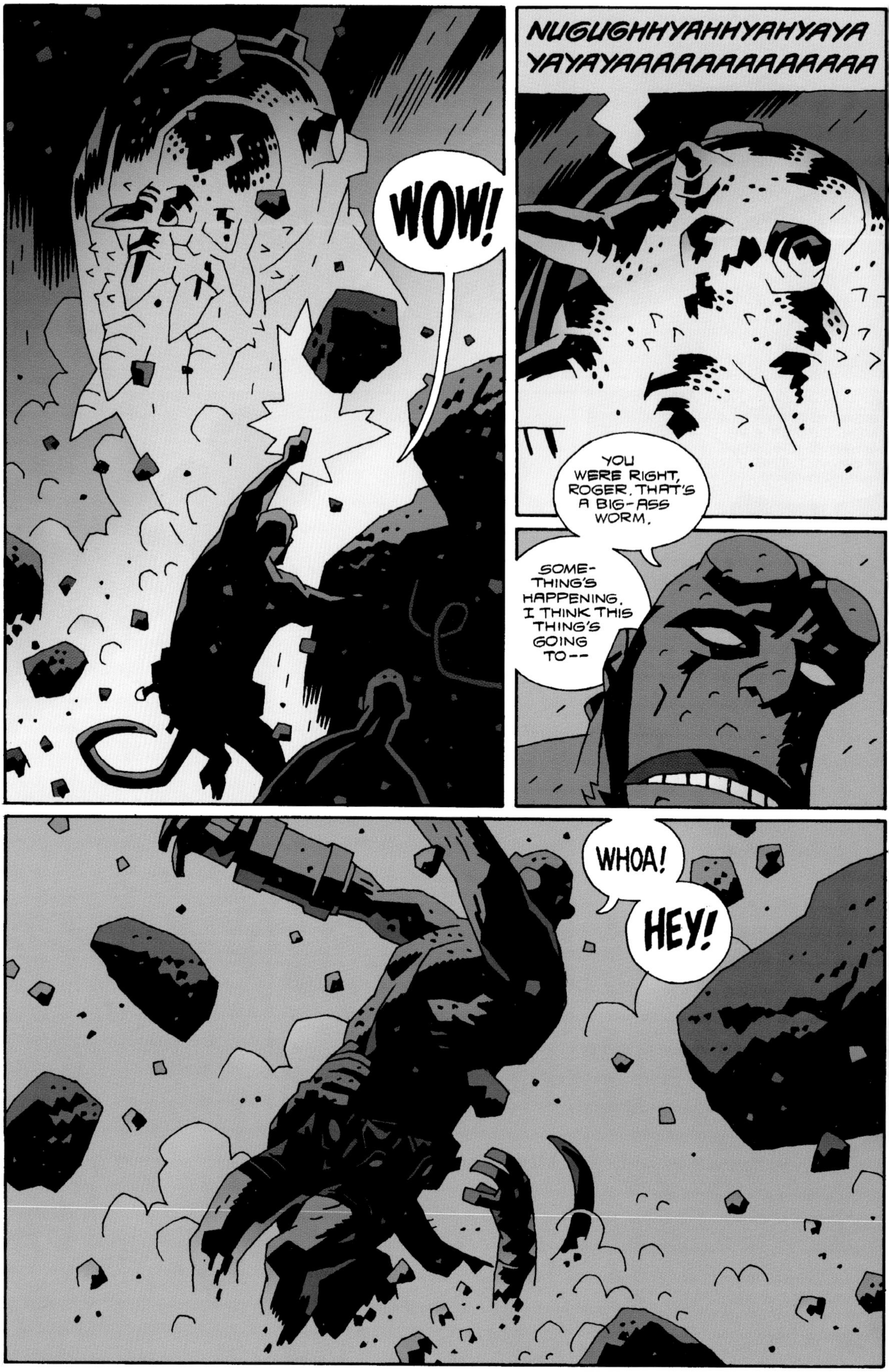
WOW!
NUGUGHHYAHHYAHYAYA YAYAYAAAAAAAAAAAAAA
YOU WERE RIGHT, ROGER. THAT'S A BIG-ASS WORM.
SOME-THING'S HAPPENING. I THINK THIS THING'S GOING TO--
WHOA!
HEY!

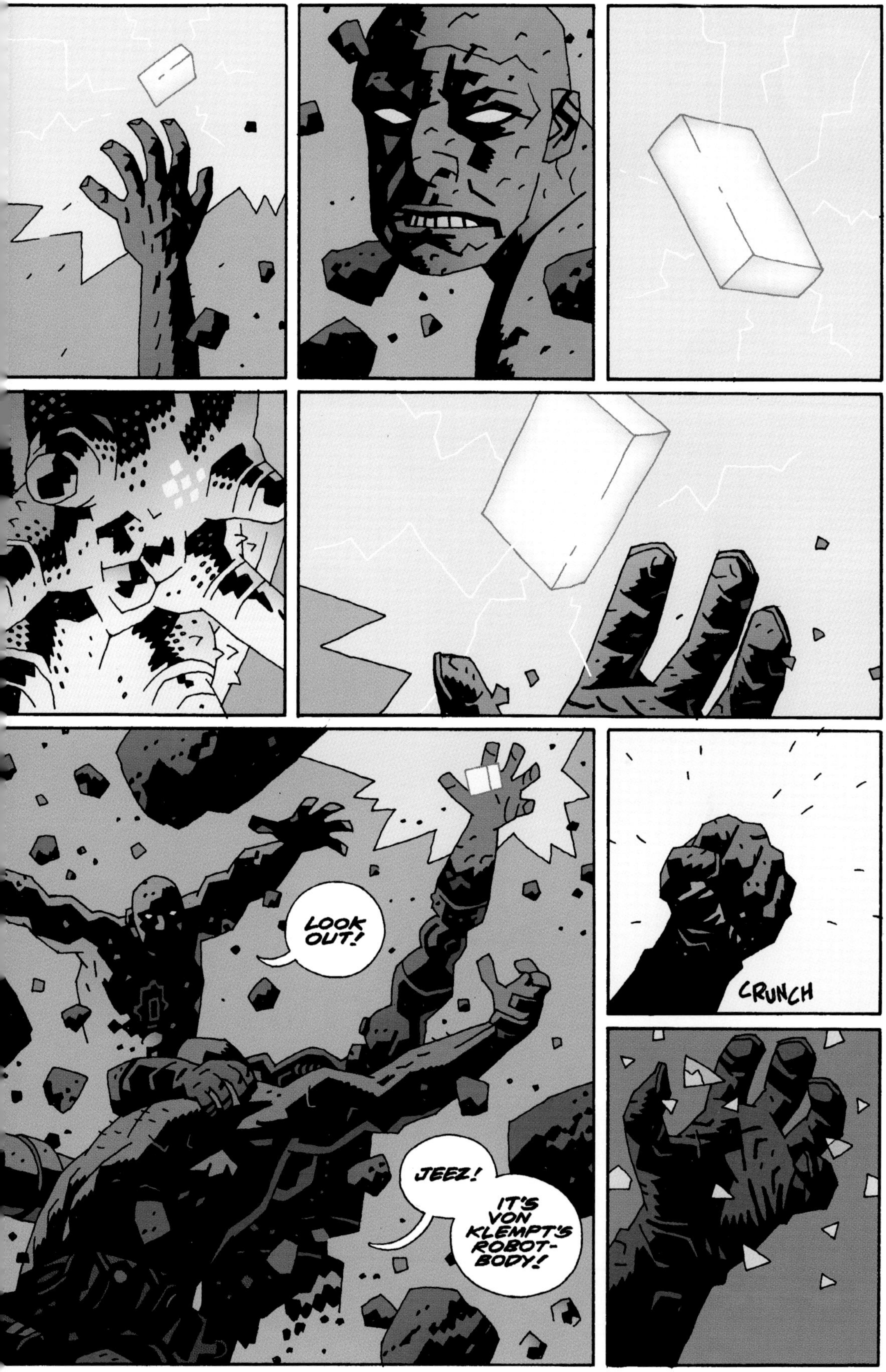
LOOK OUT!
CRUNCH
JEEZ!
IT'S VON KLEMPT'S ROBOT-BODY!

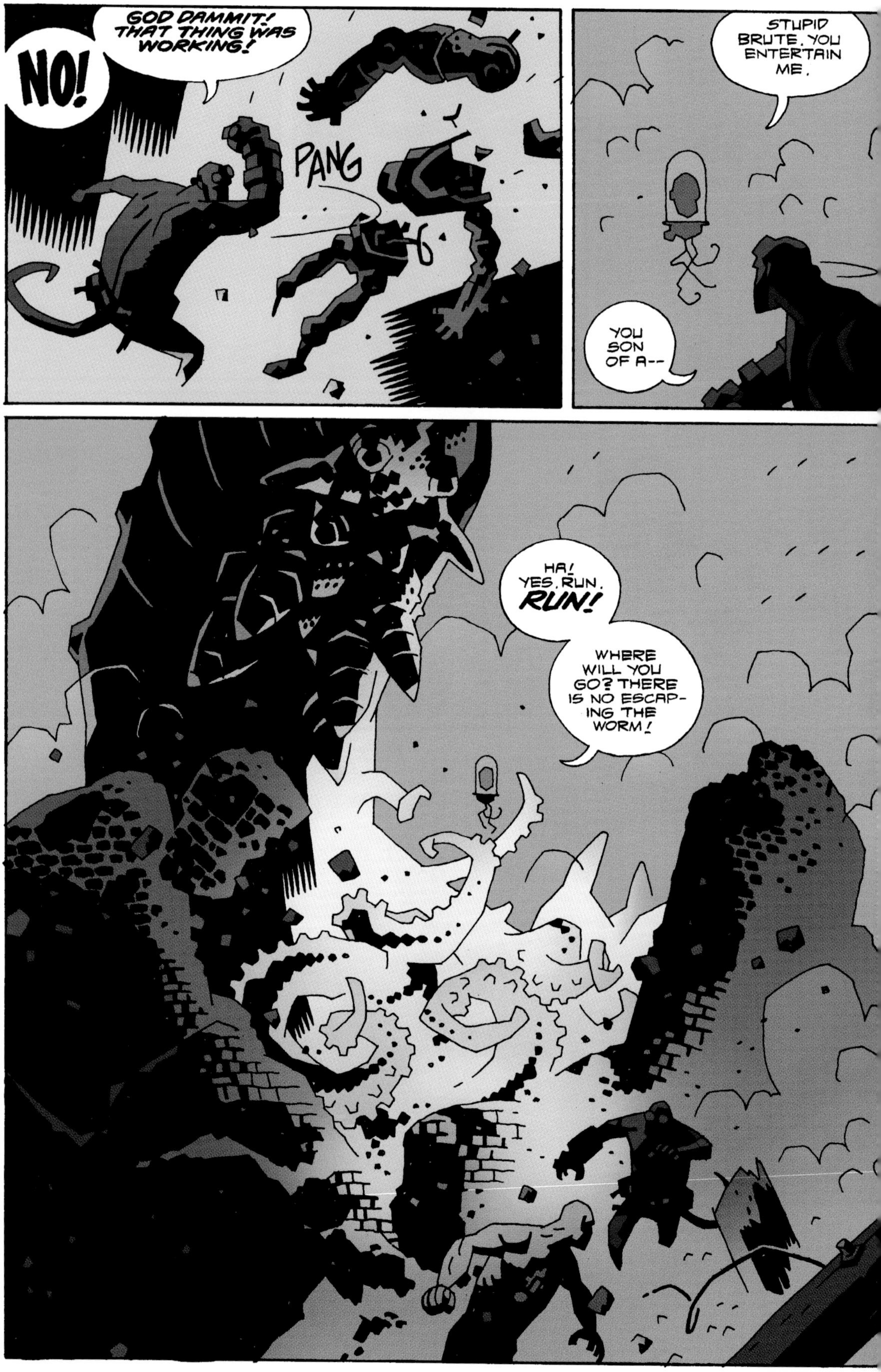
NO!
GOD DAMMIT! THAT THING WAS WORKING!
PANG
STUPID BRUTE. YOU ENTERTAIN ME.
YOU SON OF A--
HA! YES. RUN. RUN!
WHERE WILL YOU GO? THERE IS NO ESCAPING THE WORM!

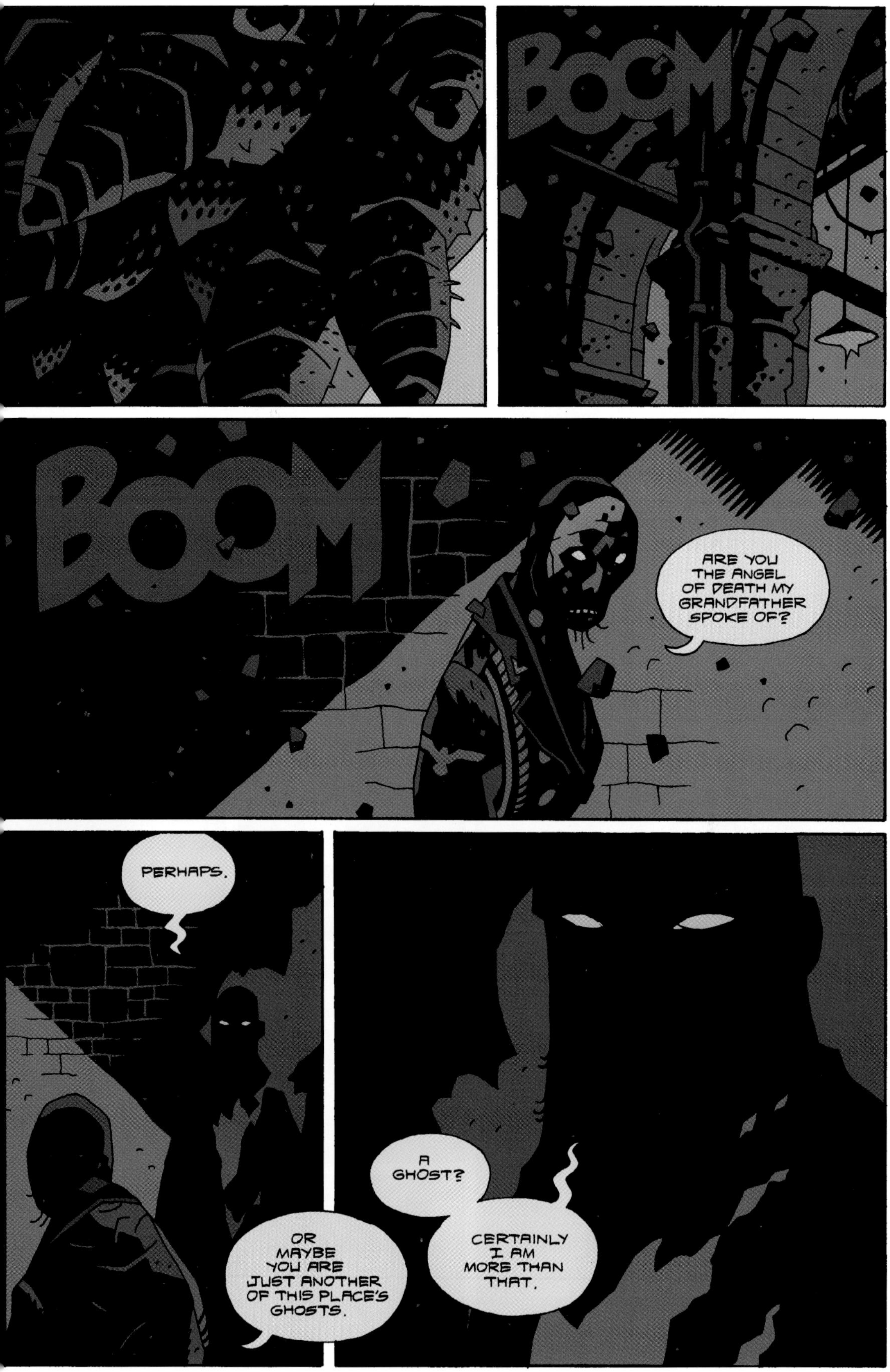
BOOM!
BOOM!
ARE YOU THE ANGEL OF DEATH MY GRANDFATHER SPOKE OF?
PERHAPS.
OR MAYBE YOU ARE JUST ANOTHER OF THIS PLACE'S GHOSTS.
A GHOST?
CERTAINLY I AM MORE THAN THAT.

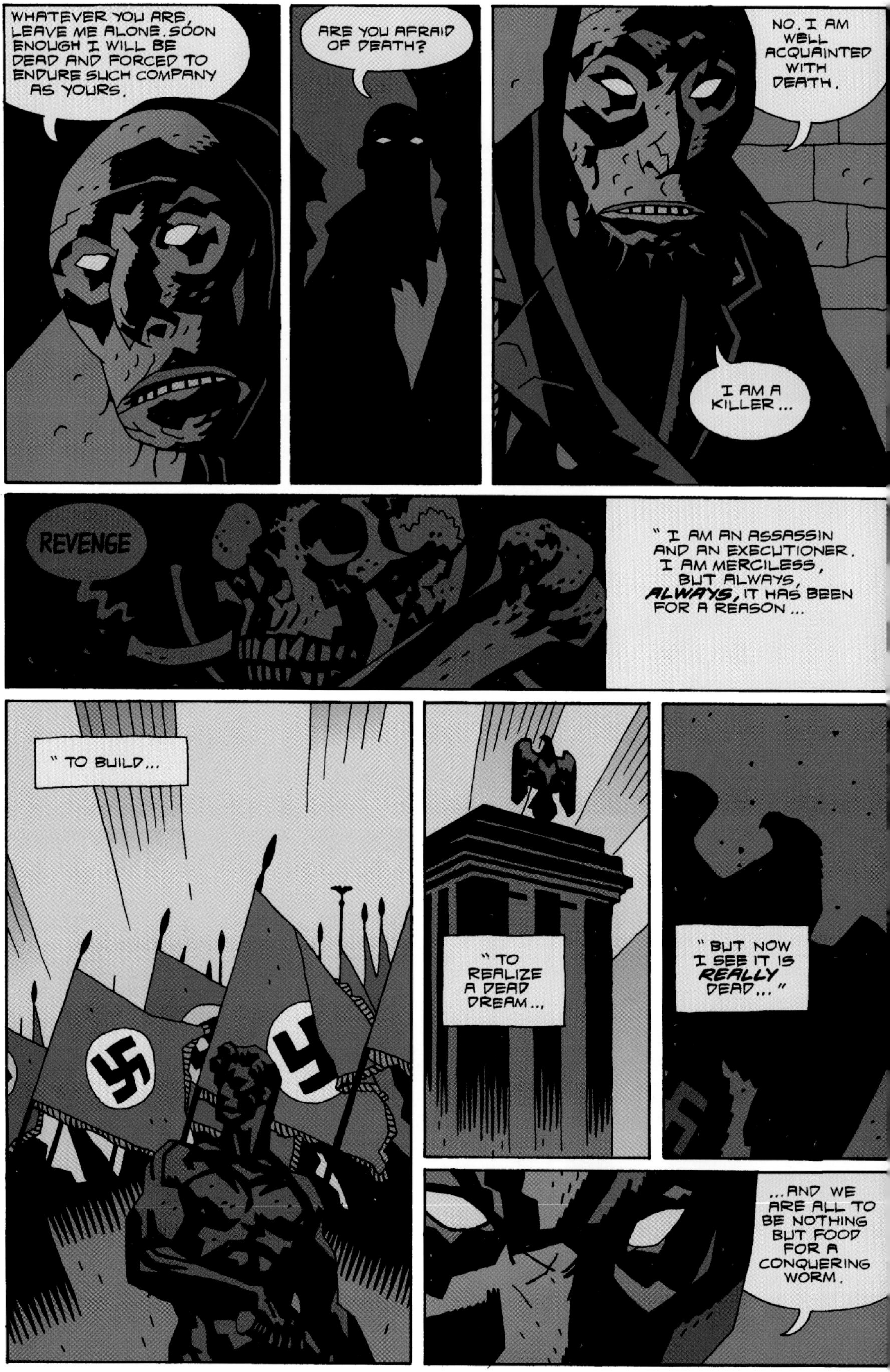
WHATEVER YOU ARE, LEAVE ME ALONE. SOON ENOUGH I WILL BE DEAD AND FORCED TO ENDURE SUCH COMPANY AS YOURS.
ARE YOU AFRAID OF DEATH?
NO. I AM WELL ACQUAINTED WITH DEATH.
I AM A KILLER...
REVENGE
"I AM AN ASSASSIN AND AN EXECUTIONER. I AM MERCILESS, BUT ALWAYS, ALWAYS, IT HAS BEEN FOR A REASON...
"TO BUILD...
"TO REALIZE A DEAD DREAM...
"BUT NOW I SEE IT IS REALLY DEAD..."
...AND WE ARE ALL TO BE NOTHING BUT FOOD FOR A CONQUERING WORM.

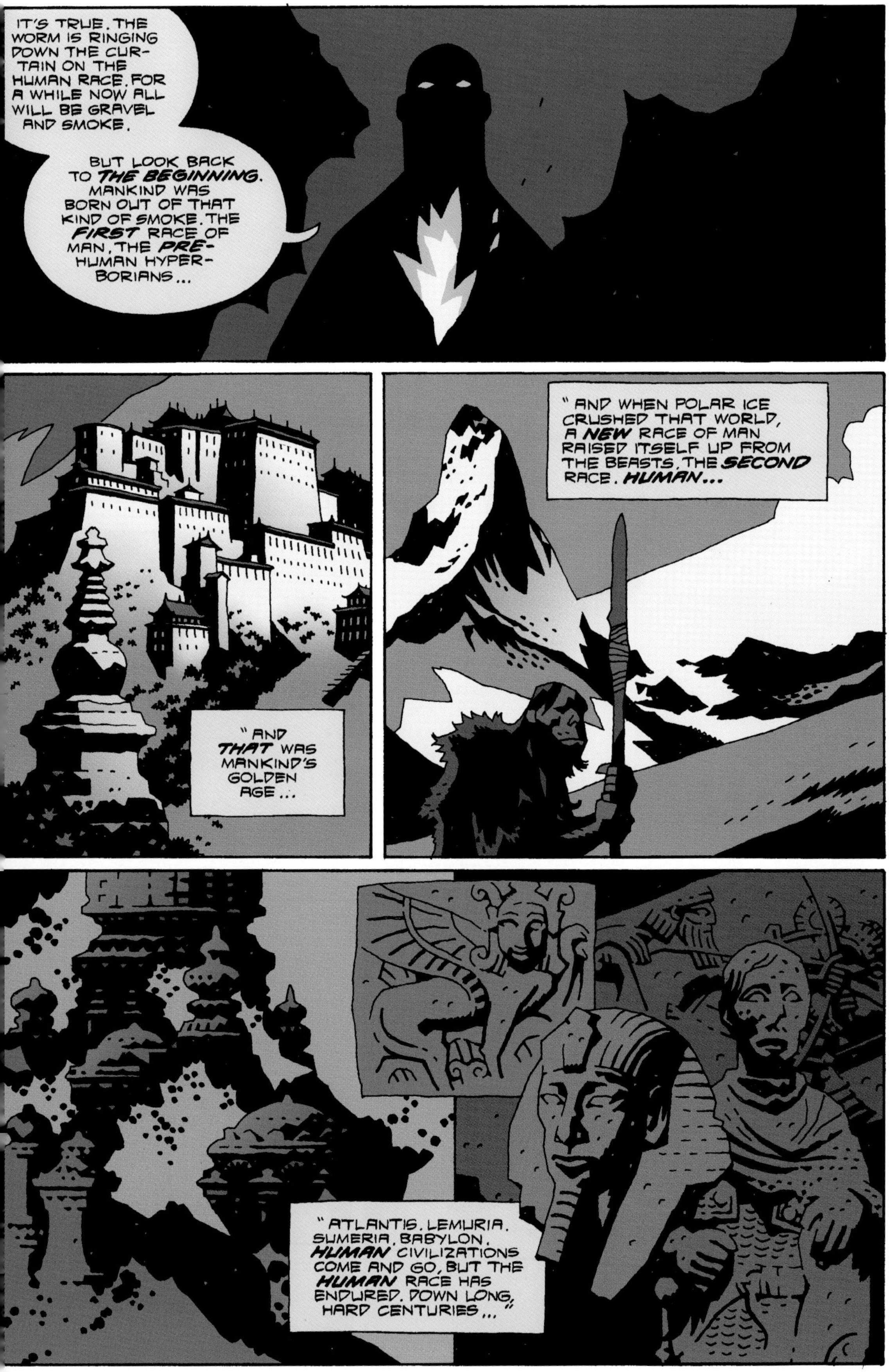
IT'S TRUE. THE WORM IS RINGING DOWN THE CUR-TAIN ON THE HUMAN RACE. FOR A WHILE NOW ALL WILL BE GRAVEL AND SMOKE.
BUT LOOK BACK TO THE BEGINNING. MANKIND WAS BORN OUT OF THAT KIND OF SMOKE. THE FIRST RACE OF MAN, THE PRE-HUMAN HYPER-BORIANS...
"AND THAT WAS MANKIND'S GOLDEN AGE...
"AND WHEN POLAR ICE CRUSHED THAT WORLD, A NEW RACE OF MAN RAISED ITSELF UP FROM THE BEASTS, THE SECOND RACE. HUMAN...
"ATLANTIS. LEMURIA. SUMERIA. BABYLON. HUMAN CIVILIZATIONS COME AND GO, BUT THE HUMAN RACE HAS ENDURED. DOWN LONG, HARD CENTURIES..."

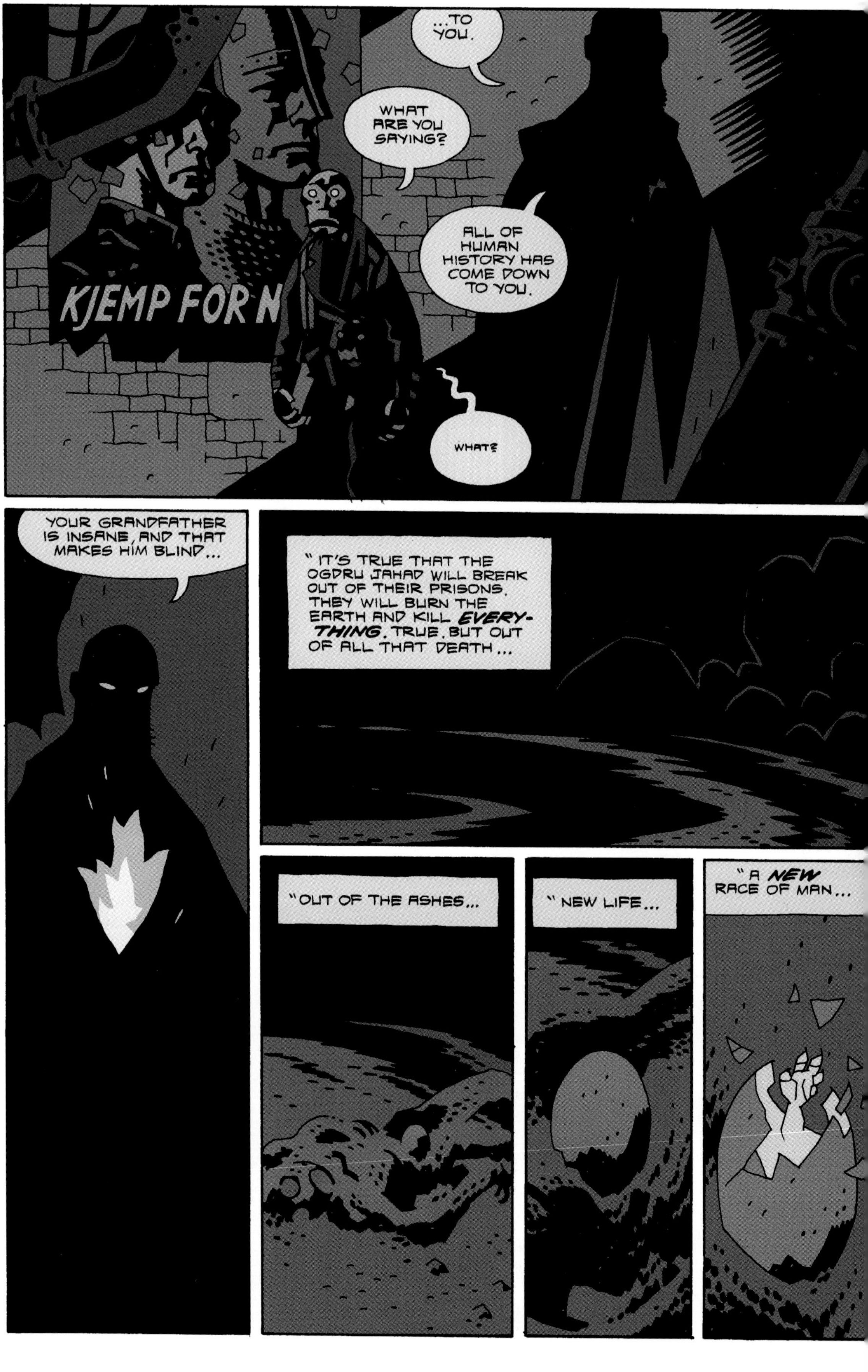

KJEMP FOR N
...TO YOU.
WHAT ARE YOU SAYING?
ALL OF HUMAN HISTORY HAS COME DOWN TO YOU.
WHAT?
YOUR GRANDFATHER IS INSANE, AND THAT MAKES HIM BLIND...
"IT'S TRUE THAT THE OGDRU JAHAD WILL BREAK OUT OF THEIR PRISONS. THEY WILL BURN THE EARTH AND KILL *EVERYTHING*. TRUE. BUT OUT OF ALL THAT DEATH...
"OUT OF THE ASHES...
"NEW LIFE...
"A *NEW* RACE OF MAN...

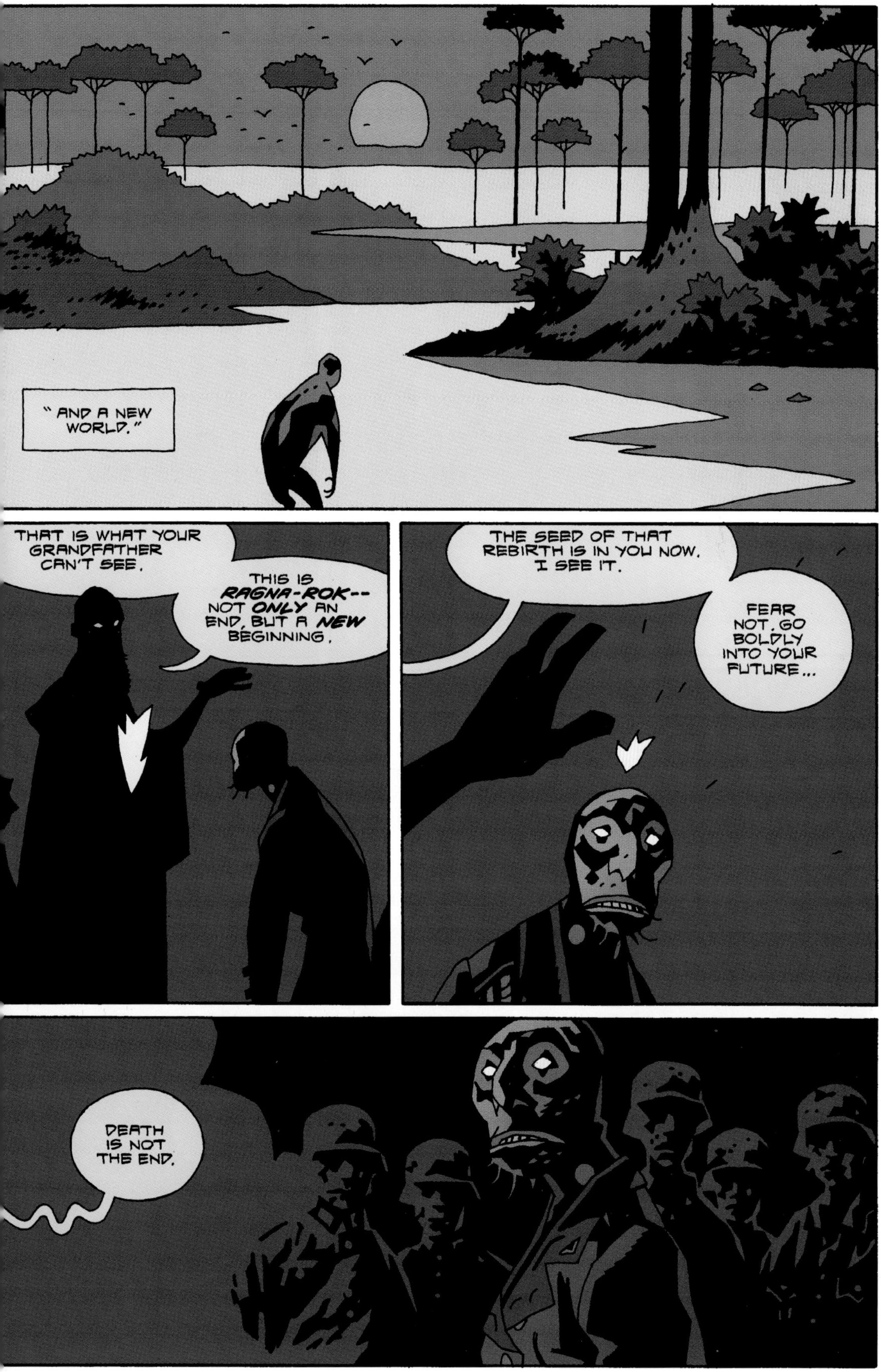
"AND A NEW WORLD."
THAT IS WHAT YOUR GRANDFATHER CAN'T SEE.
THIS IS *RAGNA-ROK*-- NOT *ONLY* AN END, BUT A *NEW* BEGINNING.
THE SEED OF THAT REBIRTH IS IN YOU NOW. I SEE IT.
FEAR NOT. GO BOLDLY INTO YOUR FUTURE...
DEATH IS NOT THE END.

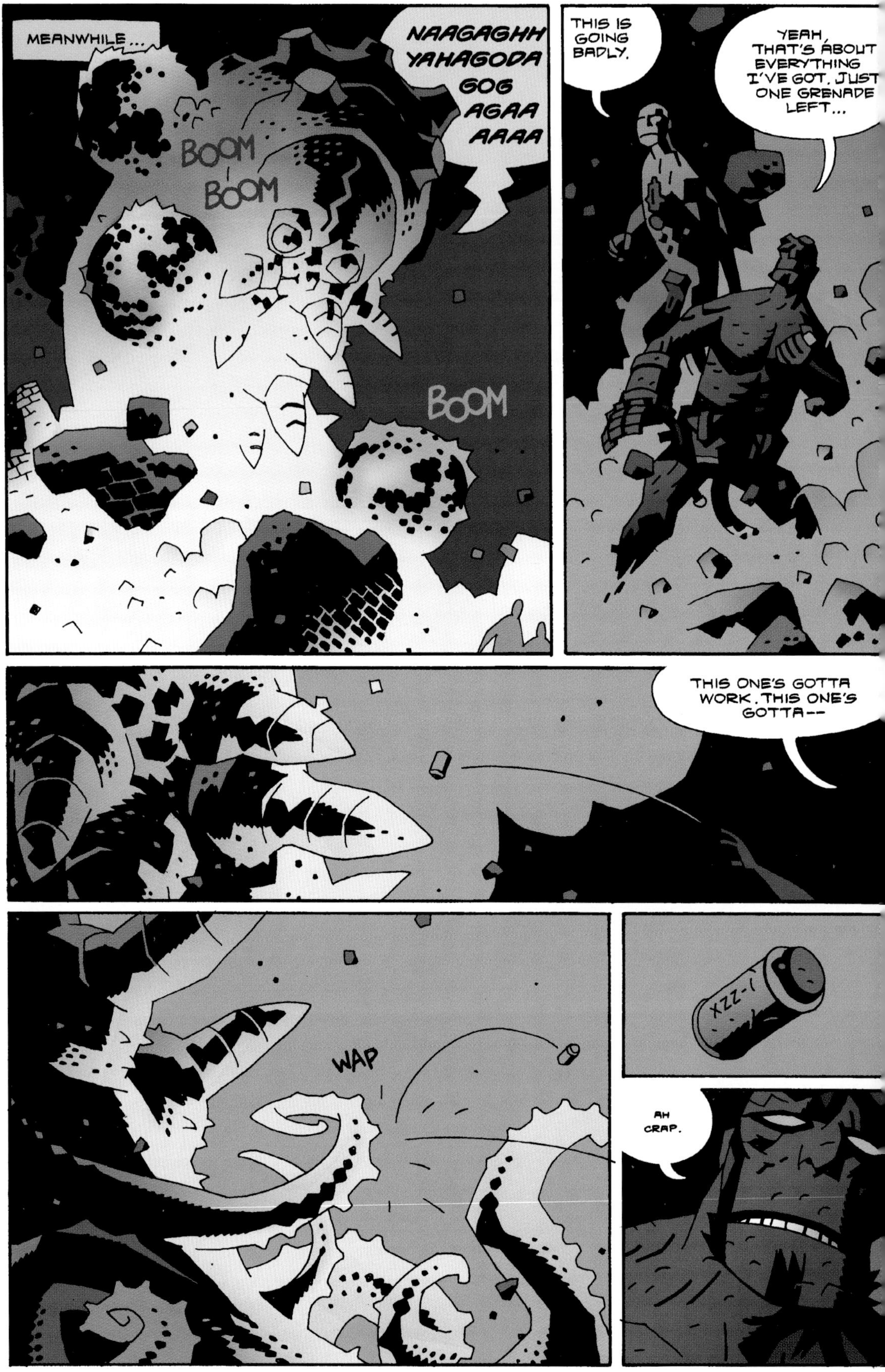
MEANWHILE...
NAAGAGHH YAHAGODA GOG AGAA AAAA
BOOM BOOM
BOOM
THIS IS GOING BADLY.
YEAH, THAT'S ABOUT EVERYTHING I'VE GOT. JUST ONE GRENADE LEFT...
THIS ONE'S GOTTA WORK. THIS ONE'S GOTTA--
WAP
XZZ-1
AH CRAP.

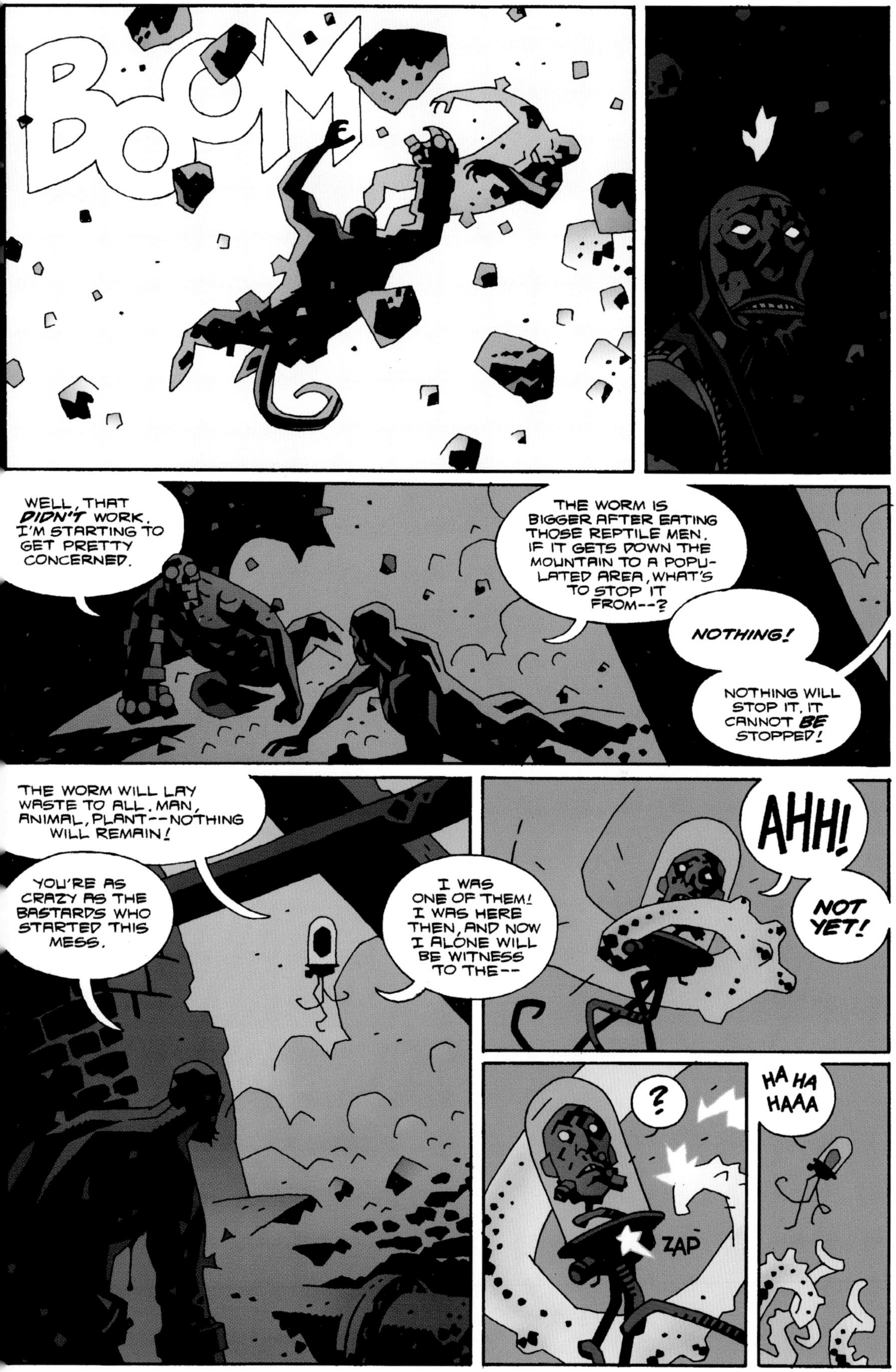
BOOM
WELL, THAT DIDN'T WORK. I'M STARTING TO GET PRETTY CONCERNED.
THE WORM IS BIGGER AFTER EATING THOSE REPTILE MEN. IF IT GETS DOWN THE MOUNTAIN TO A POPU-LATED AREA, WHAT'S TO STOP IT FROM--?
NOTHING!
NOTHING WILL STOP IT. IT CANNOT BE STOPPED!
THE WORM WILL LAY WASTE TO ALL. MAN, ANIMAL, PLANT--NOTHING WILL REMAIN!
YOU'RE AS CRAZY AS THE BASTARDS WHO STARTED THIS MESS.
I WAS ONE OF THEM! I WAS HERE THEN, AND NOW I ALONE WILL BE WITNESS TO THE--
AHH!
NOT YET!
?
ZAP
HA HA HAAA

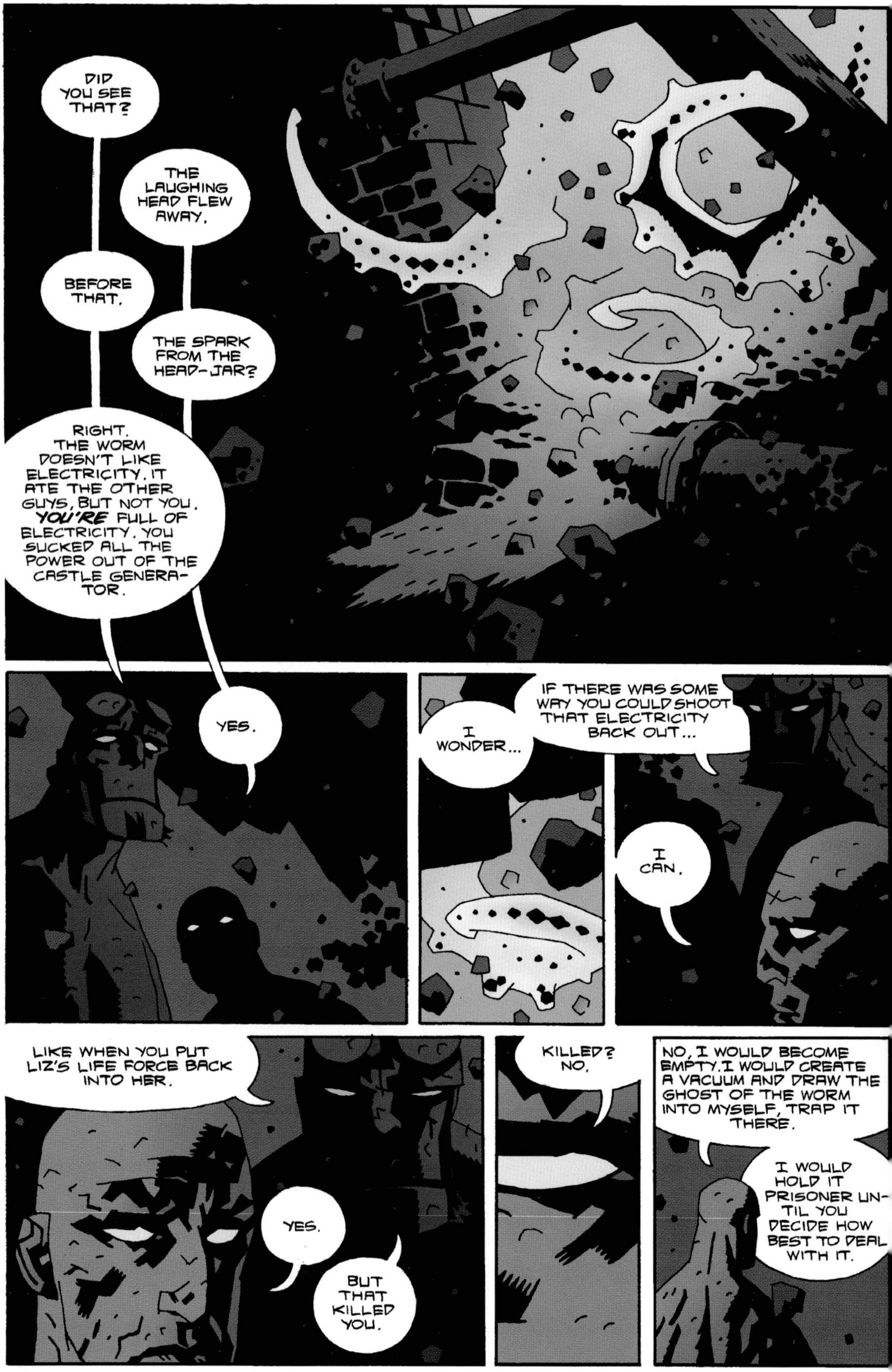
DID YOU SEE THAT?
THE LAUGHING HEAD FLEW AWAY.
BEFORE THAT.
THE SPARK FROM THE HEAD-JAR?
RIGHT. THE WORM DOESN'T LIKE ELECTRICITY. IT ATE THE OTHER GUYS, BUT NOT YOU. YOU'RE FULL OF ELECTRICITY. YOU SUCKED ALL THE POWER OUT OF THE CASTLE GENERATOR.
YES.
I WONDER...
IF THERE WAS SOME WAY YOU COULD SHOOT THAT ELECTRICITY BACK OUT...
I CAN.
LIKE WHEN YOU PUT LIZ'S LIFE FORCE BACK INTO HER.
YES.
BUT THAT KILLED YOU.
KILLED? NO.
NO, I WOULD BECOME EMPTY. I WOULD CREATE A VACUUM AND DRAW THE GHOST OF THE WORM INTO MYSELF, TRAP IT THERE.
I WOULD HOLD IT PRISONER UNTIL YOU DECIDE HOW BEST TO DEAL WITH IT.

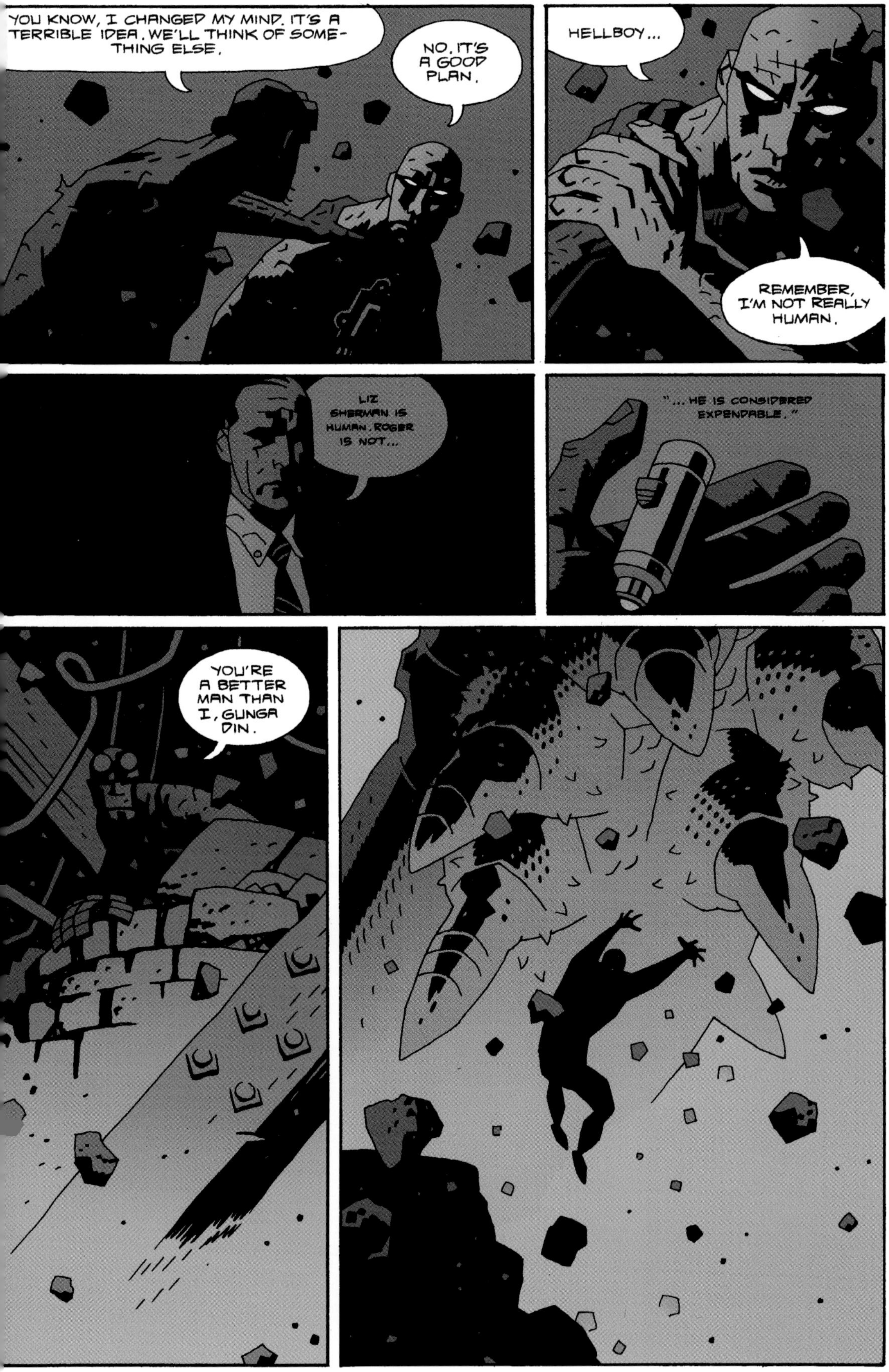
YOU KNOW, I CHANGED MY MIND. IT'S A TERRIBLE IDEA. WE'LL THINK OF SOMETHING ELSE.
NO. IT'S A GOOD PLAN.
HELLBOY...
REMEMBER, I'M NOT REALLY HUMAN.
LIZ SHERMAN IS HUMAN. ROGER IS NOT...
"...HE IS CONSIDERED EXPENDABLE."
YOU'RE A BETTER MAN THAN I, GUNGA DIN.

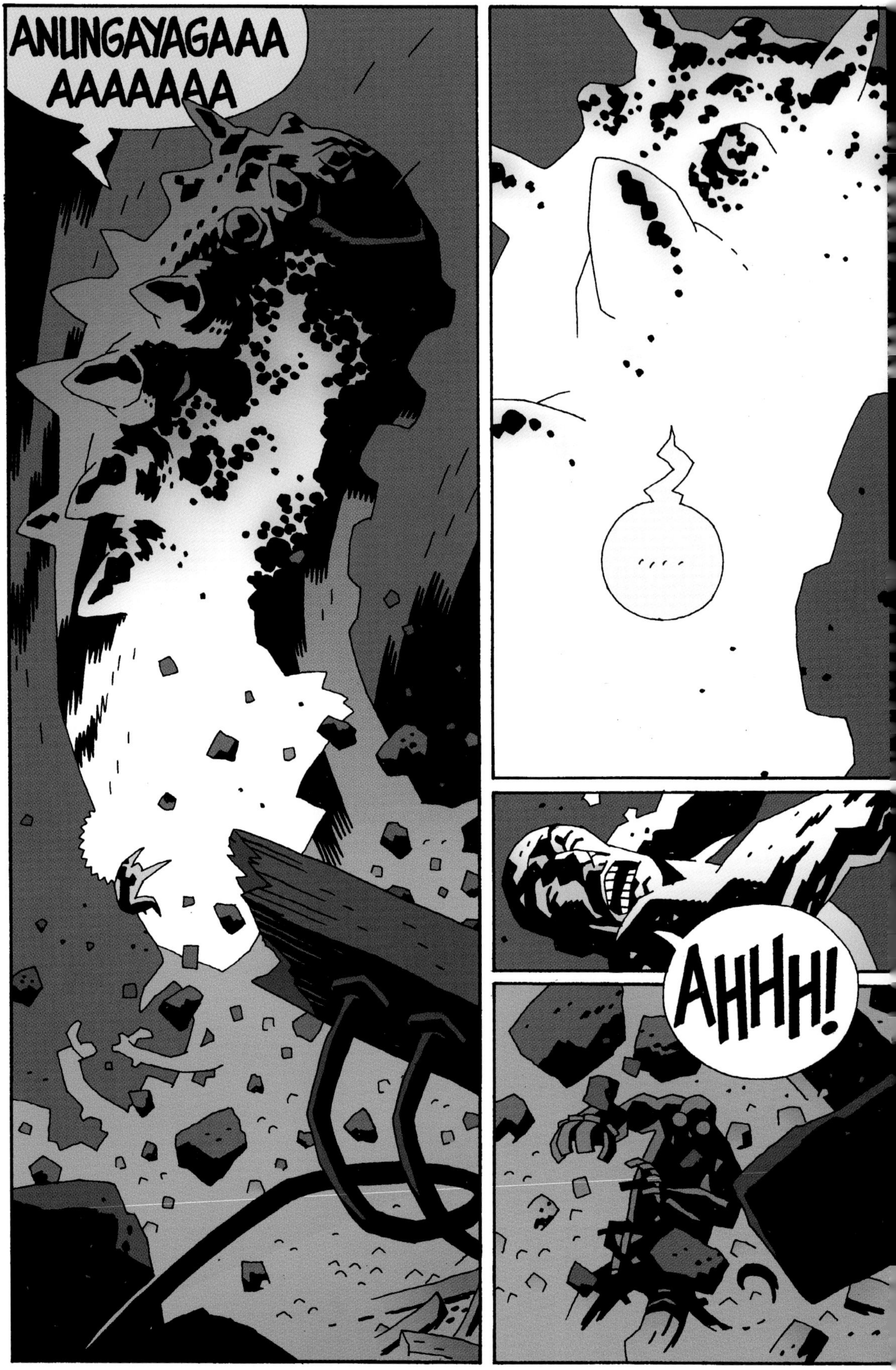
ANUNGAYAGAAA AAAAAAA
AHHH!

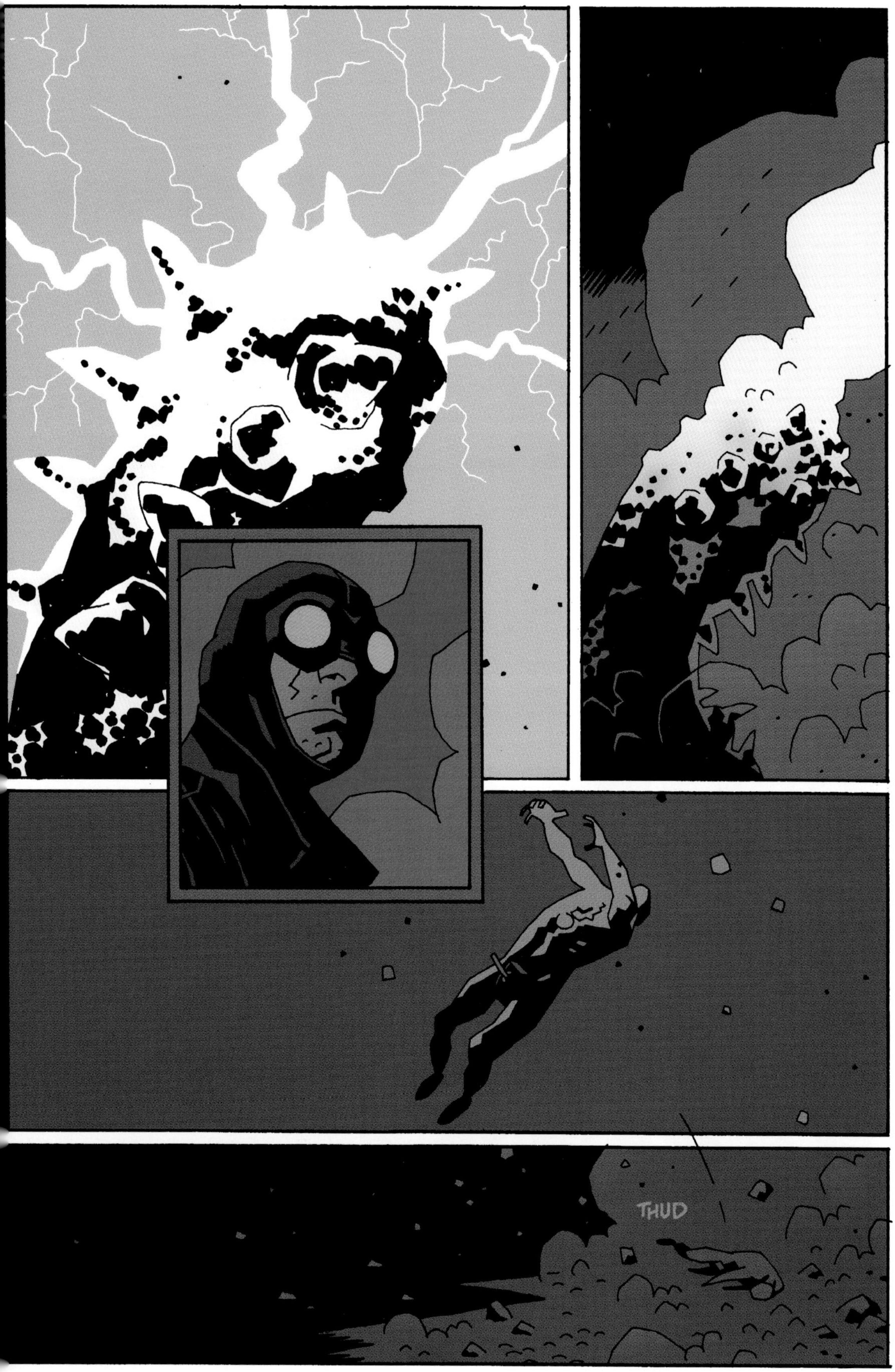
THUD

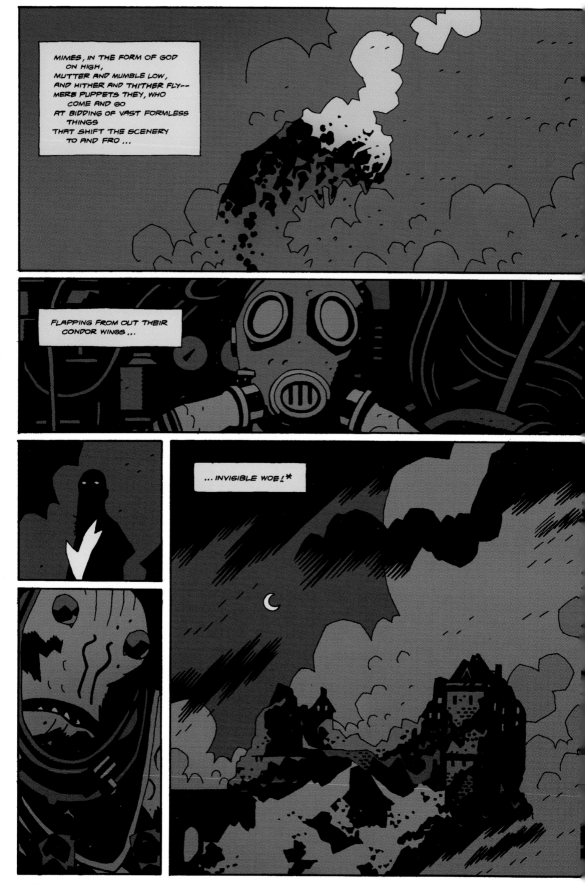

MIMES, IN THE FORM OF GOD
   ON HIGH,
MUTTER AND MUMBLE LOW,
AND HITHER AND THITHER FLY--
MERE PUPPETS THEY, WHO
   COME AND GO
AT BIDDING OF VAST FORMLESS
   THINGS
THAT SHIFT THE SCENERY
   TO AND FRO ...

FLAPPING FROM OUT THEIR
   CONDOR WINGS ...

... INVISIBLE WOE!*

* FROM "LIGEIA"

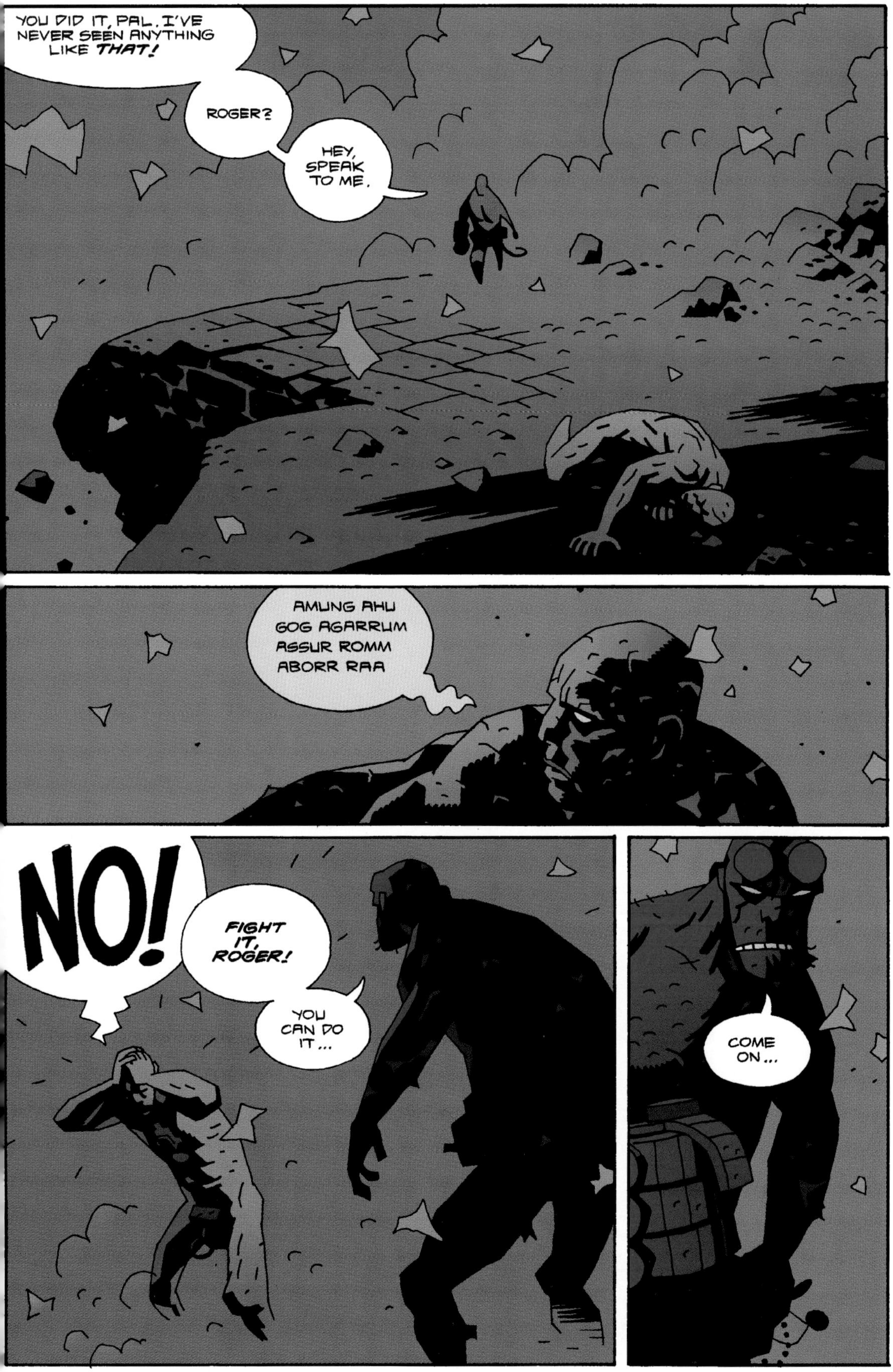
YOU DID IT, PAL. I'VE NEVER SEEN ANYTHING LIKE *THAT!*
ROGER?
HEY, SPEAK TO ME.
AMUNG AHU GOG AGARRUM ASSUR ROMM ABORR RAA
NO!
FIGHT IT, ROGER!
YOU CAN DO IT...
COME ON...

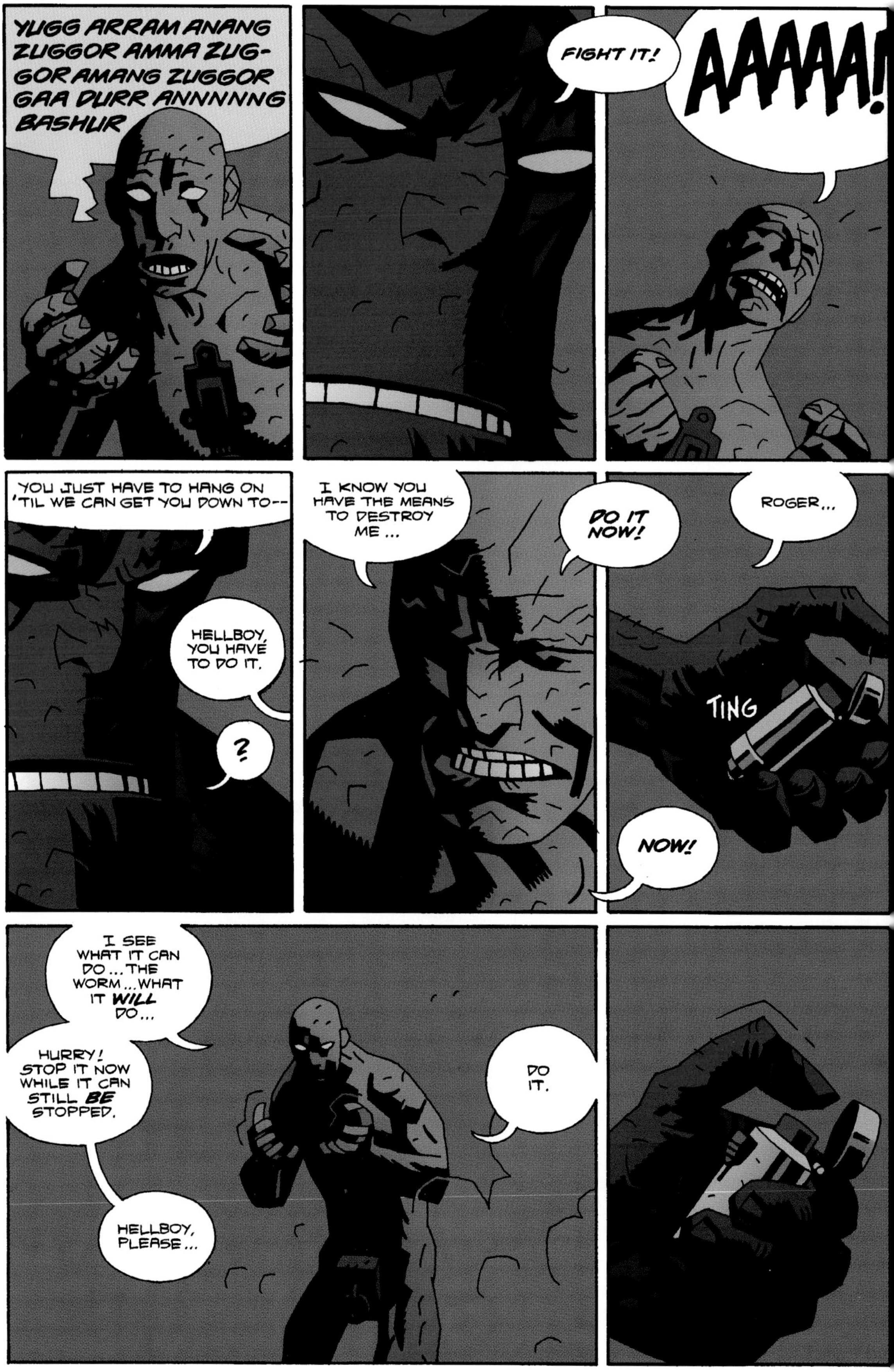

YUGG ARRAM ANANG ZUGGOR AMMA ZUG-GOR AMANG ZUGGOR GAA DURR ANNNNNG BASHUR
FIGHT IT!
AAAAAA!
YOU JUST HAVE TO HANG ON 'TIL WE CAN GET YOU DOWN TO--
HELLBOY, YOU HAVE TO DO IT.
?
I KNOW YOU HAVE THE MEANS TO DESTROY ME ...
DO IT NOW!
ROGER...
TING
NOW!
I SEE WHAT IT CAN DO ... THE WORM ... WHAT IT WILL DO ...
HURRY! STOP IT NOW WHILE IT CAN STILL BE STOPPED.
HELLBOY, PLEASE ...
DO IT.

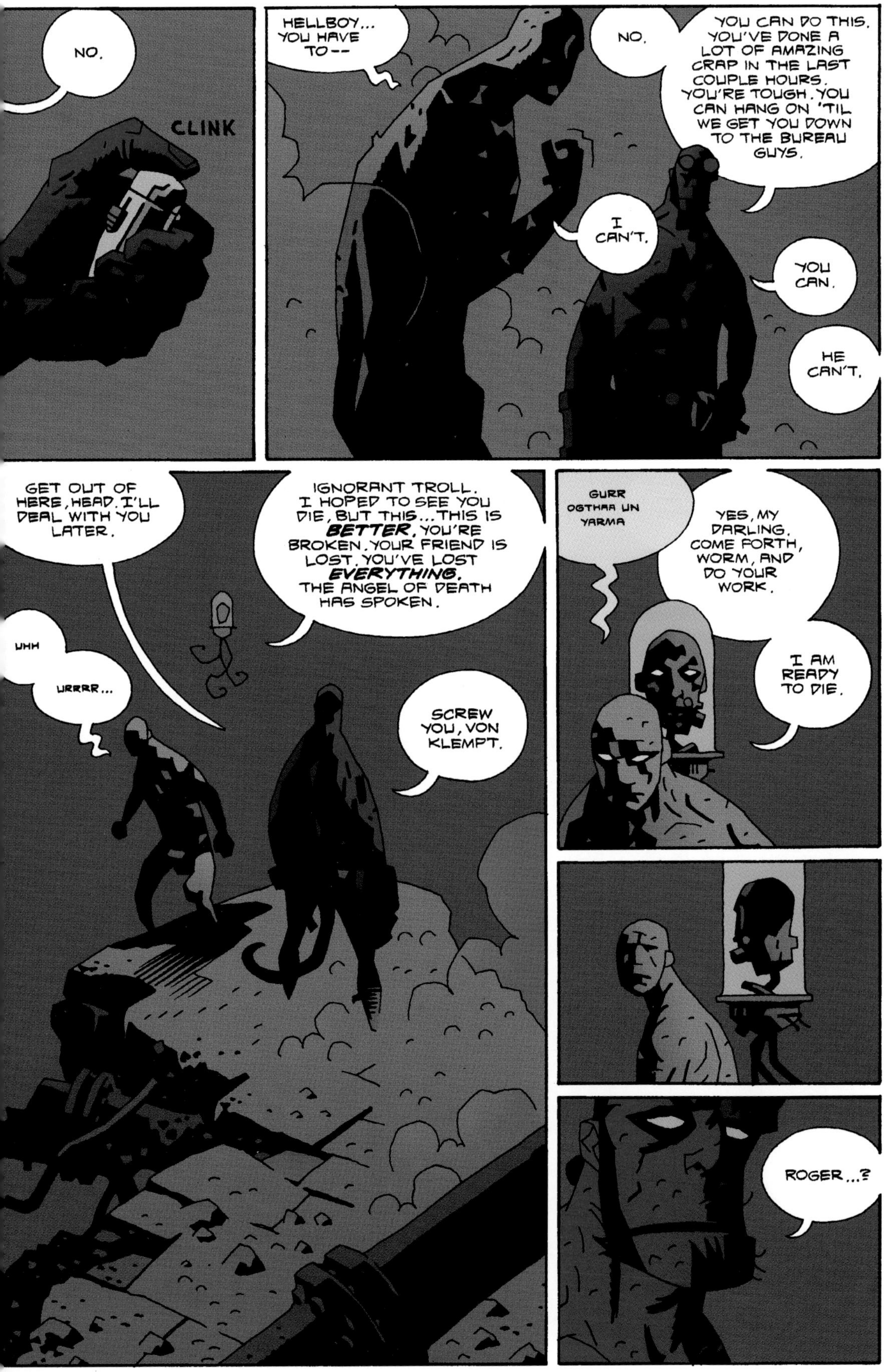
NO.
CLINK
HELLBOY... YOU HAVE TO--
NO.
YOU CAN DO THIS. YOU'VE DONE A LOT OF AMAZING CRAP IN THE LAST COUPLE HOURS. YOU'RE TOUGH. YOU CAN HANG ON 'TIL WE GET YOU DOWN TO THE BUREAU GUYS.
I CAN'T.
YOU CAN.
HE CAN'T.
GET OUT OF HERE, HEAD. I'LL DEAL WITH YOU LATER.
IGNORANT TROLL. I HOPED TO SEE YOU DIE, BUT THIS... THIS IS **BETTER.** YOU'RE BROKEN. YOUR FRIEND IS LOST. YOU'VE LOST **EVERYTHING.** THE ANGEL OF DEATH HAS SPOKEN.
UHH
URRRR...
SCREW YOU, VON KLEMPT.
GURR OGTHAA UN YARMA
YES, MY DARLING. COME FORTH, WORM, AND DO YOUR WORK.
I AM READY TO DIE.
ROGER...?

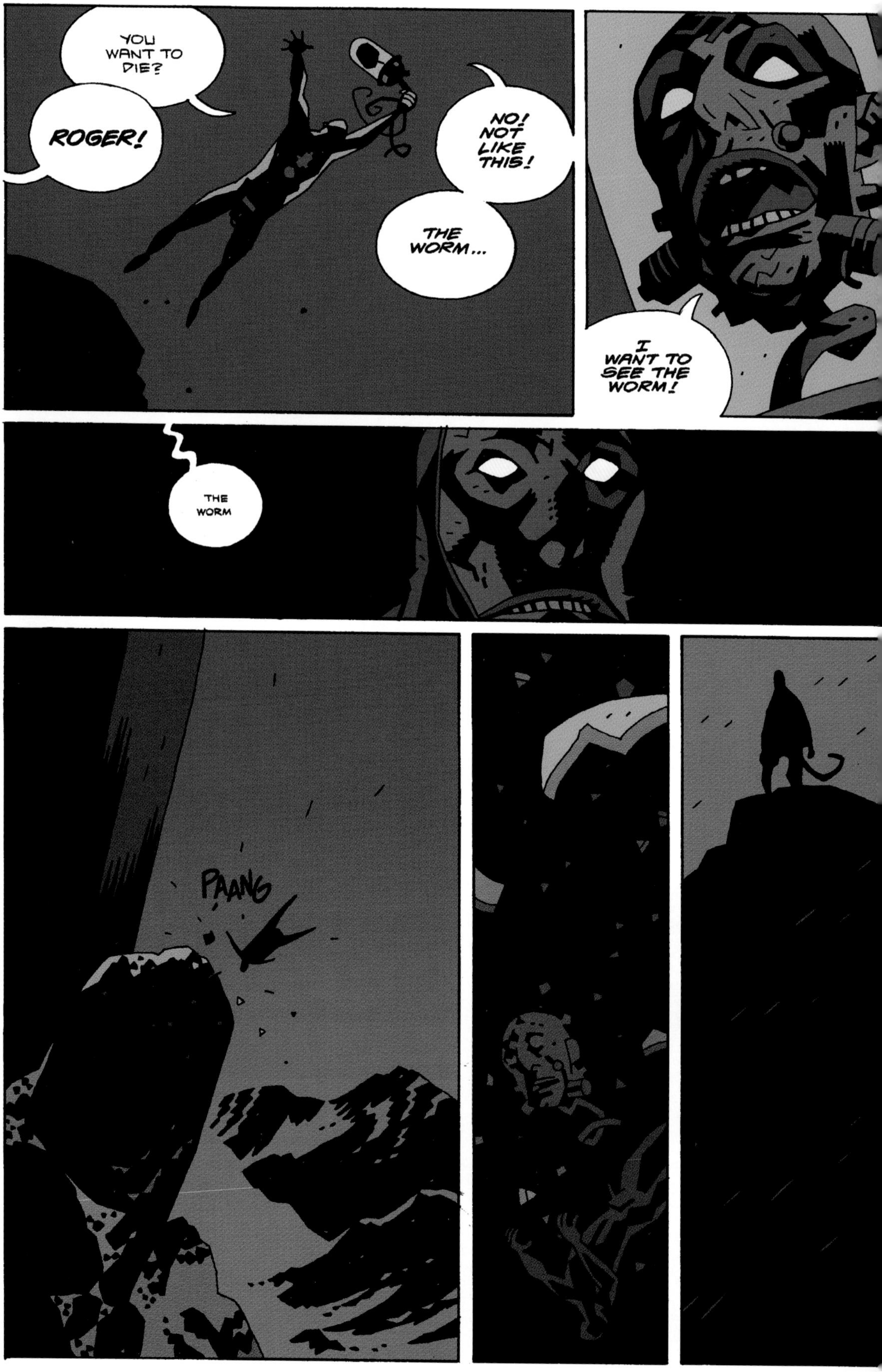
YOU WANT TO DIE?
ROGER!
NO! NOT LIKE THIS!
THE WORM...
I WANT TO SEE THE WORM!
THE WORM
PAANG

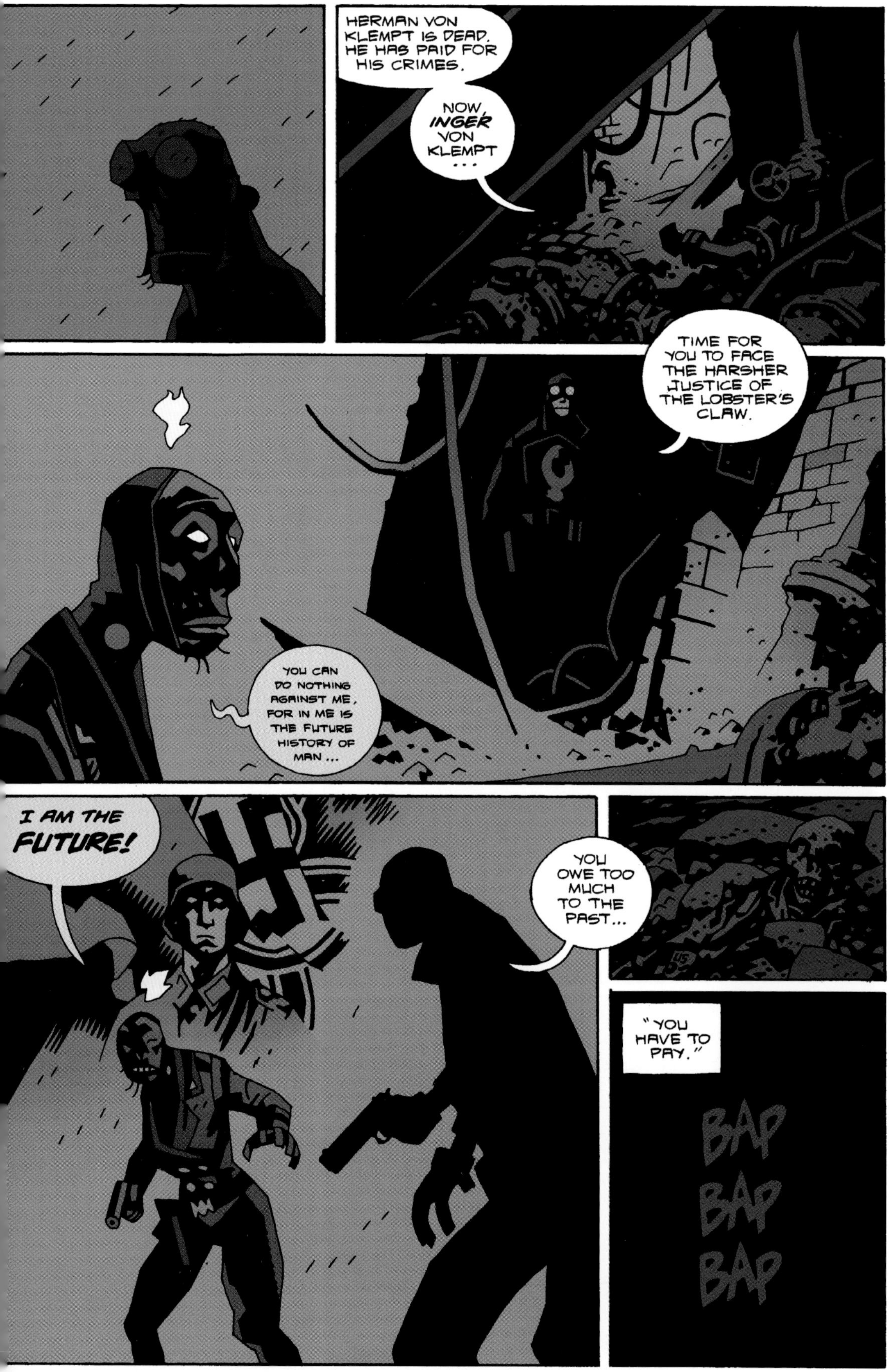
HERMAN VON KLEMPT IS DEAD. HE HAS PAID FOR HIS CRIMES.
NOW, INGER VON KLEMPT . . .
TIME FOR YOU TO FACE THE HARSHER JUSTICE OF THE LOBSTER'S CLAW.
YOU CAN DO NOTHING AGAINST ME, FOR IN ME IS THE FUTURE HISTORY OF MAN ...
I AM THE FUTURE!
YOU OWE TOO MUCH TO THE PAST...
"YOU HAVE TO PAY."
BAP
BAP
BAP

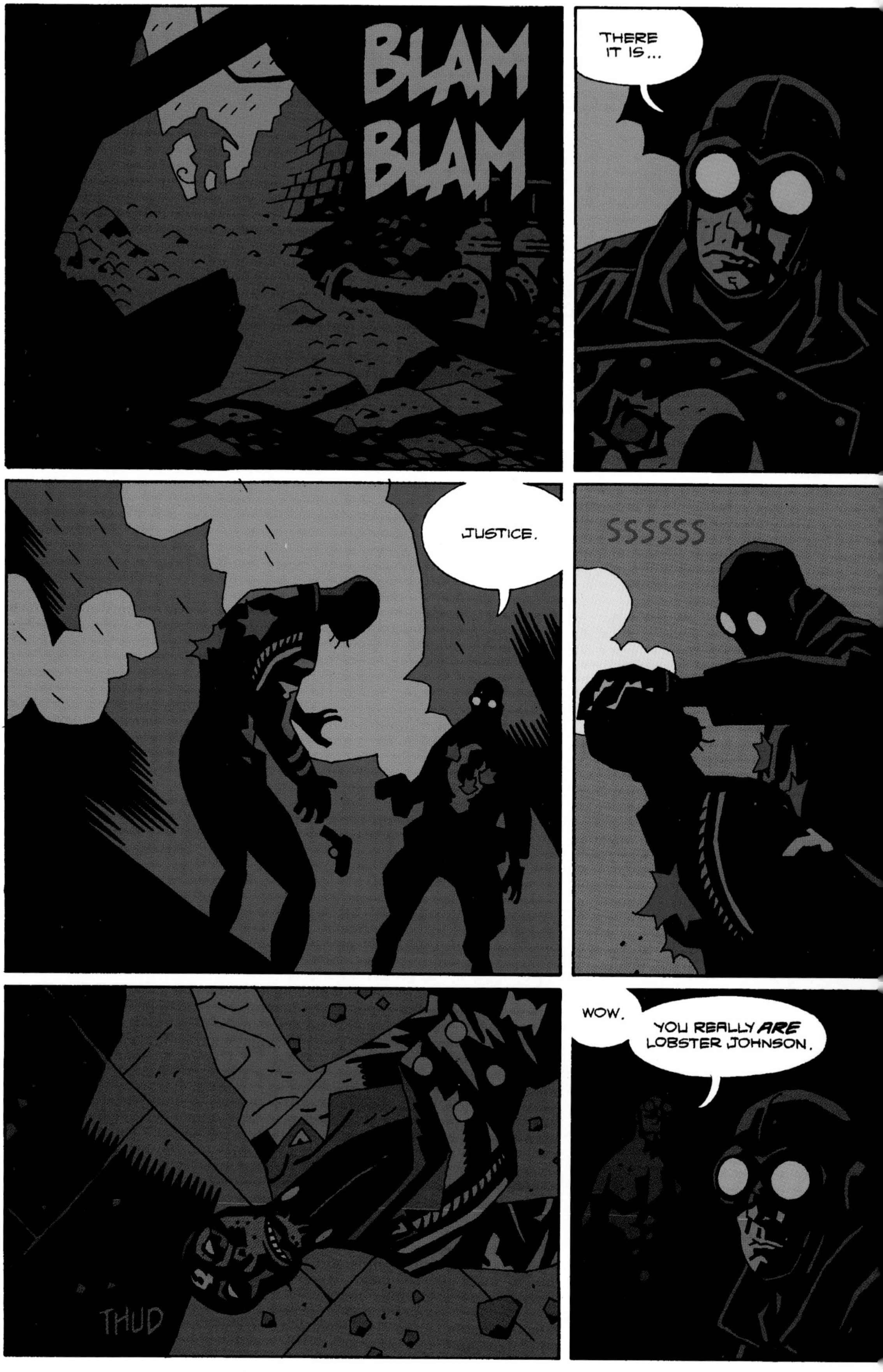

BLAM
BLAM
THERE IT IS...
JUSTICE.
SSSSSS
THUD
WOW.
YOU REALLY *ARE* LOBSTER JOHNSON.

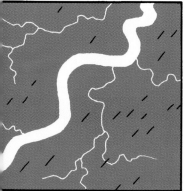

THERE HE IS!

PULL THAT COVER OFF HIS CHEST.

GOT IT!

OH, JEEZ!

POP

THE THING'S EATING HIM FROM THE IN- SIDE OUT.

LOOK OUT!

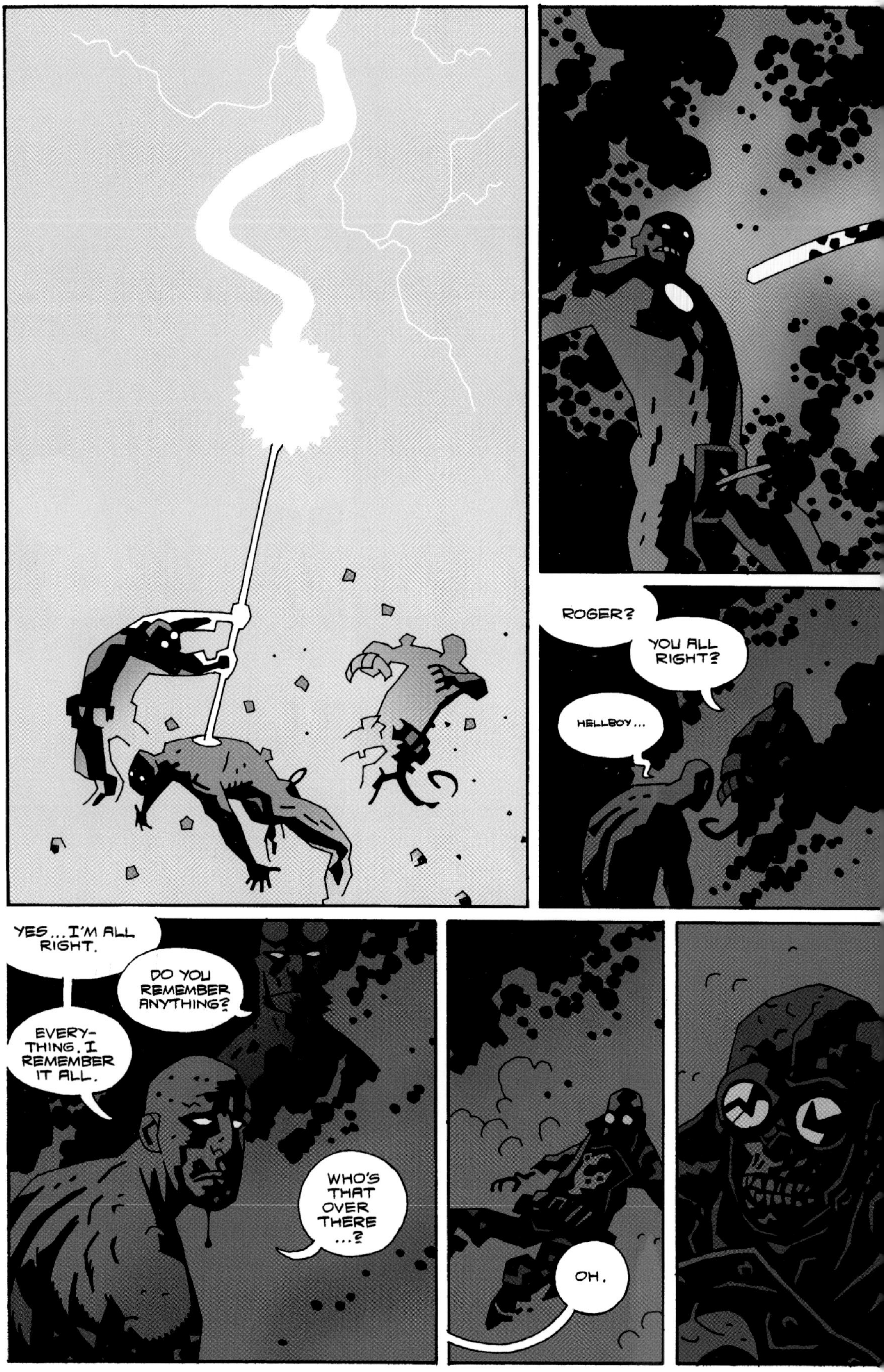
ROGER?
YOU ALL RIGHT?
HELLBOY...
YES... I'M ALL RIGHT.
DO YOU REMEMBER ANYTHING?
EVERY- THING. I REMEMBER IT ALL.
WHO'S THAT OVER THERE ...?
OH.

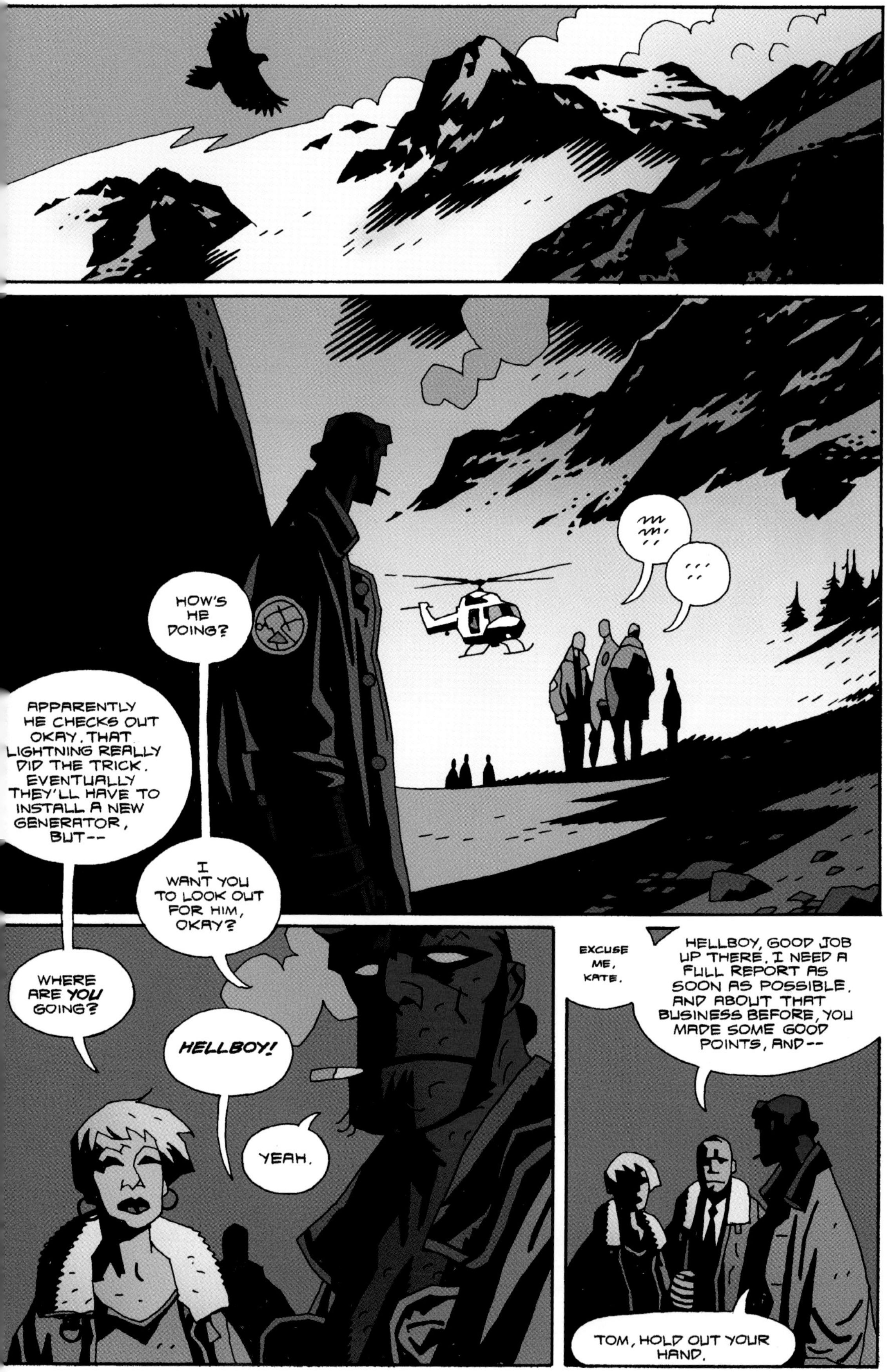
HOW'S HE DOING?
APPARENTLY HE CHECKS OUT OKAY. THAT LIGHTNING REALLY DID THE TRICK. EVENTUALLY THEY'LL HAVE TO INSTALL A NEW GENERATOR, BUT--
I WANT YOU TO LOOK OUT FOR HIM, OKAY?
WHERE ARE *YOU* GOING?
HELLBOY!
YEAH.
EXCUSE ME, KATE.
HELLBOY, GOOD JOB UP THERE. I NEED A FULL REPORT AS SOON AS POSSIBLE. AND ABOUT THAT BUSINESS BEFORE, YOU MADE SOME GOOD POINTS, AND--
TOM, HOLD OUT YOUR HAND.

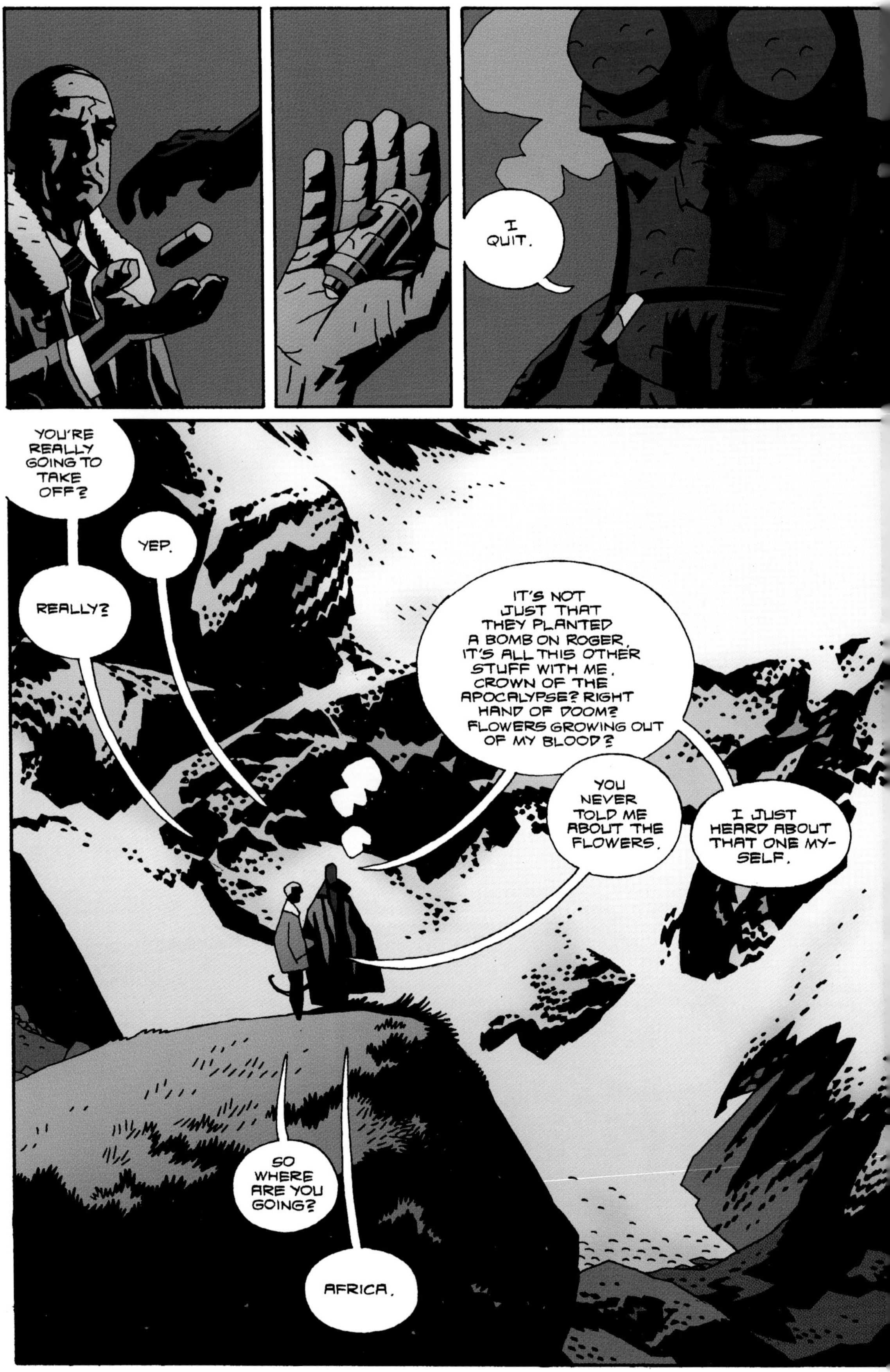
I QUIT.
YOU'RE REALLY GOING TO TAKE OFF?
YEP.
REALLY?
IT'S NOT JUST THAT THEY PLANTED A BOMB ON ROGER, IT'S ALL THIS OTHER STUFF WITH ME. CROWN OF THE APOCALYPSE? RIGHT HAND OF DOOM? FLOWERS GROWING OUT OF MY BLOOD?
YOU NEVER TOLD ME ABOUT THE FLOWERS.
I JUST HEARD ABOUT THAT ONE MY-SELF.
SO WHERE ARE YOU GOING?
AFRICA.

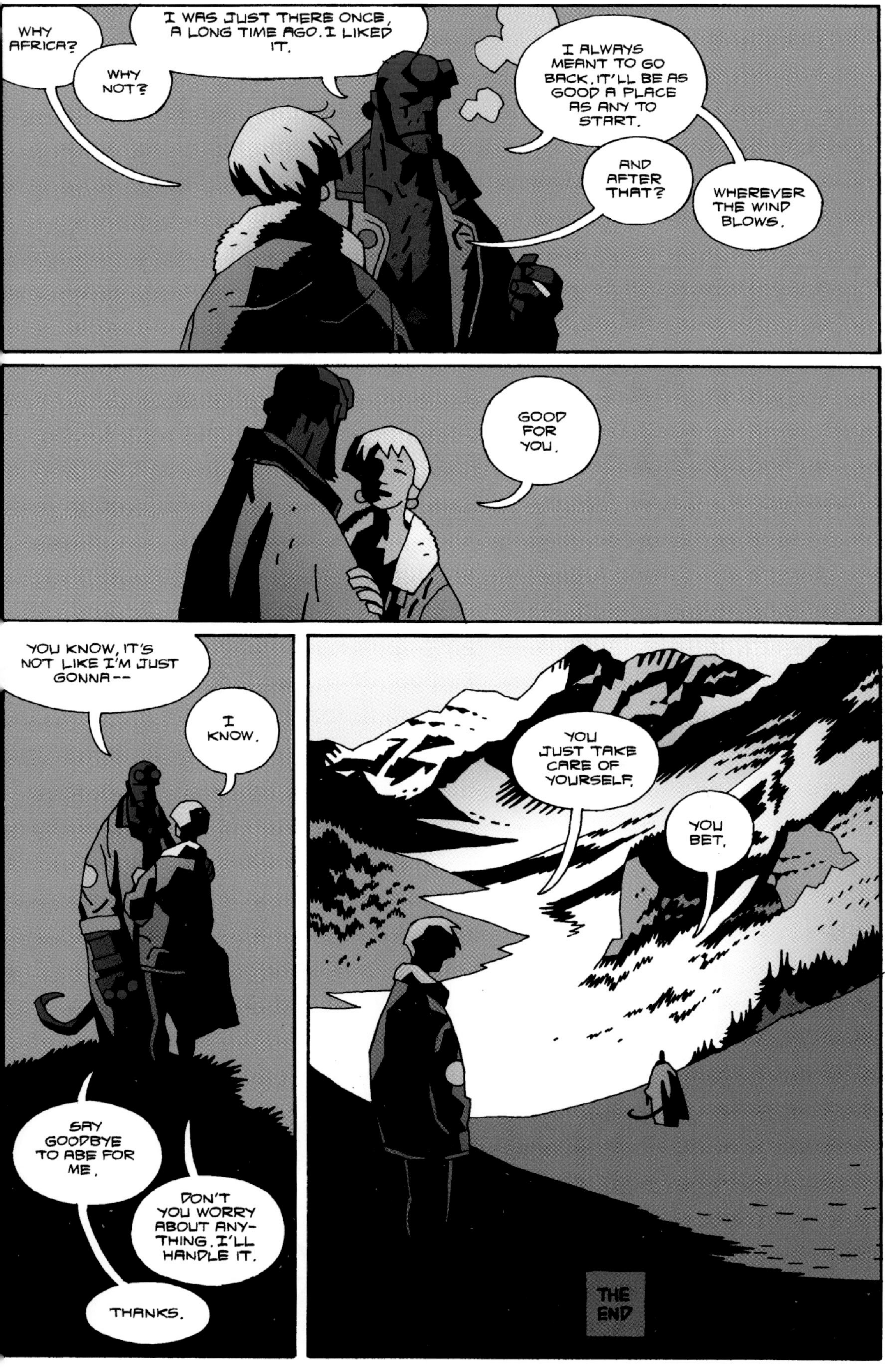
WHY AFRICA?
I WAS JUST THERE ONCE, A LONG TIME AGO. I LIKED IT.
WHY NOT?
I ALWAYS MEANT TO GO BACK. IT'LL BE AS GOOD A PLACE AS ANY TO START.
AND AFTER THAT?
WHEREVER THE WIND BLOWS.
GOOD FOR YOU.
YOU KNOW, IT'S NOT LIKE I'M JUST GONNA--
I KNOW.
SAY GOODBYE TO ABE FOR ME.
DON'T YOU WORRY ABOUT ANY-THING. I'LL HANDLE IT.
THANKS.
YOU JUST TAKE CARE OF YOURSELF.
YOU BET.
THE END

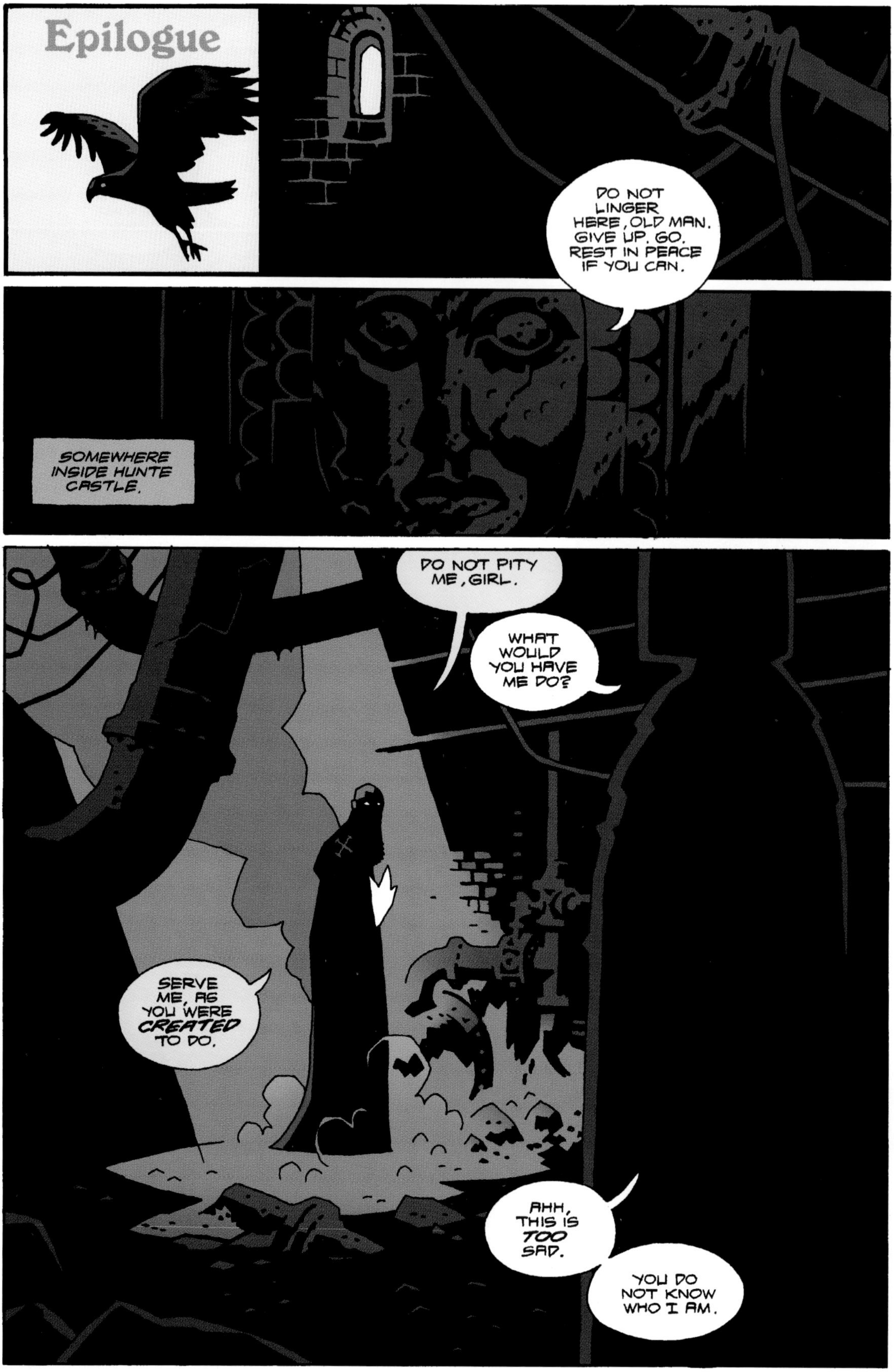
Epilogue
DO NOT LINGER HERE, OLD MAN. GIVE UP. GO. REST IN PEACE IF YOU CAN.
SOMEWHERE INSIDE HUNTE CASTLE.
DO NOT PITY ME, GIRL.
WHAT WOULD YOU HAVE ME DO?
SERVE ME, AS YOU WERE CREATED TO DO.
AHH, THIS IS TOO SAD.
YOU DO NOT KNOW WHO I AM.

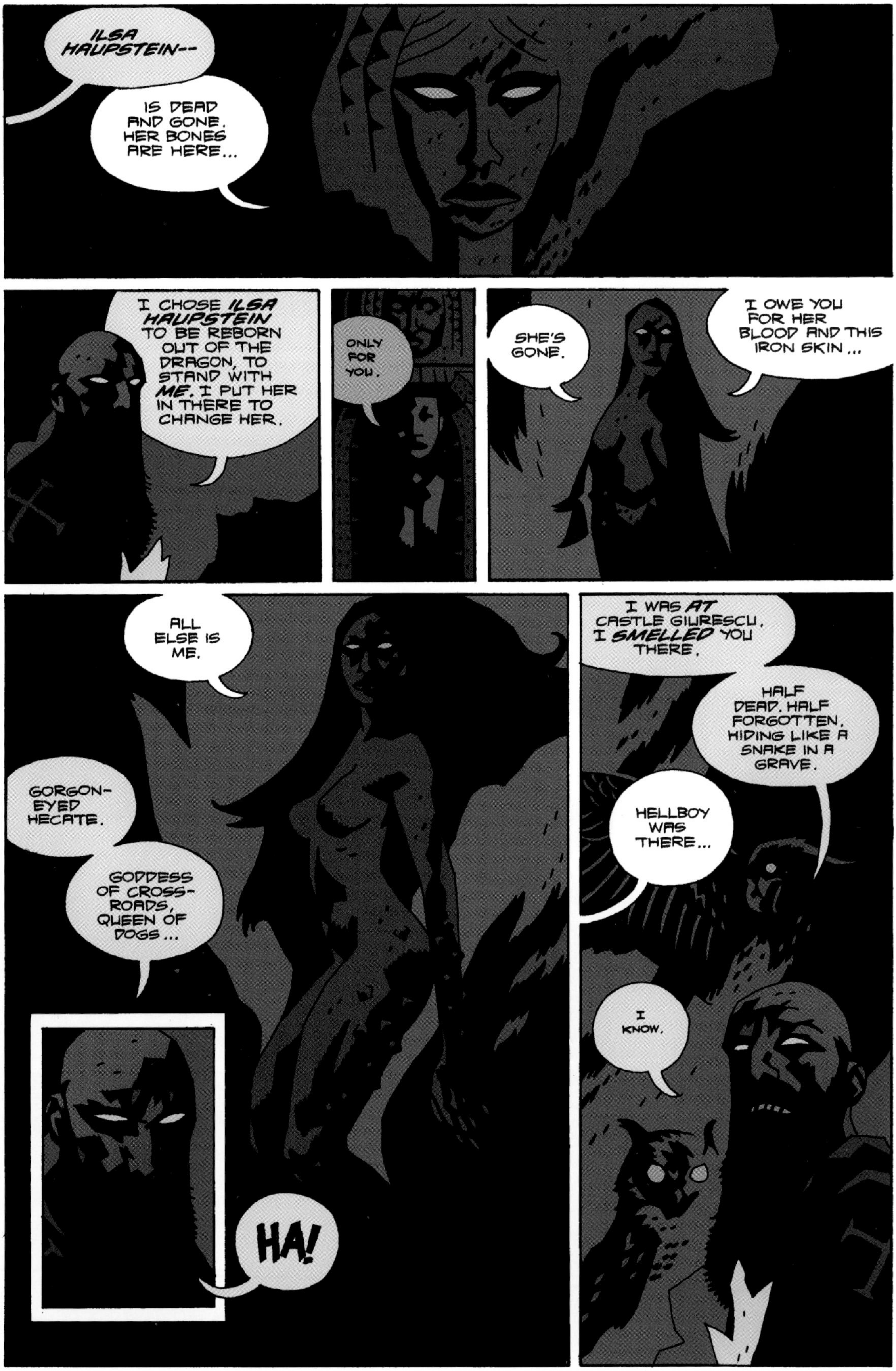

ILSA HAUPSTEIN--
IS DEAD AND GONE. HER BONES ARE HERE...
I CHOSE ILSA HAUPSTEIN TO BE REBORN OUT OF THE DRAGON, TO STAND WITH ME. I PUT HER IN THERE TO CHANGE HER.
ONLY FOR YOU.
SHE'S GONE.
I OWE YOU FOR HER BLOOD AND THIS IRON SKIN...
ALL ELSE IS ME.
GORGON-EYED HECATE.
GODDESS OF CROSS-ROADS, QUEEN OF DOGS...
HA!
I WAS AT CASTLE GIURESCU. I SMELLED YOU THERE.
HALF DEAD. HALF FORGOTTEN. HIDING LIKE A SNAKE IN A GRAVE.
HELLBOY WAS THERE...
I KNOW.

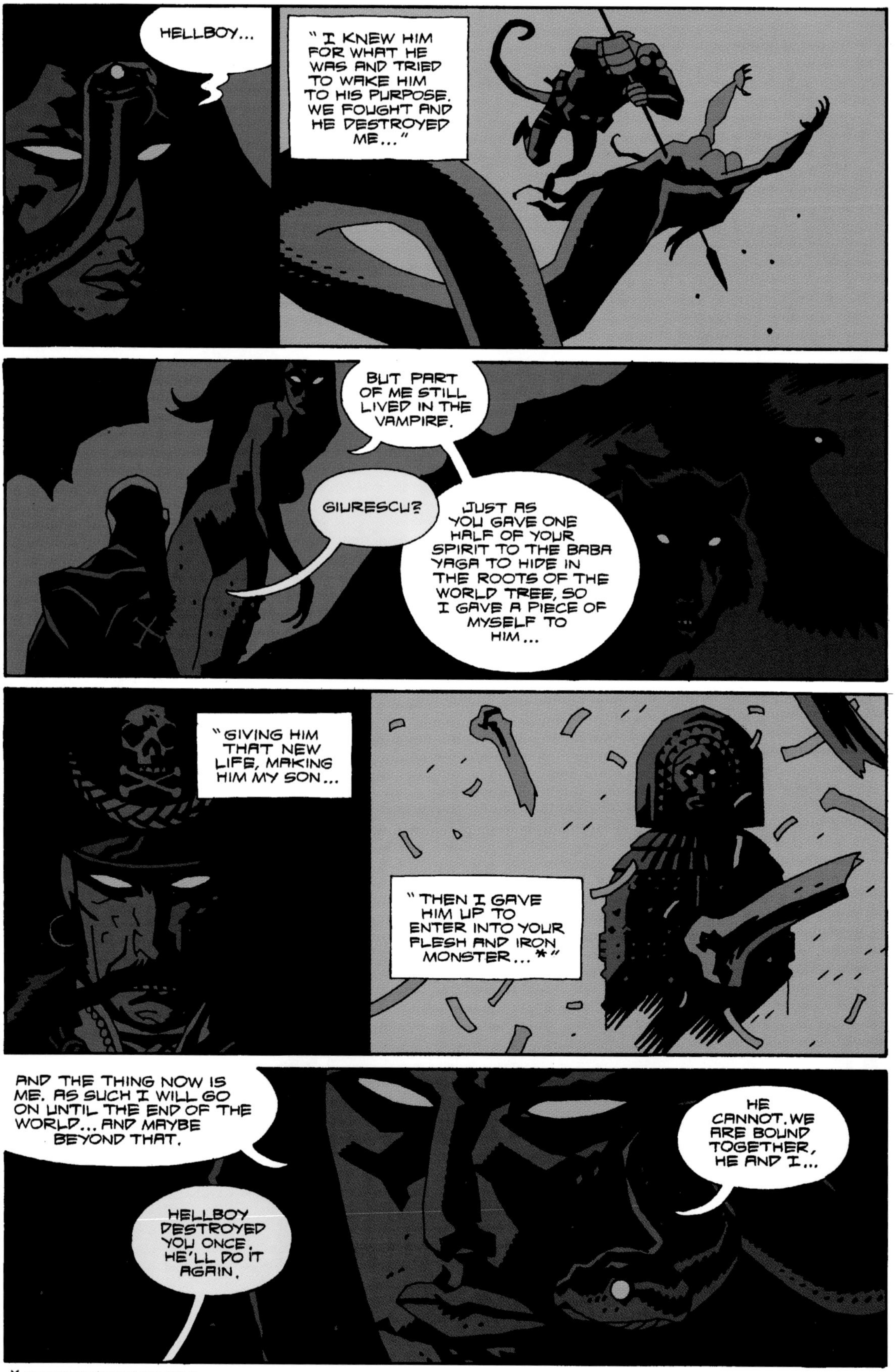
HELLBOY...
"I KNEW HIM FOR WHAT HE WAS AND TRIED TO WAKE HIM TO HIS PURPOSE. WE FOUGHT AND HE DESTROYED ME..."
BUT PART OF ME STILL LIVED IN THE VAMPIRE.
GIURESCU?
JUST AS YOU GAVE ONE HALF OF YOUR SPIRIT TO THE BABA YAGA TO HIDE IN THE ROOTS OF THE WORLD TREE, SO I GAVE A PIECE OF MYSELF TO HIM...
"GIVING HIM THAT NEW LIFE, MAKING HIM MY SON...
"THEN I GAVE HIM UP TO ENTER INTO YOUR FLESH AND IRON MONSTER...*"
AND THE THING NOW IS ME. AS SUCH I WILL GO ON UNTIL THE END OF THE WORLD... AND MAYBE BEYOND THAT.
HELLBOY DESTROYED YOU ONCE. HE'LL DO IT AGAIN.
HE CANNOT. WE ARE BOUND TOGETHER, HE AND I...

* HELLBOY: WAKE THE DEVIL

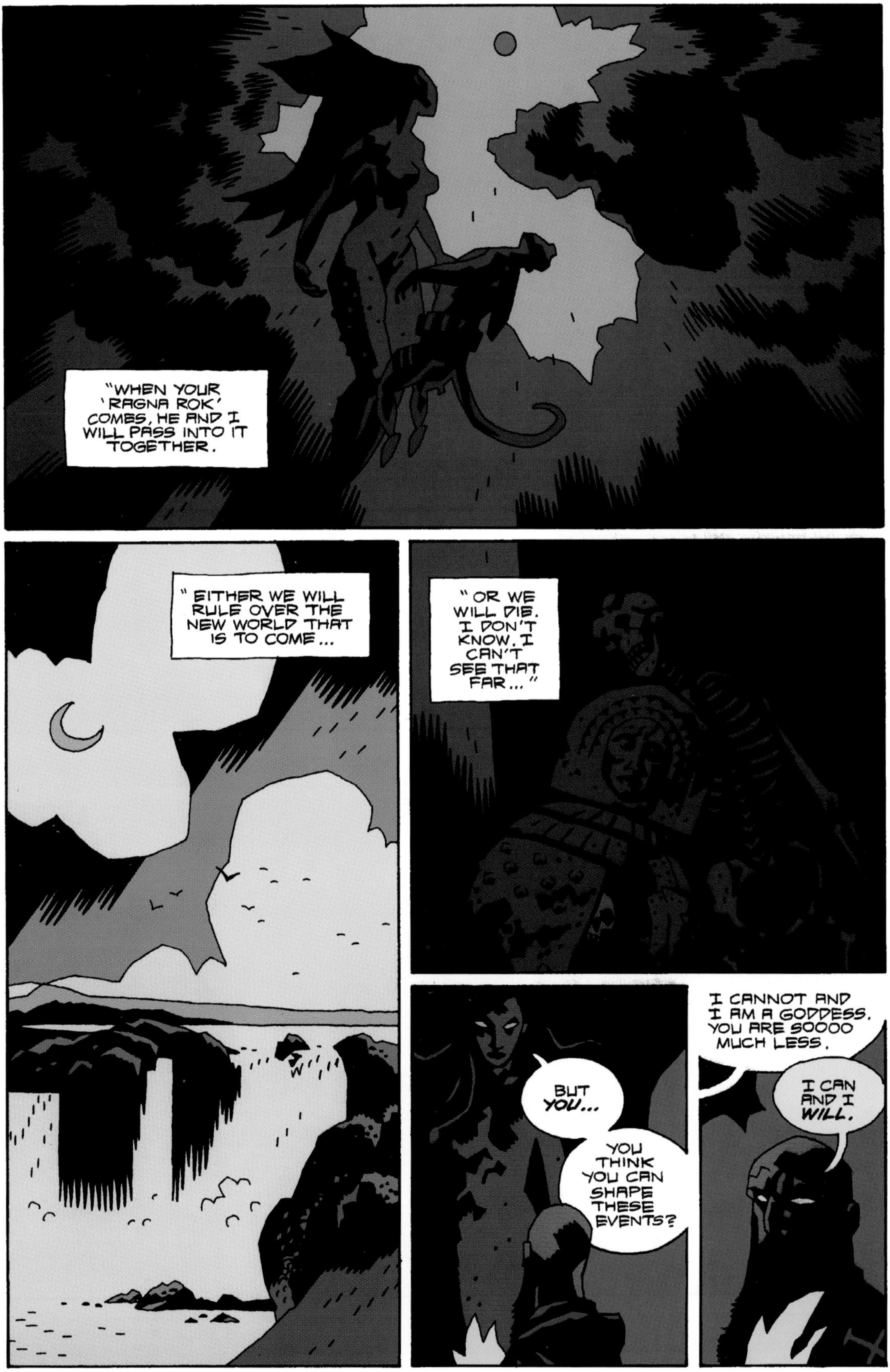
"WHEN YOUR 'RAGNA ROK' COMES, HE AND I WILL PASS INTO IT TOGETHER.
" EITHER WE WILL RULE OVER THE NEW WORLD THAT IS TO COME...
" OR WE WILL DIE. I DON'T KNOW. I CAN'T SEE THAT FAR..."
BUT *YOU*...
YOU THINK YOU CAN SHAPE THESE EVENTS?
I CANNOT AND I AM A GODDESS. YOU ARE SOOOO MUCH LESS.
I CAN AND I *WILL*.

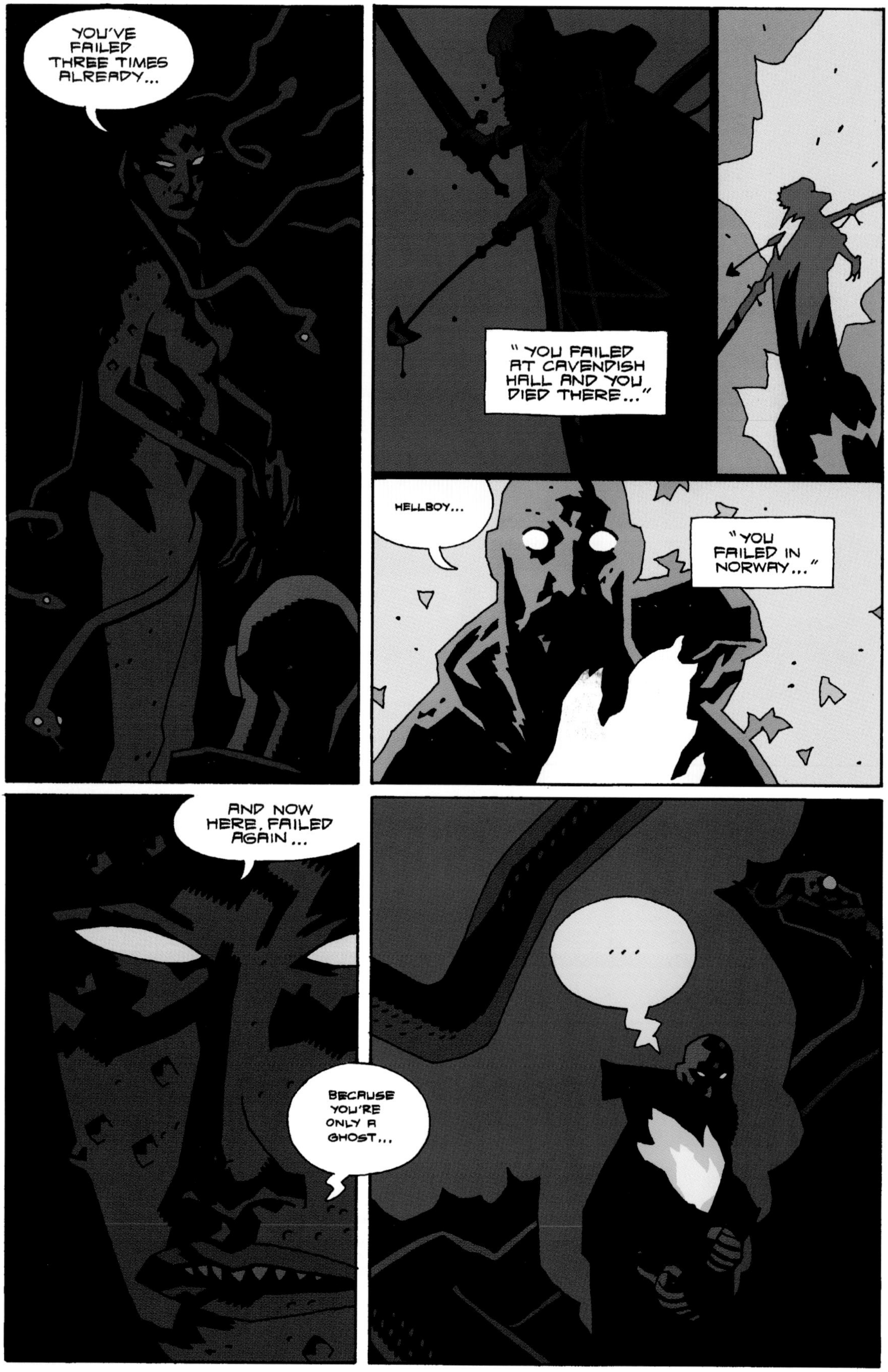
YOU'VE FAILED THREE TIMES ALREADY...
"YOU FAILED AT CAVENDISH HALL AND YOU DIED THERE..."
HELLBOY...
"YOU FAILED IN NORWAY..."
AND NOW HERE, FAILED AGAIN...
BECAUSE YOU'RE ONLY A GHOST...
...

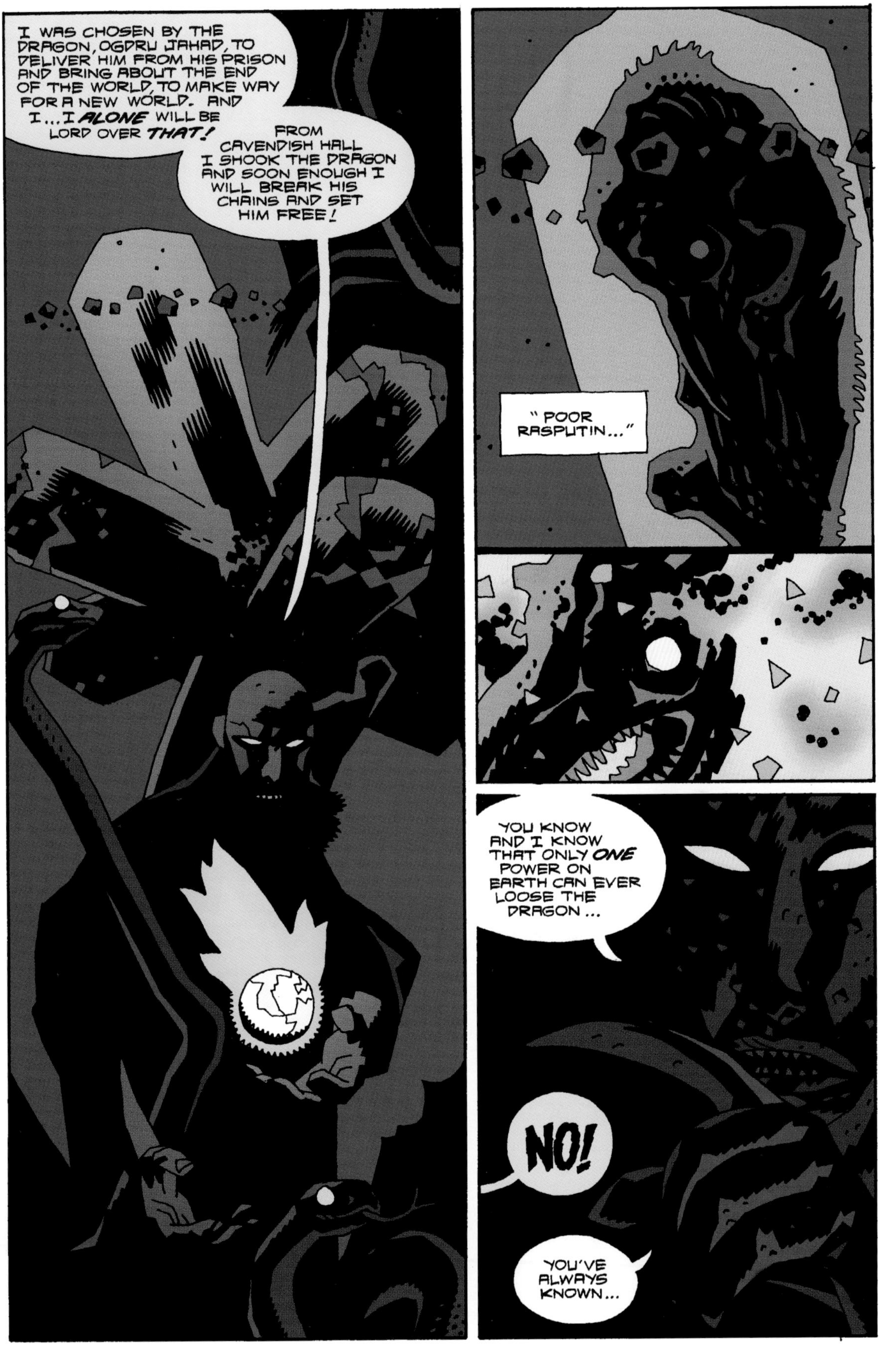
I WAS CHOSEN BY THE DRAGON, OGDRU JAHAD, TO DELIVER HIM FROM HIS PRISON AND BRING ABOUT THE END OF THE WORLD, TO MAKE WAY FOR A NEW WORLD. AND I...I ALONE WILL BE LORD OVER THAT!
FROM CAVENDISH HALL I SHOOK THE DRAGON AND SOON ENOUGH I WILL BREAK HIS CHAINS AND SET HIM FREE!
"POOR RASPUTIN..."
YOU KNOW AND I KNOW THAT ONLY ONE POWER ON EARTH CAN EVER LOOSE THE DRAGON...
NO!
YOU'VE ALWAYS KNOWN...

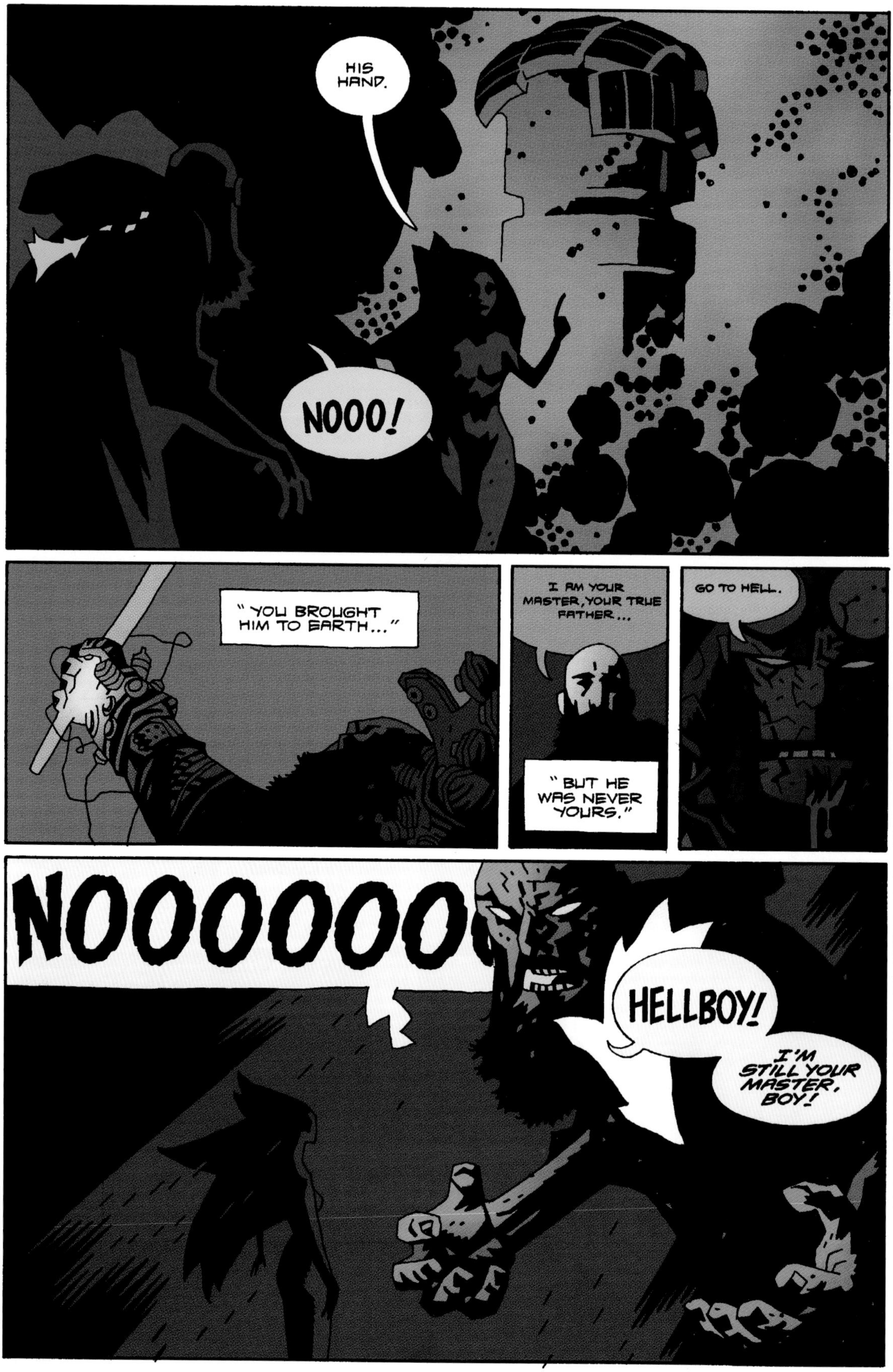
HIS HAND.
NOOO!
"YOU BROUGHT HIM TO EARTH..."
I AM YOUR MASTER, YOUR TRUE FATHER...
"BUT HE WAS NEVER YOURS."
GO TO HELL.
NOOOOOOO
HELLBOY!
I'M STILL YOUR MASTER, BOY!

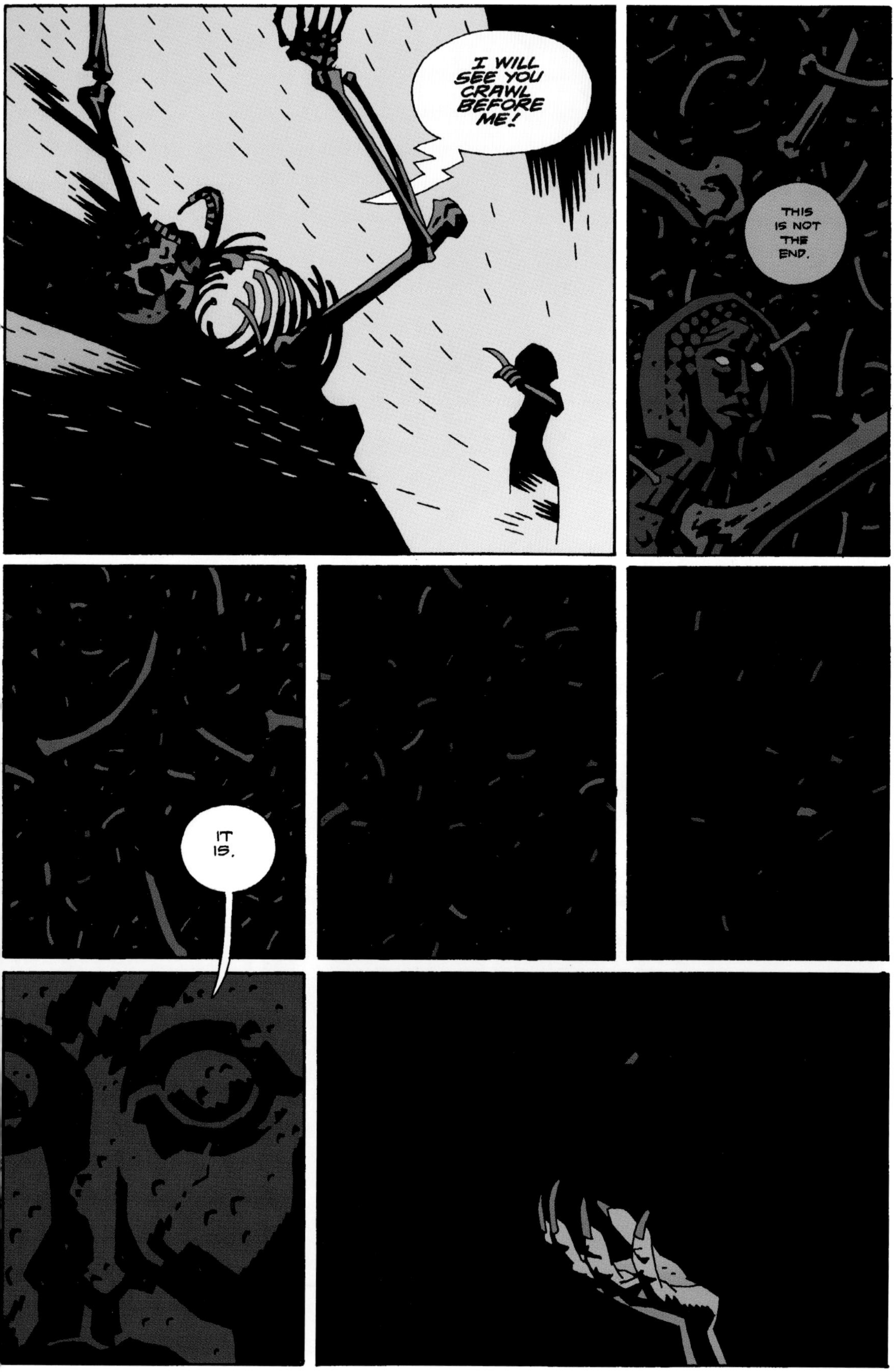
I WILL SEE YOU CRAWL BEFORE ME!
THIS IS NOT THE END.
IT IS.

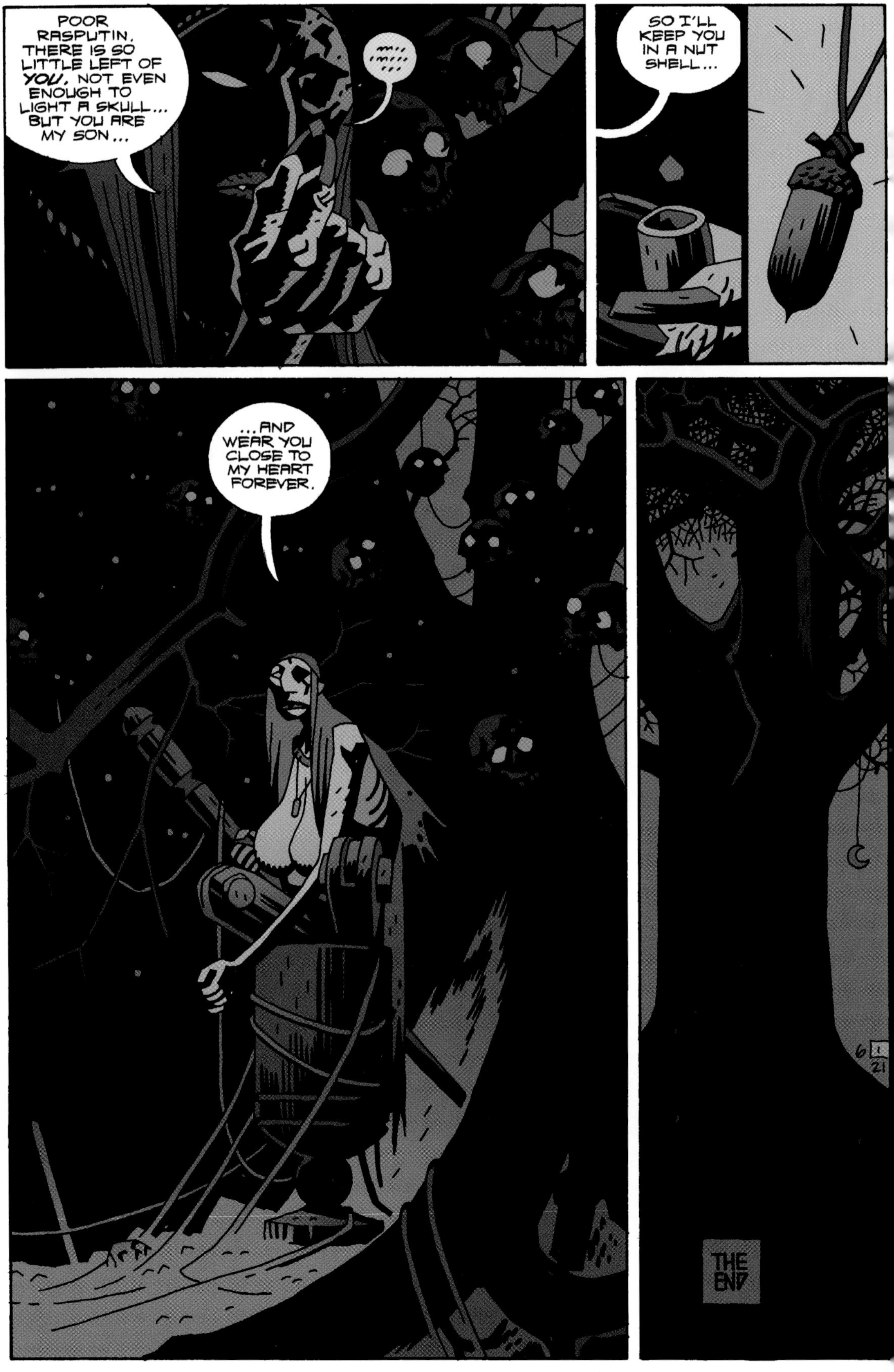
POOR RASPUTIN. THERE IS SO LITTLE LEFT OF *YOU*, NOT EVEN ENOUGH TO LIGHT A SKULL... BUT YOU ARE MY SON...
SO I'LL KEEP YOU IN A NUT SHELL...
...AND WEAR YOU CLOSE TO MY HEART FOREVER.
THE END

HELLBOY™

SKETCHBOOK

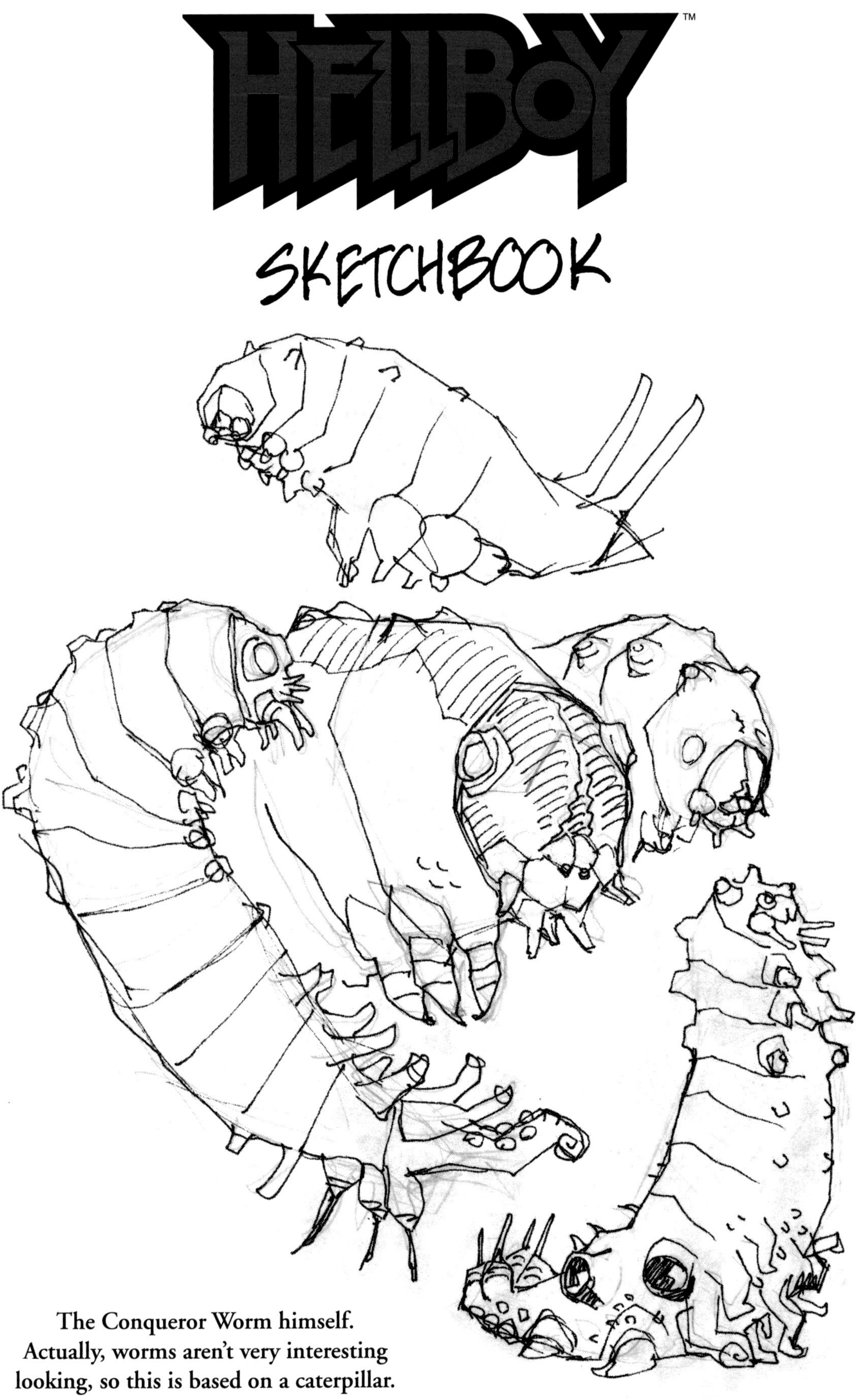

The Conqueror Worm himself.
Actually, worms aren't very interesting looking, so this is based on a caterpillar.

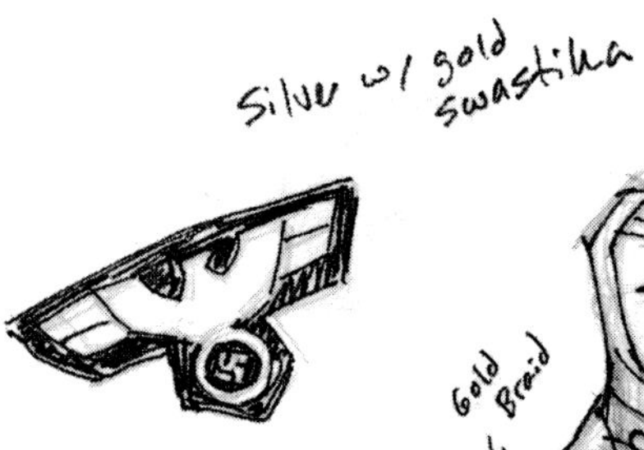
Silver w/ gold swastika

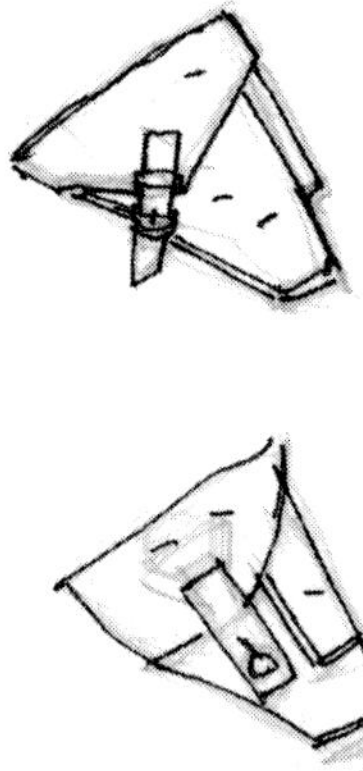

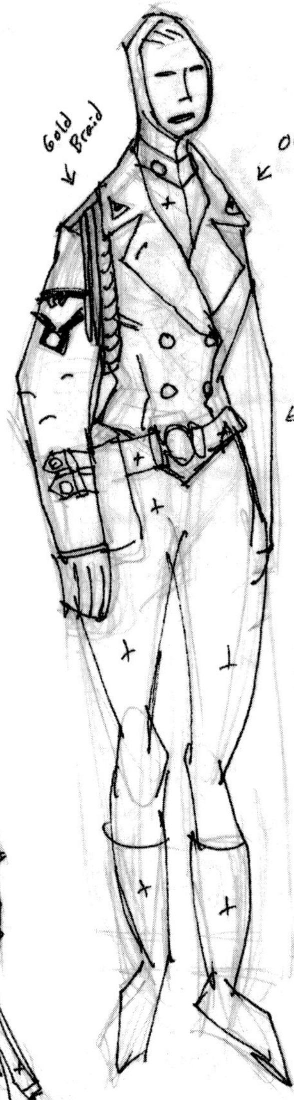
Gold Braid
orange collar tips
Brown Holster & Belt

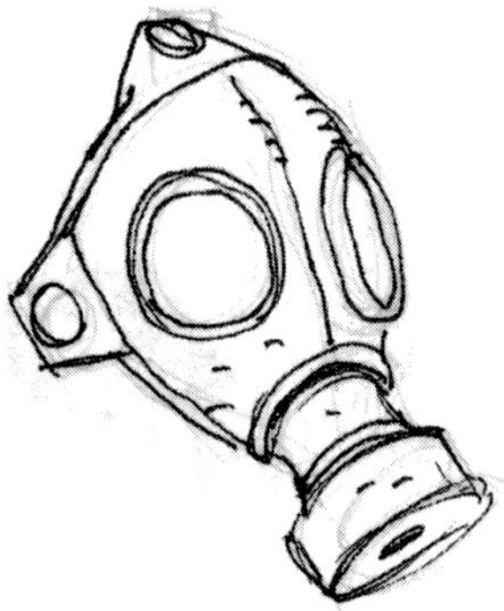

Inger von Klempt. I tried to avoid the stereotypical skin-tight, black leather, comic-book Nazi superwoman look.

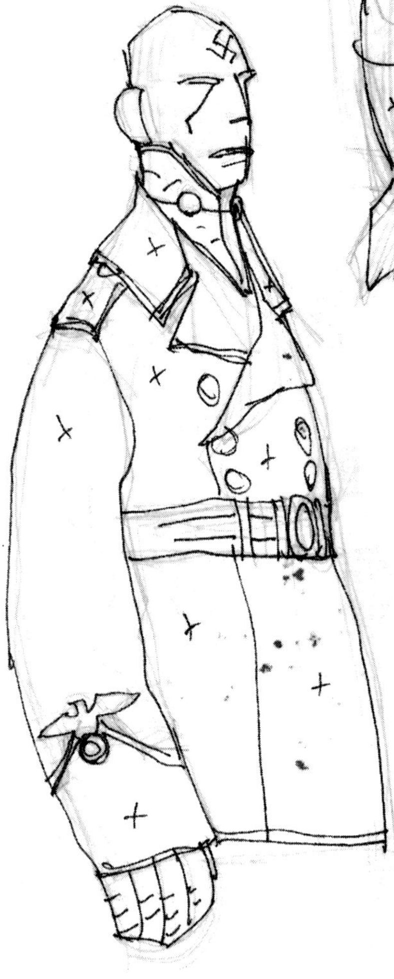

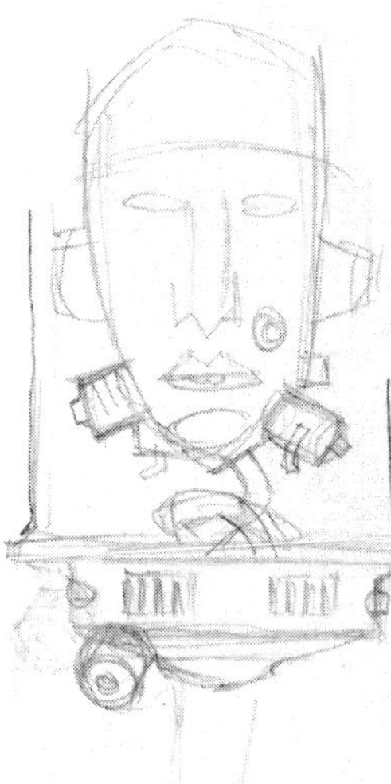

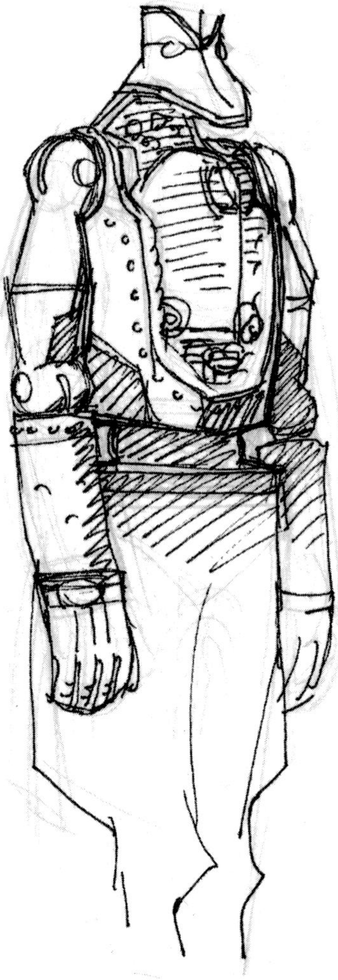

Herman von Klempt, his head jar, and robot body.

Nazi designs:
Human and reptile.

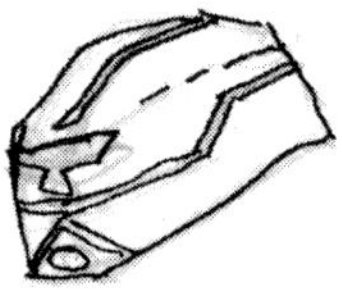

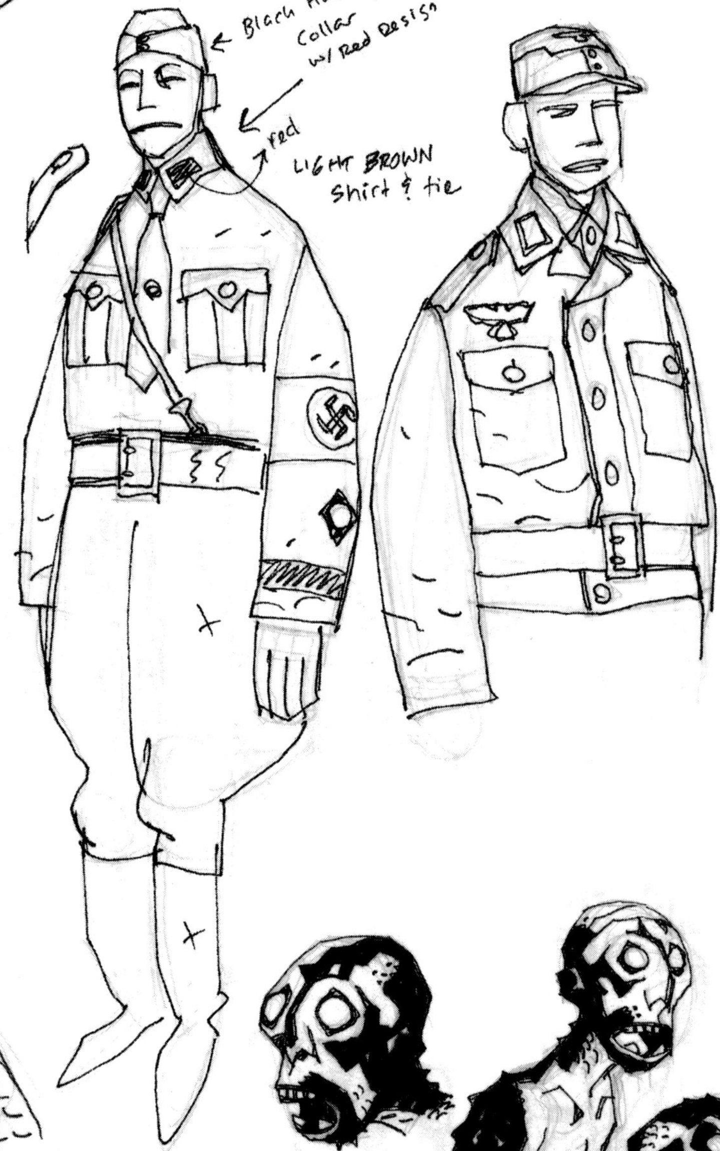

Black Hat & Collar w/ Red Design
red
LIGHT BROWN Shirt & tie
Black Pants - Dark Brown Belt

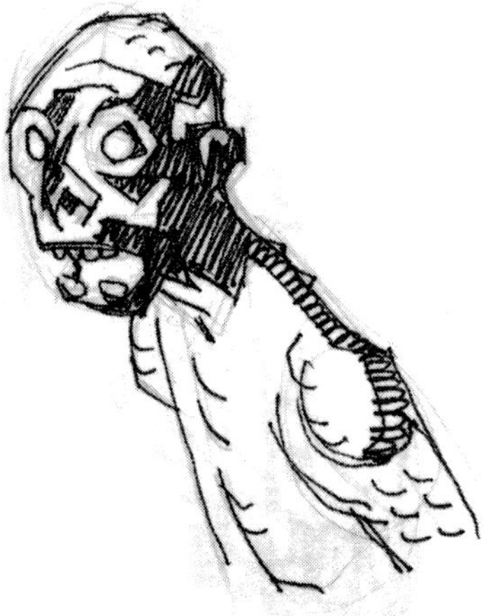

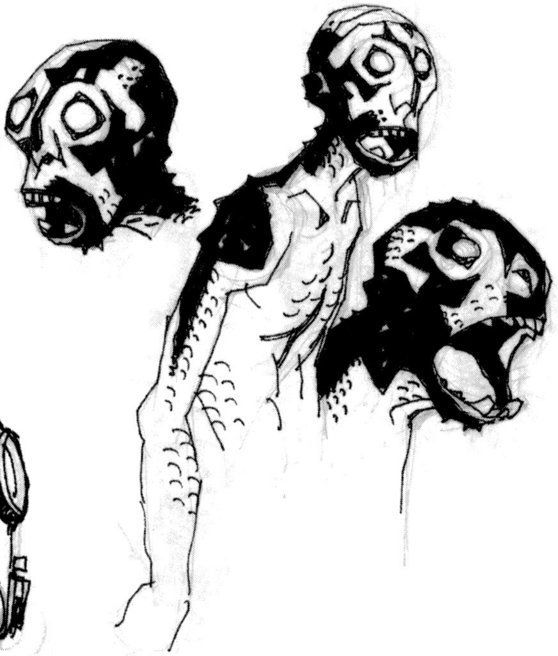

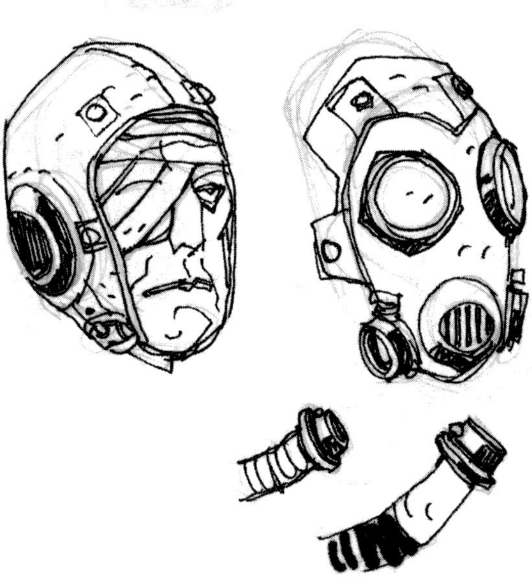

Study for Doctor Oeming in his space capsule. I added a mustache to avoid confusion with Lobster Johnson.

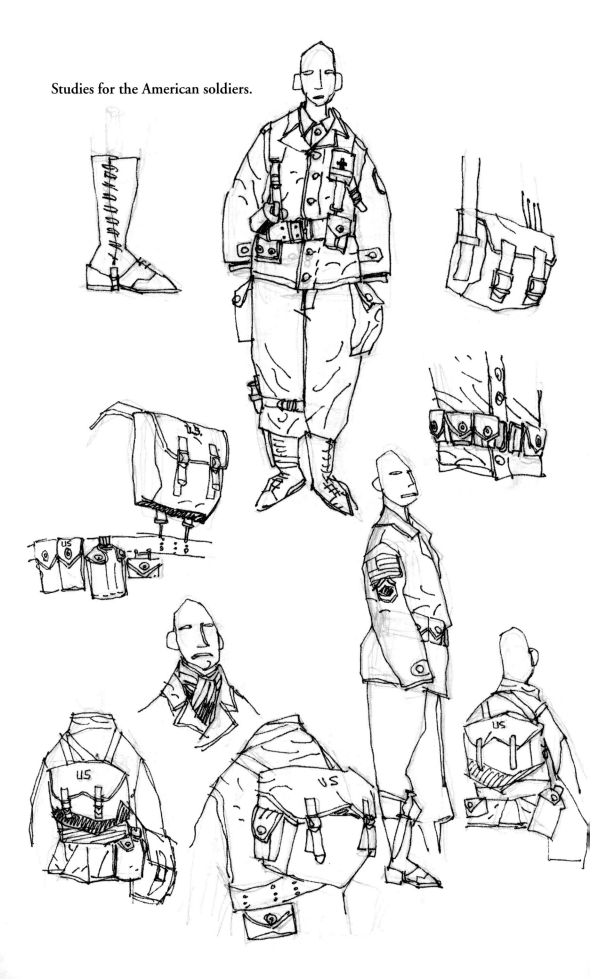

Studies for the American soldiers.

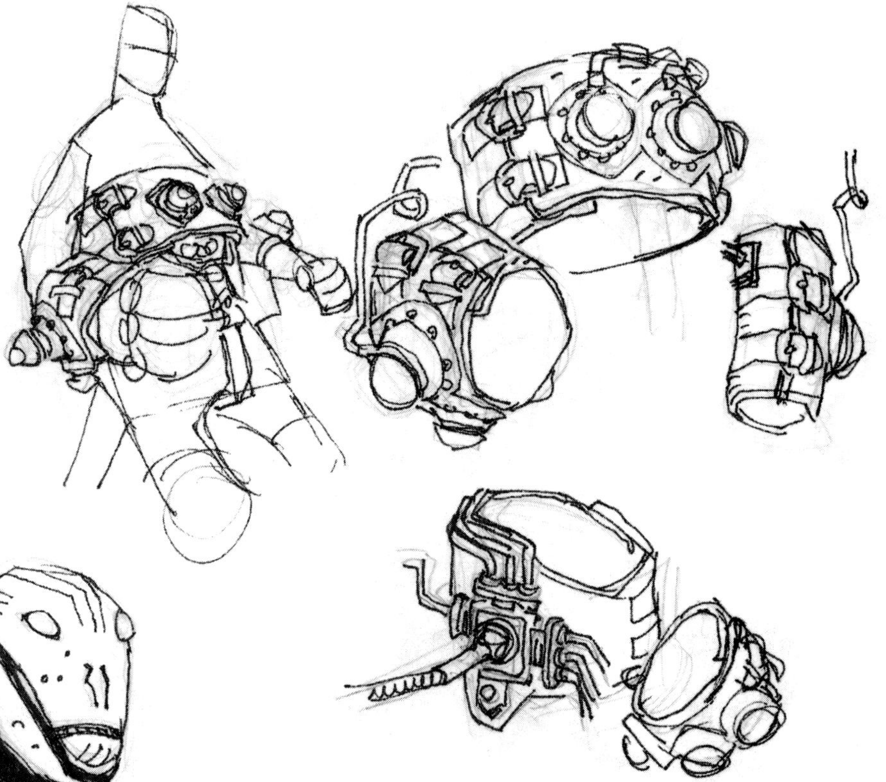

The "torture harness" (above) and its control box (below) which was based on the parking meter outside my apartment.

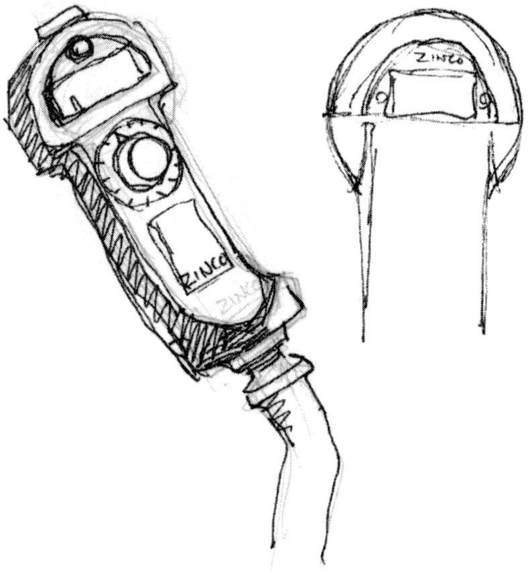

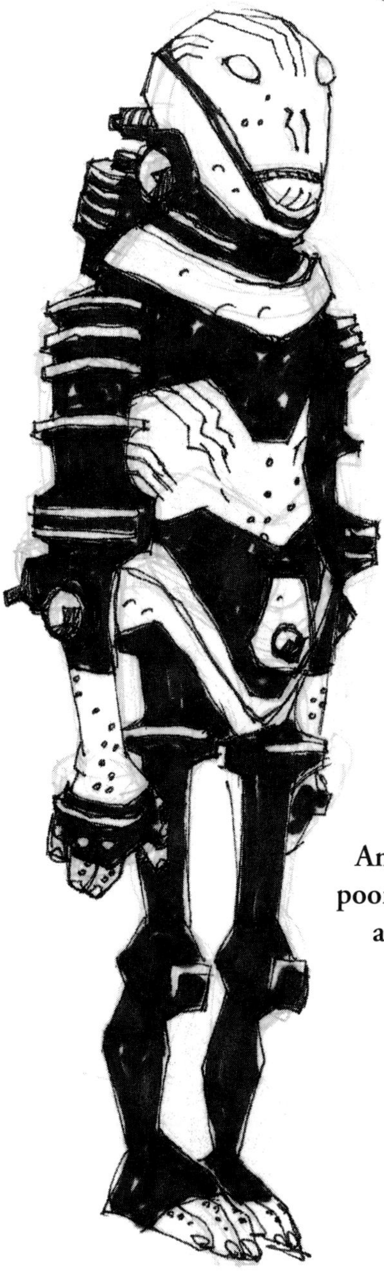

And finally the poor dead alien in all his glory.

There you go.

MIKE MIGNOLA

Mike Mignola
New York City

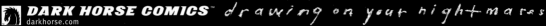